Law of Evidence

The M & E Handbook Series

Law of Evidence

L B Curzon
Barrister

Second edition

1986

Pitman Publishing
128 Long Acre, London WC2E 9AN

A Division of Longman Group UK Limited

First published in 1978
Second edition 1986
Reprinted 1990

© Longman Group UK Ltd 1986

British Library Cataloguing in Publication Data

Curzon, Leslie Basil
    Law of evidence.—2nd ed.—(M & E
    handbook series, ISSN 0625-8828)
    1. Evidence (Law)—England
    I. Title
    344.207'6   KD7499

ISBN 0 7121 0675 8

Printed in England by Clays Ltd, St Ives plc

Contents

administrative matters; Official seals, signatures, gazettes; Some problems relating to judicial notice

Preface to the second edition

This text has been prepared for students who are making a first approach to the law of evidence and for those who require a rapid scheme of revision prior to a first examination in this subject. Specifically, students working for the bar, solicitors', LL.B. and similar examinations, and police officers preparing for promotion examinations have been kept in mind.

The text follows the format of the HANDBOOK series and comprises study notes, progress tests and specimen examination papers. It is not intended as a replacement for any one of the standard textbooks (*see* Appendix 1); it is intended, rather, as a supplement and guide.

A study of the law of evidence is highly demanding: its complexities and subtleties may come as a surprise to students. Some of the reasoning behind its principles is tortuous; some of the intricacies underlying concepts such as hearsay or the burden of proof may appear to be unnecessarily obscure. But the real significance of evidence in the English legal process should not be forgotten: the very complexities of the rules and the underlying rationale have often reflected a continuing awareness of the need to ensure that our system of trial shall be as fair as possible. A statement from the *Thirteenth Report of the Law Reform Committee* is worth keeping in mind: "Rules of evidence are not an end in themselves and are justified only in so far as they assist the court by which they are applied to reach a just determination in the matter upon which it has to adjudicate."

This second edition mirrors recent changes in the law resulting from statute and judicial decision. Extensive reference has been made, in particular, to the important Police and Criminal Evidence Act 1984. The table of cases has been pruned so as to provide space for references to recent cases, and a table of statutes has been added. Helpful suggestions made by readers of the first edition have been taken into consideration during the preparation of this new edition.

The following planned study scheme, using this HANDBOOK, is recommended to the reader.

(a) The *first reading* should begin with a *detailed study of Chapters 1 and 2 only*, followed by a *swift reading* of the remainder of the text, so that an *overall view of the subject area* is obtained.

(b) The *second reading* should be made up of a *detailed study of the entire text*, in methodical fashion, chapter by chapter. Principles, definitions and supporting material must be comprehended. (Where possible, leading cases ought to be studied in the reports.) The progress tests should be attempted and answers checked against the text.

(c) The *third reading* should take the form of a *general revision*.

(d) Finally, the *three test papers* which make up Appendix 3 should be attempted under strict examination conditions.

A note on techniques of learning may be appropriate here. "Rote-learning" (the mere memorisation of material with little effort devoted to the process of assimilation and comprehension) will be totally unproductive for students of the law of evidence. Subject mastery in this area necessitates a thorough understanding of principles, their inter-relationship and the premises from which they are derived. A systematic study programme, timed and spaced with care, the comprehension of principles through the process of applying them to cases, and a planned revision which seeks to organise those principles into a unified whole—these are the constituents of a productive self-study scheme. Coke's words, written some three and a half centuries ago, are of relevance:

"For then only can we be said to know the law when we apprehend the reasons of it; that is, when we bring the reason of the law so to our own reason that we perfectly understand it as our own; and then, and never before, have we such an excellent and inseparable property and ownership therein, as we can neither lose it, nor can any man take it from us; and these reasons being fully apprehended in one case will direct us (the learning of the law is so chained together) in many other like cases. But if by your study and industry you make not the reason of the law your own it is not possible for you long to retain it in your memory" (*Coke upon Littleton*, 1628).

I wish to thank the Senate of the University of London for permission to reprint in Appendix 3 a selection of questions set for its LL.B. examinations. In addition, I would like to record my gratitude to Helen Bond of Lancashire Polytechnic for comments on an early draft of this new edition and Emlyn Williams for his help in updating, his meticulous attention to detail and his careful editing of the text.

L.B.C.

NOTE

The cross references in the table of cases, table of statutes and text of this book consist of the relevant chapter number in roman, followed by the section number in bold.

Table of cases

Table of statutes

Part one
Introductory matters

1

The nature of evidence

Preliminary matters

1. The place of evidence in the English legal system. In general, trials under English law reflect the *adversary system*, as contrasted with the *inquisitorial system* which is characteristic of many Continental systems of law.

(*a*) Under the *adversary system*, based on "accusatorial procedure" and the important presumption of innocence (*see* 10:**16**) which prevail in common law legal systems, parties and their representatives have the primary responsibility for finding and presenting evidence. Cases are tried on evidence adduced by the parties. The judge does not generally investigate the facts; he acts as an umpire between parties, rather than as an inquisitor. "The judge's part . . . is to hearken to the evidence, only himself asking questions of witnesses when it is necessary to clear up any point that has been overlooked or left obscure; to see that the advocates behave themselves seemly and keep to the rules laid down by law; to exclude irrelevancies and discourage repetition; to make sure by wise intervention that he follows the points that the advocates are making and can assess their work; and at the end to make up his mind where the truth lies": *per* Denning, L. J. in *Jones* v. *N.C.B.* (1957).

(*b*) Under the *inquisitorial system* the judge plays a highly active role in the discovery of facts, the examination of documents and the interrogation of the accused.

(*c*) "Generally, continental methods emphasise more strongly the legal value of utility. The state takes a more active part in the exploration of truth, both in civil and criminal matters. Anglo-

American law, on the other hand, emphasises security, and the individual litigant or defendant has not only more elaborate safeguards, which not infrequently compel the acquittal of obviously guilty persons, but he also exerts a bigger influence on the course of proceedings": Friedmann, *Legal Theory*.

(*d*) The importance of the presentation of evidence by parties under the adversary system, the significance of the jury in that system—one writer on jurisprudence speaks of the law of evidence as "the child of the jury"—and the attempts to prevent the jury from the consequences of being misled have resulted in the creation of a host of rules and regulations, often highly technical and complex, relating to what evidence may or may not be presented, and what is or is not sufficient proof. "The English rules are stricter than those of other systems in ruling out certain types of evidence, this being due partly to the fact that the jury was so extensively used as the fact-finding body and judges feared that the jury might place undue weight on certain types of evidence which are notoriously untrustworthy": Paton, *Jurisprudence*.

2. The keystones of our system of evidence. A number of basic principles may be discerned in our law of evidence, holding together the structure of the trial, civil and criminal.

(*a*) *The parties are to be treated fairly throughout the proceedings.* Both sides must be heard (*audi alteram partem*), so that it has become a vital principle of so-called "natural justice" that a party shall not be condemned unheard. *See Local Government Board* v. *Arlidge* (1915); *Ridge* v. *Baldwin* (1964) (in which the House of Lords declared void—because it was contrary to natural justice—a dismissal which took place in the absence of the dismissed party who had, therefore, been unable to present his case).

(*b*) *The principle of orality is dominant.* At the very heart of the English system of trial is the oral examination of witnesses. It should be noted, however, that evidence may be given on affidavit (*see* 5:4); persons who cannot attend court because of an infirmity may give their evidence out of court, in the presence of the parties, to an "examiner" (*see* 5:4 (*a*)). *See also* the Criminal Justice Act 1967, s. 9; *Lister* v. *Quaife* (1983); *R*. v. *Rathbone, ex p. Dikko* (1985). *See also* oral evidence at 2:17 (*a*).

(c) *The burden of proof (see Chap. 6) generally rests on the person who positively asserts facts.* "It is an ancient rule founded on considerations of good sense and it should not be departed from without strong reasons": *per* Viscount Maugham in *Joseph Constantine Steamship Line Ltd.* v. *Imperial Smelting Co. Ltd.* (1942). *See Woolmington* v. *D.P.P.* (1935); *Abrath* v. *N. E. Railway Co.* (1886).

(d) *Matter which a party wishes to adduce in relation to proof must be relevant to the facts in issue (see 2:4) (see,* for example, *Boldron* v. *Widdows* (1824)) and must be admissible (i.e. it must not infringe any exclusionary rules): *see R.* v. *Quinn and Bloom* (1962).

3. Rules of legal evidence: a preliminary comment. Specified formal and procedural rules must be observed when evidence is offered in court. The basic rules of evidence, which will emerge throughout the text, may be said to have been formulated and to have evolved so as to assist in the determination of four principal problems:

(a) *Upon whom rests the burden of proving facts? See* 2 (c) above and Chap. 6. This is not always a clear-cut matter. Thus, A accuses B of stealing his money—the burden of proof is clearly on A. X is accused of murder and pleads insanity—here is a special case in which the burden of proof of X's insanity may be on X (unless the Crown chooses to raise the issue): *see R.* v. *Windle* (1952); Criminal Procedure (Insanity) Act 1964, s. 6. *See* 6:21.

(b) *What facts must be proved?* In general, a party must establish proof of every material fact upon which he intends to rely by sufficient evidence. Thus, D is accused of murdering E; the prosecution must establish by sufficient evidence that E was killed unlawfully by D *and* with malice aforethought. Exceptions to this strict rule occur, for example, in the case of facts of which the court takes judicial notice (*see* 9:14) or, in the case of civil proceedings, where formal admissions of facts are made upon the pleadings or (orally) in court (*see* 9:7).

(c) *What facts ought to be excluded from the court's cognisance? See* 2 (d) above. Not all facts relating to a matter may be presented to the court. In general, proof of facts in issue and of facts having relevance to the issue (*see* 13:12) is allowed. Thus, as a general rule, parties to a civil action are not allowed to give evidence of a general reputation for their good character (*see* 14:21).

(*d*) *What modes of proof are acceptable?* As a general rule, English law recognises particular kinds of proof only, e.g. proof by *real evidence* (*see* 2:17 (*c*)), by *documentary evidence* (*see* 2:17 (*b*)) and by *oral evidence* (*see* 2:17 (*a*)). The exceptions to this rule are discussed at appropriate places in the text.

4. Evidence as part of the adjective law. The law of evidence forms part of the *adjective law* (concerned with procedure and practice in the courts) as contrasted with *substantive law* (concerned with the determination of rights, duties, liabilities, etc.).

(*a*) Questions of the particular court to which a litigant ought to apply, the form of the pleadings to be filed, are matters of procedure (which are closely related to the law of evidence). Questions of the mode of proof, admission or rejection of evidence, etc. are clearly part of the law of evidence.

(*b*) It is occasionally difficult to differentiate some rules of evidence and substantive law. Thus, it has been suggested that "questions as to *what* facts must be proved to give rise to a cause of action or to a defence thereto, or as to *what* facts may not be proved, are questions of substantive law . . .": Law Reform Committee 1966 (Cmnd. 2964). Further, it has been pointed out by some writers that irrebuttable presumptions (*see* 10:8 (*a*)) may, in some cases, effectively bring into existence or remove rights or duties and, hence, may amount to rules of law.

Definition of evidence

5. The problem of definition. The problem of definition arises, fundamentally, from: the need to differentiate the restricted, technical use of the term "evidence" in law and its use in popular speech ("his clothes are evidence of his good taste"); the need to subsume under one general heading a variety of disparate matters, e.g. the burden of proof, the admissibility of confessions, corroboration of an accomplice's evidence.

6. Some important definitions. The following are some of the definitions of evidence put forward by legal writers:

(a) "Facts which are legally admissible and the legal means of attempting to prove such facts": Nokes.

(b) "Firstly, the means, apart from argument and inference, whereby the court is informed as to the issues of fact as ascertained by the pleadings; secondly, the subject matter of such means . . . Evidence, in the first sense, means the testimony, whether oral, documentary or real, which may be legally received in order to prove or disprove some fact in dispute": Phipson.

(c) "The evidence received by courts of justice in proof or disproof of facts, the existence of which comes in question before them": Best.

(d) "That which demonstrates, makes clear, or ascertains the truth of the very fact or point in issue, either on the one side or on the other": Blackstone.

(e) "All the legal means, exclusive of mere argument, which tend to prove or disprove any matter of fact, the truth of which is submitted to judicial investigation": Taylor.

(f) "The usual means of proving or disproving a fact or matter in issue": Halsbury's *Laws of England*.

(g) "One fact is evidence of another when it tends in any degree to render the existence of that other probable. The quality by virtue of which it has such an effect may be called its 'probative force', and evidence may therefore be defined as any fact which possesses such force": Salmond.

(h) "Any species of proof, or probative matter, legally presented at the trial of an issue, by the act of the parties and through the medium of witnesses, records, documents, concrete objects, etc., for the purpose of inducing belief in the minds of the court or jury as to their contention": Black.

7. A working definition. For the purpose of this text, evidence is considered as *the legally admissible facts into which the court will enquire, the legal means of attempting to prove or disprove those facts before the court and the resultant corpus of rules of law attaching thereto.*

Content of the law of evidence

8. Main sources. Our law of evidence derives in large measure from common law rules, resulting from the gradual withdrawal of the determination of problems of fact from the judges and the transfer of those problems to lay juries, so that it became necessary to formulate *exclusionary rules* "lest minds untrained in legal niceties be led astray". Statute (*see* 12 below) has also contributed largely to the development of the law of evidence. Recently-formulated rules reflecting the impact of contemporary technology on the collecting and recording of information (e.g. computers—*see* 17:16 and 19:23, tape recorders—*see* 5:10 (*a*), 8:7 (*b*), 20:21) indicate that the boundaries of the law of evidence are not fixed. (*See also* the report (*The Times*, 3rd December 1976) of the first use in an English court of videotape recordings as evidence tendered by a police photographer, and *Kajala* v. *Noble* (1982).)

9. Main divisions of the law of evidence. Based on the writings of lawyers, the decisions of the courts and statutory provisions, the law of evidence tends to be studied under the following main headings:

(*a*) Problems of classification of judicial evidence.

(*b*) Problems relating to proof and its standards.

(*c*) Matters of relevancy and admissibility.

(*d*) Problems of hearsay and documentary evidence.

10. Plan of this Handbook. The plan of this text is based on **9** above; it is built, therefore, around four parts:

(*a*) *Part One* is concerned with the basis of evidence, its essential nature and classification. It considers the definition of evidence, the functions of judge and jury, the competence and compellability of witnesses and the manner and mode of their examination before the court.

(*b*) *Part Two* examines problems of proof; in particular, the burden and standard of proof, problems relating to corroboration and the main difficulties arising from the presentation of documentary evidence.

(*c*) *Part Three* continues the examination of problems of proof; in particular, those matters of which proof is not required or not allowed and those matters which may be proved in judicial proceedings.

(*d*) *Part Four* looks into the problem of the hearsay rule, its scope and the exceptional circumstances in which hearsay evidence is admissible in civil and criminal proceedings.

11. Studying the law of evidence: some caveats. Students of the law of evidence should consider carefully the following cautions, together with their implications for a course of study:

(*a*) Some knowledge of *procedure* is essential before undertaking a study of evidence. In the pages which follow, that knowledge is presumed. (An outline of procedure ought to be revised prior to a study of this text.)

(*b*) The *vocabulary* of the law of evidence is highly technical. Its main terms almost invariably differ in meaning from similar terms employed in everyday usage. "Facts", "proof", "document", "presumption", "character", have precise meanings within the context of the law of evidence; the student must be on guard against confusing these meanings with those attached to common usage.

(*c*) The *"unitary nature"* of the law of evidence can present problems to the student. Evidence is "all of a piece" and it is impossible to select only particular problems for study while totally ignoring others. Thus, it may be possible, as a feature of one's study of the criminal law, to exclude an examination of, say, treason or blasphemy; it is not possible, in one's study of the law of evidence, to ignore *any* aspect. Hearsay evidence, for example, runs like a thread through the entire fabric of the law of evidence. Relevance, admissibility, burden of proof, cannot be excluded from one's study of that law. An overall view of the subject matter should be obtained, therefore, before a detailed study is undertaken.

12. Statutory reforms in the law of evidence. Among the more important of the statutes in the law of evidence have been the following:

(*a*) Evidence Act 1843, allowing persons who had any interest in the outcome of proceedings to testify.

(*b*) Evidence Act 1851, abolishing, in civil cases, the restrictive common law rule whereby parties to the proceedings were not competent to give evidence.

(*c*) Criminal Evidence Act 1898, allowing the accused to give evidence on his own behalf.

(*d*) Evidence Act 1938, relating to the admissibility of evidence based on statements made in a document.

(*e*) Civil Evidence Act 1968, amending the law of evidence in relation to hearsay evidence of statements of fact in civil proceedings and in relation to the privilege against self-incrimination.

(*f*) Civil Evidence Act 1972, amending the law of evidence in relation to hearsay statements of opinion admissible in evidence in civil proceedings and in relation to the admissibility of opinion evidence.

(*g*) Police and Criminal Evidence Act 1984, amending the law of evidence in relation to documentary evidence in criminal proceedings, competence and compellability of an accused's spouse, and confessions.

Evidence in civil and criminal cases

13. The general rule. The law of evidence is, in general, the same for civil *and* criminal proceedings.

14. Exceptions. Among the more important exceptions to the general rule are the following (which are dealt with at appropriate points in the text):

(*a*) In criminal cases it is necessary to prove a case beyond reasonable doubt. In civil cases a preponderance of probability may suffice.

(*b*) In criminal cases dying declarations may be admissible in trials for murder and manslaughter. In civil cases such declarations are not admissible.

(*c*) In criminal cases the good character of the accused is usually admissible. In civil cases the good character of either party is generally inadmissible.

(*d*) In criminal cases admissions are admissible only if voluntary. In civil cases admissions are almost always admissible.

(e) In criminal cases unsworn evidence may be admissible. In civil cases evidence is received only when given on oath or affirmation.

(f) In criminal cases the spouse of the accused may not always be a compellable witness. In civil cases the parties' spouses are almost always compellable witnesses.

Progress test 1

1. Distinguish the "adversary" and the "inquisitorial" systems. (**1**)

2. Upon whom does the burden of proof generally rest? (**2**)

3. In general, what facts must a party prove at a trial? (**3**)

4. Why may evidence be considered a part of the adjective law? (**4**)

5. Define evidence. (**5–7**)

6. In what sense is the law of evidence considered as possessing a "unitary nature"? (**11**)

7. Enumerate some of the more recent statutes in the development of the law of evidence. (**12**)

8. In what ways does the law of evidence differ in civil and criminal cases? (**14**)

2
Basic classifications

Preliminary matters

1. The necessity for classification. There is no single, accepted classification of the fundamental types of evidence. Nevertheless, reference is made in the cases and literature to schemes of classification. It is important to note, however, that classifications tend to reflect a textbook writer's individual preferences; they have no reference to any statutory classification. The classifications in **3–31** below refer in particular to the important areas of:

    (*a*) facts (*see* **3–8** below);
    (*b*) types of evidence (*see* **9–31** below).

2. Difficulties of classification. Problems may arise because of nomenclature and overlap, and these should be kept in mind in studying the classifications set out in this chapter.

   (*a*) *Nomenclature.* There is no recognised terminology, so that, for example, the term "direct evidence" has more than one meaning, "hearsay" and "derivative evidence" are both referred to by some writers as "second-hand evidence".

   (*b*) *Overlap.* Types of evidence may not always fall neatly into separate categories, for purposes of classification. So-called "parol evidence", for example, may spill over into the categories of "oral" or "extrinsic" evidence.

Classification of facts

3. **General classification.** The term "facts" is applied broadly to "whatever is the subject of perception or consciousness" (Phipson). The fact which is evidence is known as an "evidential fact"; the fact of which it is evidence is known as the "principal fact". The term "fact" when used in this fashion in the law of evidence must be differentiated clearly from its meaning in common usage ("that which has actual existence"). The following types of fact are considered below:

(a) *Facts in issue* (*see* 4 below);

(b) *Other relevant or "evidential" facts* (*see* 5–8 below).

4. **Facts in issue.** *See* 13:6–11. This term refers to all those facts ("main" or "principal") which *must be proved* by the party making an allegation (plaintiff, prosecutor) in order to succeed, and the facts that defendant (or accused) *must prove* in order to establish his defence. They usually emerge from the pleadings and the substantive law and are a matter which the judge determines. Generally, they must be proved by evidence.

(a) In a criminal case "whenever there is a plea of not guilty, everything is in issue, and the prosecution has to prove the whole of their case, including the identity of the accused, the nature of the act and the existence of any necessary knowledge or intent": *per* Lord Goddard in *R.* v. *Sims* (1946).

(b) A fact admitted expressly or by implication is generally not in issue.

(c) An example of "facts in issue" is as follows: X is accused of the murder of Y. X pleads not guilty. "Facts in issue" include the killing of Y by X and the existence of malice aforethought on the part of X. Should X raise the defence of provocation, that becomes a fact in issue.

(d) "Subordinate" or "collateral" facts in issue may refer to facts affecting the admissibility of evidence and the credibility of witnesses.

5. **Facts relevant to the issue.** *See* 13:12. This term, referred to as "evidential facts" or "logically probative facts" in some textbooks,

relates to facts from which facts in issue or relevant facts may be inferred.

(*a*) Facts of this nature are those which are so related to the facts in issue that they render the latter either probable or improbable.

"Evidence is relevant if it is logically probative or disprobative of some matter which requires proof. It is sufficient to say, even at the risk of etymological tautology, that relevant (i.e. logically probative or disprobative) evidence is evidence which makes the matter which requires proof more or less probable": *per* Lord Simon in *DPP* v. *Kilbourne* (1973).

(*b*) *Example:* X is accused of unlawfully wounding Y with a knife. Z, a witness, testifies that he saw X leaving Y's house, in which Y had been found wounded, brandishing a knife. After Z's evidence is adduced, the prosecution will attempt to show that Z is telling the truth and will invite the jury to *infer* that the knife seen by Z was used by X in the wounding of Y.

6. Alternative nomenclature. Other terms applied to facts in issue and evidentiary facts are:

(*a*) *Facta probanda* (sing: *factum probandum*)=facts in issue.
(*b*) *Facta probantia* (sing: *factum probans*)=evidentiary facts.

7. Proof of facts in issue and evidentiary facts. In general, these facts may be proved by: testimony; admissible hearsay statements; documents; things.

8. Primary facts. This term was defined in *British Launderers' Research Association* v. *Hendon Rating Authority* (1949), thus: "Primary facts are facts which are observed by witnesses and proved by oral testimony, or facts proved by the production of a thing itself, such as original documents. Their determination is essentially a question of fact for the tribunal of fact, and the only question of law that can arise on them is whether there was any evidence to support the finding. The conclusions from primary facts are, however, inferences deduced by a process of reasoning from them."

Classification of types of evidence

9. General classification. The following classification is adopted below:

(*a*) Direct and hearsay evidence (*see* **11–13** below);
(*b*) Direct and circumstantial evidence (*see* **14–16** below);
(*c*) Oral, documentary and real evidence (*see* **17–21** below);
(*d*) Primary and secondary evidence (*see* **22–27** below);
(*e*) Other classifications (*see* **28–31** below).

10. Problems of classification. *See* **2** above. It should be noted that the divisions set out below are "traditional"; although referred to in the courts and the textbooks they do not form, in any sense, universal, immutable categories.

Direct and hearsay evidence

11. Definitions. These terms are defined as follows:

(*a*) *Direct* (or "*original*" or "*testimony*") *evidence*. Testimony concerning a fact actually perceived by a witness with one of his senses.
(*b*) *Hearsay* (or "*indirect*", "*second-hand*") *evidence*. Evidence of some fact not actually perceived by a witness with one of his own senses, but proved by him to have been stated by some other person. *See* Part 4.

12. Examples of direct evidence. The following should be noted:

(*a*) The fact in issue is whether X had been driving on the wrong side of the road. Y gives evidence of seeing X driving his car at the time in question on the wrong side of the road.
(*b*) The fact in issue is whether A and B were present when C signed his will. D gives evidence of having seen A and B together with C at a table on which was a document which C was signing.

13. Examples of hearsay evidence. *See* Chap. 16. The following should be noted:

(*a*) A is accused of the murder of B. C testifies to the effect that he heard B shout out a few moments before a shot was heard, "For Heaven's sake, A, put down that gun!" This is hearsay evidence intended to prove *the truth* of what B had stated, namely, that A was about to shoot him.

(*b*) The contents of a police officer's notebook referring to the statement of a witness to an accident on the highway are produced as evidence. They constitute hearsay evidence of the accident in question.

NOTE: Some writers refer to direct and hearsay evidence collectively as "testimonial evidence".

Direct and circumstantial evidence

14. Definitions. These terms are defined as follows:

(*a*) *Direct evidence* (another meaning of the term which was used at **11** above). Evidence of a fact actually in issue.

(*b*) *Circumstantial (or "indirect" or "presumptive") evidence.* Evidence of some fact not actually in issue, but relevant to a fact in issue, from which a fact in issue may be inferred. (Note Bentham's definition: "Circumstantial evidence is that deduced from the existence of a fact, or a group of facts, which, being directly applicable to the principal fact, lead to the conclusion that the latter exists.")

15. Examples of direct evidence. The following should be noted:

(*a*) The fact in issue is whether X stole Y's purse. Z's evidence that he had observed X putting his hand in Y's pocket and taking out a purse may be adduced as direct evidence of X's having appropriated Y's property.

(*b*) The fact in issue is X's libelling Y. Z's evidence that he saw X posting on a wall a defamatory cartoon which he had drawn, relating to Y, may be adduced as direct evidence of X's having published the matter complained of by Y.

16. Examples of circumstantial evidence. The following should be noted:

(*a*) X gives evidence that skid marks made by the tyres of Y's motor-cycle were on the wrong side of the road. This may be circumstantial evidence from which a fact in issue—Y's driving on the wrong side of the road—can be inferred. *See*, e.g., *Elliott* v. *Loake* (1983); *Coles* v. *Underwood* (1984).

(*b*) X is accused of Y's murder by shooting. Z swears that he saw a revolver in X's possession shortly after Y's death. Z's evidence is direct evidence as to X's possession of a revolver; it is no more than circumstantial evidence relating to the fact in issue, namely, whether X shot Y with that weapon.

Oral, documentary and real evidence

17. Definitions. These terms are defined as follows:

(*a*) *Oral* (or *"parol"*) *evidence*. The testimony of a witness, usually on oath or affirmation, given by his word of mouth in the witness box.

(*b*) *Documentary evidence*. Evidence derived by the court from the inspection of some document (*see* 8:3 (*b*)) produced to it.

(*c*) *Real* (or *"objective"* or *"demonstrative"*) evidence. Evidence derived by the court from the examination of physical objects, other than documents, produced for inspection. *See also* **31** below.

18. Examples of oral evidence. The following should be noted:

(*a*) X declares in court, on oath, in answer to a question put by counsel for Y: "Y has never given me any money at any time."

(*b*) A, a police officer, being questioned in court by counsel for B, states: "B struck me when I attempted to arrest him."

19. Examples of documentary evidence. *See* Chaps. 8, 19. The following should be noted:

(*a*) The fact in issue is the content of a letter alleged to have been written by X and sent to Y. Y produces the letter in court and reads an extract from it.

(*b*) The fact in issue is A's indebtedness to B. A computer print-out on which evidence of the debt is recorded is produced for inspection by the court. *See* the Civil Evidence Act 1968, s. 5 (1) (*see* **17:16**).

(c) For examples in recent legislation of "evidence by certificate", *see:* Food Act 1984, s. 97 (certificate of a public analyst in the prescribed form); Road Traffic Regulation Act 1984, s. 113 (certificate in the prescribed form, certifying that a person specified in the certificate stated to the constable who signed the certificate that a particular motor vehicle was being driven or used by, or belonged to, that person on a particular occasion, shall be admissible evidence for the purpose of determining by whom the vehicle was being driven or used, etc.); Video Recordings Act 1984, s. 19 (certificate admissible as evidence of the fact that, on a specified date, no classification certificate had been issued in respect of video work in question). *See also* **18:19**.

20. Examples of real evidence. The following should be noted:

(a) In an action relating to injuries caused by a "fierce and mischievous dog", the animal is produced for examination by the court: *see Line* v. *Taylor* (1862).

(b) Evidence of the course of ships was derived from examination of a filmed record of radar echoes: *The Statue of Liberty* (1968). *See* also *Castle* v. *Cross* (1985) in which a print-out of the reading of a breath-testing device was admitted as *real* evidence.

21. Some points concerning real evidence. The following points should be considered:

(a) The term "real evidence" covers not only material objects and the general appearance of persons but also the demeanour of a witness, and a view out of court, i.e. an inspection by judge and jury of some object or place outside the court when the characteristics of that object or place constitute facts from which facts in issue may be inferred. *See* O. 35, r. 8.

(i) "I think that a view is part of the evidence just as much as an exhibit. It is real evidence": *per* Denning, L. J., in *Goold* v. *Evans & Co.* (1951).

(ii) See Buckingham v. *Daily News Ltd.* (1956); *Salsbury* v. *Woodland* (1970); *Tito* v. *Waddell* (1975); *R.* v. *Gurney* (1977).

(b) In general, oral evidence is required to introduce or explain real evidence.

(c) The non-production of a physical object by a party who could produce it may lead to the court's discrediting his evidence relating to it: *see Armory* v. *Delamirie* (1722).

(d) The non-production of a physical object which might have been conveniently produced for inspection will not render inadmissible any oral evidence relating to it: *R.* v. *Francis* (1874).

(e) Whether a document is to be considered as documentary or real evidence will depend on the purpose for which it is produced (e.g. as evidence of the document's existence or of the matter contained therein).

Primary and secondary evidence

22. **Definitions.** These terms are defined as follows:

(a) *Primary (or "best") evidence.* Evidence which itself suggests that, in the circumstances, it is the best, or is such that it does not in itself suggest the existence of any better evidence. (Note that the term is also applied to evidence given by a witness testifying to facts within his own knowledge.)

(b) *Secondary (or "inferior") evidence.* That which, in itself, suggests the existence of other and better evidence.

23. **Examples of primary evidence.** The following should be noted:

(a) The fact in issue is the content of a document prepared by X. The original document is produced in court.

(b) The fact in issue is the extent of damage to X's property, under the Criminal Damage Act 1971. X's damaged property is produced in court.

24. **Examples of secondary evidence.** *See* **8:9.** The following should be noted:

(a) The fact in issue is the content of a letter alleged to have been written by X. A copy of the letter is produced in court. *See R.* v. *Nowaz* (1976).

(b) The content of A's lost will is in question. A's daughter gives oral (i.e. secondary) evidence as to its contents: *see Sugden* v. *Lord St. Leonards* (1876).

NOTE: There are *no degrees* of secondary evidence: *Brown* v. *Woodman* (1834). *See also* 8:**9**.

The "best evidence" rule

25. Statement of the rule. "There is but one general rule of evidence, the best that the nature of the case will admit": *per* Lord Hardwicke in *Omychund* v. *Barker* (1745). *See also Macdonell* v. *Evans* (1852); *Greenaway* v. *Homelea Fittings* (1985).

26. The rule as it was in practice. The operation of the rule may be discerned in the following cases:

(a) *Chenie* v. Watson (1797). Oral evidence was offered relating to a bushel measure. It was not accepted; it was held that the measure itself should have been produced.

(b) *Williams* v. *E. India Co.* (1802). Damage had resulted from goods placed on board a ship. Plaintiff was nonsuited after failing to call as a witness the defendant's officer who had loaded the goods on board.

27. The rule today. The rule no longer applies in practice since the court admits all relevant evidence: *Kajala* v. *Noble* (1982). (In that case, the court suggested that the old rule was limited to written documents "in the strict sense of the term", and had no relevance to tapes or films.) *See R.* v. *Wayte* (1983)—photostat copies of documents are admissible where relevant and the originals have been lost.

Other classifications

28. Insufficient, prima facie and conclusive evidence. These terms are defined as follows:

(a) *Insufficient evidence*. Evidence so weak and unsure that it would not support any reasonable person in deciding the issue in favour of the party adducing it. *See Hawkins* v. *Powells Tillery Steam Coal Co.* (1911).

(*b*) *Prima facie evidence.* Evidence in support of a fact in issue, necessitating acceptance of proof of that fact in the absence of further contradictory evidence (e.g. that a share certificate is prima facie evidence of good title: *see* the Companies Act 1985, s. 186). *See Smithwick* v. *N.C.B.* (1950); Prevention of Terrorism (Temporary Provisions) Act 1984, Sch. 3, para. 7(2); Prosecution of Offences Act 1985, s. 26 (signed consents for the institution of criminal proceedings to be admissible as prima facie evidence without further proof); Companies Act 1985, s. 361 (register of members is prima facie evidence of any matters which are by the Act directed or authorised to be inserted in it).

(*c*) *Conclusive evidence.* Evidence arising, for example, from some statutory provision which obliges the court to accept it as complete proof of some fact and to reject evidence adduced in an attempt to disprove it (e.g. the irrebuttable presumptions—*see* 10:**11**). *See Kerr* v. *John Mottram Ltd.* (1940); Civil Evidence Act 1968, s.13 (1)—evidence of a subsisting criminal conviction shall be conclusive evidence of the commission of the offence for purposes of libel and slander actions.

29. Original and derivative evidence. These terms are defined by Best, thus:

(*a*) *Original evidence.* "That which has an independent probative force of its own."

(*b*) *Derivative evidence.* "That which derives its force from some other source."

30. Judicial and extra-judicial evidence. Salmond speaks of:

(*a*) *judicial evidence.* "That which is produced to the court." It comprises those evidential facts (*see* **3** above) brought to the personal knowledge and observation of the court; *and*

(*b*) *extra-judicial evidence.* "That which does not come directly under judicial cognisance, but nevertheless constitutes an intermediate link between judicial evidence and the fact requiring proof."

31. Personal and real evidence. Salmond distinguishes these terms as follows:

(a) *Personal evidence (i.e. "testimony").* "All statements, verbal or written, judicial or extra-judicial . . . possessed of probative force."

(b) *Real evidence.* "The residue of evidential facts."

Progress test 2

1. What is meant by a "fact in issue"? (4)
2. X is accused under the Theft Act 1968, s. 8 (1) of robbing Y. State some of the likely "facts in issue". (4)
3. Explain (a) *factum probandum*; (b) *factum probans*. (6)
4. Define hearsay evidence. (11)
5. What is meant by circumstantial evidence? (14)
6. Define documentary evidence. (17)
7. It is alleged that D's dog has savaged P's lambs. Are there any circumstances in which the dog may properly be produced for inspection by the court? (20)
8. Is the view of a place outside the court ever accepted as real evidence? (21)
9. Explain the best evidence rule and comment on its significance today. (25–27)

3

The functions of judge and jury in relation to evidence

Preliminary matters

1. Problems to be considered. The general problems considered below turn on the following matters:

(a) The general rule relating to the separation of the functions of judge and jury (*see* **3–4** below).

(b) Exceptions to the general rule (*see* **5–8** below).

(c) Judge sitting alone (*see* **9–10** below).

(d) Judicial control of the jury (*see* **11–15** below).

(e) The concept of judicial discretion (*see* **16–19** below).

2. The problem of procedure. A general knowledge of procedure in criminal and civil proceedings is assumed in this chapter. In particular, the role and functions of the jury and other related procedural matters should be known.

The general rule

3. Statement of the rule. *In general, matters of law fall to be determined by the judge; matters of fact, by the jury. See Mechanical Inventions* v. *Austin* (1935). In other words, the question of whether something *can be* (in law), is for the *judge*; whether (in fact) something *is* falls to the *jury*.

4. Examples of the rule in practice. The following examples should be noted:

(*a*) In the case of *libel*, it will fall to the *judge* to decide whether certain words *are capable of bearing* a defamatory meaning. It is for the *jury* to decide whether in fact those words *did bear* that defamatory meaning. *See Nevill* v. *Fine Art Co.* (1897); *Broome* v. *Agar* (1928).

(*b*) In a case relating to *negligence*, it is for the *judge* to say whether negligence *can* be inferred from given circumstances.

"It has always been considered a question of law to be determined by the judge, subject, of course, to review, whether there is evidence which, if it is believed, and the counter evidence, if any, not believed, would establish the facts in controversy. It is for the jury to say whether and how far the evidence is to be believed": *per* Willes, J. in *Ryder* v. *Wombwell* (1868), cited by Lord Blackburn in *Metropolitan Railway Co.* v. *Jackson* (1877).

(*c*) In a case relating to an *agreement to supply goods to a minor*, it is for the *judge* to decide whether there is a possibility that goods supplied *can be* necessaries. The *jury* should decide whether the goods in question *actually are* necessaries. *See Nash* v. *Inman* (1908).

Exceptions to the general rule

5. Matters relating to the admissibility of evidence. The existence of those facts upon which admissibility of evidence depends is a matter of fact which, exceptionally, is determinable by the *judge*. *See Bartlett* v. *Smith* (1843).

(*a*) Whether a confession is voluntary (*see* 20:11) is determined by the *judge*. *See R.* v. *Chadwick* (1934). If he holds that it *is* admissible, its *weight* is a matter for the *jury*: *see R.* v. *Murray* (1951).

(*b*) Whether privilege attaches to the answering of a question is determined by the *judge*. *See Stace* v. *Griffith* (1869).

(*c*) Whether a document, for example, a bill of exchange, is properly stamped is determined by the *judge*: *Bartlett* v. *Smith* (1843).

NOTE: The construction of a document is generally a question of *law* for the *judge*; but where extrinsic evidence is allowed in explanation that evidence is for the *jury*: *Morrell* v. *Frith* (1838).

6. Matters relating to "reasonableness". In some cases the question of whether a course of conduct is reasonable or not is determined, not by the jury, but by the *judge*.

(*a*) In an action for false imprisonment or malicious prosecution, the *judge* decides whether the facts operating on the mind of defendant constituted reasonable cause in the circumstances. "It is well settled that the question of the absence of reasonable and probable cause is for the judge. At the same time it is, I think, clear that the question is one of fact and not law": *per* Lord Atkin in *Herniman* v. *Smith* (1938). *See* also *Lister* v. *Perryman* (1870).

(*b*) Whether a covenant in restraint of trade is reasonable is decided by the *judge. See Dowden & Pook Ltd.* v. *Pook* (1904).

(*c*) Whether a complaint (in the case of an alleged sexual offence)—*see* 13:22—was made "at the first reasonable opportunity" (i.e. "as speedily as can reasonably be expected") is a question to be answered by the *judge. See R.* v. *Cummings* (1948).

7. Matters relating to foreign law. Foreign law includes all law except English law. Thus, Scots law and the law of the Commonwealth are considered to be foreign law (*see further*, 9:22 (*a*) (*ii*)). Such law is a matter of fact to be determined by the *judge. See* the Civil Evidence Act 1972, s. 4 (1); County Courts Act 1984, s. 68; County Court Rules 1981, O. 20, r. 25; and *R.* v. *Hammer* (1923).

8. Matters affecting punishment after conviction. Where, after conviction, there emerges a matter of fact which might bear on the appropriateness of punishment, this forms a question to be determined by the *judge*.

Judge sitting without a jury

9. The case of trial by judge alone. Where the judge sits alone and, therefore, combines the functions of judge and jury, the general rule (*see* 3 above) nevertheless applies, so that *qua* judge he "notionally directs himself" as to questions of law, and *qua* jury he will determine questions of fact.

10. Result of these circumstances. On appeal from the decision of a judge sitting without a jury, the Court of Appeal will not, in general, overturn the findings of the judge acting *qua* jury (just as it will hesitate to interfere with a jury's findings following a correct decision by the judge). *See*, however, *Watt* v. *Thomas* (1947); *Yuill* v. *Yuill* (1945).

Judicial control of the jury

11. The general position. Judicial control of the jury emerges, for example, in the exceptions to the general rule that matters of fact are to be determined by the jury (*see* **3** above). Other aspects of that general control are touched upon at **12–15** below.

12. Presumptions. *See* Chap. 10. Presumptions of law, as explained by the judge to the jury, can act, in practice, as specific limitations of a jury's power to find facts.

13. Withdrawal of an issue from the jury. Where the judge believes that there is insufficient evidence of some essential fact in the case put forward by the prosecution or plaintiff, he may withdraw the question from the jury, or he may instruct the jury to return a verdict in favour of the opponent. He may also rule that there is "no case to answer". *See Bridges* v. *N. London Railway Co.* (1874); *Vye* v. *Vye* (1969) (in which it was stated that it is "a fundamental principle" of English judicature that until all the evidence for a complainant has been heard, magistrates may not dismiss that complaint by accepting a submission of "no case to answer"); *R.* v. *Abbott* (1955); *R.* v. *Galbraith* (1981).

14. The judge's summing up. Following the closing speeches in a trial, the judge will sum up, directing the jury on relevant points of law, reviewing the evidence and drawing attention to its value. This will almost certainly influence the subsequent findings of the jury.

15. On appeal. Judicial control is also exercised through the power of the Court of Appeal to allow appeals, so that, effectively, jury verdicts may be set aside because the Court of Appeal considers them unsatisfactory. *See* the Criminal Appeal Act 1968, s. 2 (1).

NOTE: Note also the judge's power to call witnesses (*see* 5:7 (*b*)) and to order a witness to leave court (*see* NOTE at 4:**19**).

The concept of judicial discretion

16. The essence of judicial discretion. Judicial discretion can be viewed as a power, which resides in the court, of deciding a question in circumstances where some latitude of judgment is allowed. Note the following points.

(*a*) "A person entrusted with a discretion must direct himself properly in law. He must call his own attention to the matters which he is bound to consider. He must exclude from his consideration matters which are irrelevant to the matter he has to consider": *Associated Picture Houses Ltd.* v. *Wednesbury Corporation* (1947).

(*b*) For examples of the exercise of judicial discretion *see*: the right to withdraw issues from a jury if insufficiently supported by appropriate evidence (*see* **13** above); the right to disallow questions in cross-examination (*see* 5:**11**) if considered oppressive: *see R.* v. *Flynn* (1972); the right to weigh conflicting public interests in relation to public policy cases (*see Conway* v. *Rimmer* (1968) at 12:**9**); the right to exclude evidence admissible under the "similar fact principle" if considered to be of a prejudicial nature (*see Noor Mohamed* v. *R.* (1949)); the discretion to allow evidence to be given by statement if the alternative might be to oblige a party to call an opponent or his past and present employees (*see* O. 38, r. 29 (2); *Greenaway* v. *Homelea Fittings Ltd.* (1985)).

(*c*) Note the "inclusionary discretion" of the Civil Evidence Act 1968, s. 8 (*see also* O. 38, rr. 21–31, and *Ford* v. *Lewis* (1971)) and the "exclusionary discretion" of s. 18 (5) (*see* **17** below).

17. Excluding evidence in civil cases. Note the Civil Evidence Act 1968, s. 18 (5): "Nothing in this Act shall prejudice (*a*) any power of a court, in any legal proceedings, to exclude evidence (whether by preventing questions from being put or otherwise) at its discretion . . ." There appears to be no general discretion in civil cases to exclude relevant evidence even though obtained improperly: *see Lloyd* v. *Mostyn* (1842); *Calcraft* v. *Guest* (1898). Note, however, the recent case of *ITC Film Distributors* v. *Video Exchange Ltd.* (1982), in which it was stated that the general rule allowing secondary evidence of privileged documents to be adduced, even though obtained improperly, did *not* extend to documents brought into court and obtained by the other side as the result of stealth or a trick.

18. Excluding evidence in criminal cases: *R.* v. *Sang* (1980). Prior to the decision in *R.* v. *Sang*, the general rule seems to have been that the courts had an unfettered discretion to exclude evidence which they considered to have been obtained improperly or unfairly. *See*, e.g., *Jeffrey* v. *Black* (1978)—reference to the exercise of discretion to exclude evidence which "had been obtained by police officers by trickery, oppressive conduct, unfairly or as a result of behaviour which was morally reprehensible": *per* Lord Widgery, C. J. In *R.* v. *Sang* (1980), the House of Lords seemed to limit the judge's general discretion. It was stated that the judge in a criminal trial has a general discretion to refuse to admit evidence if in his opinion its probable prejudicial effect so outweighs its true probative value as to render its reception unfair to the accused, *and*, except with regard to evidence consisting of admissions and confessions and other evidence obtained from the accused after the commission of the offence, the judge has *no discretion* to refuse to admit relevant and otherwise admissible evidence on the ground of its having been obtained by unfair or improper means.

19. Excluding evidence in criminal cases: Police and Criminal Evidence Act 1984, s. 78. The 1984 Act affirms the court's discretion to exclude some types of prosecution evidence. Specifically, under s. 78 (1), the discretion may be exercised if it appears to the court that, *having regard to all the circumstances, including the circumstances in which the evidence was obtained*, the admission of such evidence would have such an adverse effect on the fairness of the proceedings that the court ought not to admit it. The subsection does not confine the exclusionary discretion to evidence obtained from the defendant, and seems to embrace prosecution evidence drawn from all sources. Note that: "nothing in this section shall prejudice any rule of law requiring a court to exclude evidence": s. 78 (2).

Progress test 3

1. What is the general rule, in relation to judge and jury, regarding the determination of matters of law? (**3**)

2. To whom do questions fall for decision relating to (*a*) the voluntary nature of a confession and (*b*) privilege attaching to the answering of a question? (**5**)

3. Where a question arises as to whether a document is stamped properly, is the jury entitled to decide? (**5**)

4. Consider the functions of judge and jury in an action for false imprisonment. (**6**)

5. What is meant by "foreign" law? Are matters relating to foreign law decided by judge or jury? (**7**)

6. Enumerate some of the ways in which judicial control of the jury is achieved. (**11–15**)

7. Comment on the discretion to disallow evidence in a criminal case. (**18, 19**)

4

Witnesses (1): competency, compellability, testimony on oath and affirmation

Preliminary matters

1. Matters to be covered. Chapters 4 and 5 outline some of the problems of the law of evidence as they relate to witnesses. The following specific topics are mentioned:

(*a*) The competency and compellability of witnesses (*see* **3–12** below).

(*b*) Oath, affirmation, etc. (*see* **13–15** below).

(*c*) Unsworn evidence (*see* **16–19** below).

(*d*) The examination of witnesses (*see* Chap. 5).

2. Preliminary definitions. The following definitions should be noted carefully:

(*a*) *Witness*. One who gives *formal or sworn evidence* at a hearing.

(*b*) *Testimony*. The *statement of a witness in court, generally sworn,* and offered as evidence of the truth of that which he asserts.

(*c*) *Competency*. The capacity *to be lawfully called to offer evidence.*

(*d*) *Compellability*. The capacity *to be lawfully obliged to give evidence.*

The competency of witnesses

3. The general rule. Evidence must be given by *legally competent witnesses*, and all persons are competent (and compellable) as witnesses in judicial proceedings. In essence, a witness is "competent" if, under the appropriate rules of law, his evidence is receivable by a court in the proceedings in question.

(a) At one time, the following categories of persons were generally considered incompetent: non-Christians (*see Omychund* v. *Barker* (1745)); convicts; persons with a proprietary or pecuniary interest in the outcome of the hearing. These restrictions have been progressively abolished: *see* Civil Rights of Convicts Act 1828; Evidence Act 1843; Evidence Act 1851.

(b) The judge decides questions of competency or incompetency, usually on preliminary examination (known as *voir dire*) in open court, in the jury's presence where the case is being tried by jury: *R.* v. *Dunne* (1929).

(c) Where incompetency of a witness becomes apparent, the judge will exclude the evidence: *see R.* v. *Moore* (1892).

4. Exceptions to the general rule. The following exceptions to the rule stated at **3** above are outlined below:

(a) persons of defective intellect (*see* **5** below);
(b) children (*see* **6** below);
(c) the accused person (*see* **7** below);
(d) the spouse of the accused (*see* **8** below).

5. Persons of defective intellect. Insanity and drunkenness amounting to temporary loss of reason will generally be held to have destroyed competency. (For details of confessions of the mentally handicapped, *see* 20:**15** (*b*).)

(a) An insane person may be competent, however, during a lucid interval. Where his insanity relates to one matter only, and he understands an oath, he may be considered capable of giving evidence on other matters: *see R.* v. *Hill* (1851).

(b) It is for the judge to decide whether a witness is incompetent because of defective intellect: *see Toohey* v. *Metropolitan Police Commissioner* (1965).

6. Children. In general, infancy does not render a witness incompetent. However, *see R.* v. *Wallwork* (1958).

(*a*) *In civil cases*, a child who, in the opinion of the court, cannot understand the nature and consequence of an oath, may not give evidence. There is no age limit below which a child is not competent; competency will depend on understanding rather than age: *see R*. v. *Brasier* (1779).

(*b*) *In criminal cases*, there is power under statute to allow a child of tender years to give unsworn testimony, *provided that* he has sufficient intelligence and understands the duty of telling the truth: Children and Young Persons Act 1933, s. 38 (1).

(*i*) The trial judge will determine whether a child has the necessary intelligence and understanding: *R*. v. *Surgenor* (1940).

(*ii*) A child's unsworn evidence must be corroborated by sworn evidence. *See* 7:**34**.

(*iii*) *See also* the Magistrates' Courts Act 1980, s. 103 (proceedings relating to sexual offences, e.g., any offence under the Sexual Offences Act 1956 or Indecency with Children Act 1960 or Protection of Children Act 1978, or any attempt to commit such an offence).

7. The accused person. Three situations are noted:

(*a*) *Accused as a witness for the prosecution*. The general rule under common law is that the accused person is *incompetent* as a witness for the prosecution. He may not, therefore, be called by the prosecution to give evidence against a co-prisoner. (Note, however, the effect of a co-prisoner "turning Queen's evidence", i.e. confessing his guilt and offering evidence against a co-prisoner, thereby becoming a competent witness. Note also the similar effect of the filing of a *nolle prosequi* in respect of an accused person: *see R*. v. *Payne* (1950).) Where an issue of competence of a prosecution witness is raised, the onus will be on the prosecution to prove that witness is competent: *R*. v. *Yacoob* (1981).

(*b*) *Accused as a witness for himself (i.e. the defence)*. The Criminal Evidence Act 1898, s. 1, renders the accused "a competent witness for the defence at every stage in the proceedings whether the person so charged is charged solely or jointly with any other person."

(*i*) Accused must be informed of his right to give evidence: *R*. v. *Villars* (1927).

(*ii*) Failure of the accused to give evidence can be commented on by the court (*see R*. v. *Sparrow* (1973)) but *not* by the prosecution: 1898 Act, s. 1 (*b*).

(*iii*) "If the co-defendant goes into the witness box and gives evidence in the course of a joint trial, then what he says becomes evidence for all the purposes of the case including the purpose of being evidence against his co-defendant": *per* Humphreys, J. in *R.* v. *Rudd* (1948).

(*iv*) The accused had a right at common law to make an unsworn statement from the dock, without cross-examination, but this was abolished by the Criminal Justice Act 1982, s. 72. (*See* **18** below.)

(*c*) *Accused as a witness for a co-accused.* In general, the accused is a competent witness for a co-accused.

8. The spouse of the accused. When the Police and Criminal Evidence Act 1984, s. 80, becomes operative, the position relating to the competency of spouses to give evidence in criminal proceedings will be as follows.

(*a*) The spouse of the accused *will be competent* to give evidence *for the prosecution*: s. 80 (1) (*a*).

(*b*) The spouse of the accused *will be competent* to give evidence *on behalf of the accused* or *any person jointly charged* with the accused: s. 80 (1) (*b*).

(*c*) There is an *exception* where husband and wife are *jointly charged* with an offence. In such a case neither spouse will be competent (or compellable) under s. 80 to give evidence for the prosecution unless he or she is not, or is no longer, liable to be convicted of that offence at the trial (whether as a result of pleading guilty, or for any other reason): s. 80 (4).

(*d*) *Former spouses* are *competent* (and compellable) to give evidence as if they had never been married to each other: s. 80 (5).

(*e*) The prosecution is forbidden to comment on any failure of the husband or wife of the accused to give evidence: s. 80 (8). (It will be noted that this restriction does not apply to the judge or counsel for the defence.)

The compellability of witnesses

9. The general rule. In general, persons who are competent witnesses are also compellable to give evidence in judicial proceedings.

(*a*) The attendance of a witness at a magistrates' court is compelled by summons or warrant; at the Crown Court by witness order or witness summons; in the High Court by subpoena. *See* the Civil Procedure (Attendance of Witnesses) Act 1965.

(*b*) In a civil case a party cannot be compelled by the court to call a witness, nor may the court itself call a witness. In criminal proceedings, however, the court may call any witness without the consent of the parties.

(*c*) Although a witness is compellable, he may not always be compelled to answer certain types of question: *see* 12:**15** and 15:**14**.

(*d*) Some exceptions to the general rule are considered at **10–12** below.

10. The accused. Under the Criminal Evidence Act 1891, s. 1 (*a*) (partially repealed by the Police and Criminal Evidence Act 1984, s. 119, Sch. 7, Part V), a person charged with an offence "shall not be called as a witness in pursuance of this Act except upon his own application". He is not a compellable witness for any co-prisoner.

11. The spouse of the accused. When the Police and Criminal Evidence Act 1984, s. 80, becomes operative, the position relating to the compellability of spouses to give evidence in criminal proceedings will be as follows.

(*a*) The spouse of the accused *will be compellable* to give evidence *on behalf of the accused*, subject to s. 80 (4) (*see* 8 (*c*) above).

(*b*) The spouse of the accused *will be compellable*, subject to s. 80 (4), to give evidence *for the prosecution or on behalf of any person jointly charged with the accused* only if the offence involves:

(*i*) assault on, or injury, or threat of injury, to the spouse of the accused or a person under 16; or

(*ii*) a sexual offence (i.e. under the Sexual Offences Act 1956, the Indecency with Children Act 1960, the Sexual Offences Act

1967, the Criminal Law Act 1977, s. 54, or the Protection of Children Act 1978) alleged to have been committed on a child under 16; or

(*iii*) attempting, or conspiring to commit, or aiding, abetting, counselling, procuring or inciting the commission of an offence within (*i*) or (*ii*) above: s. 80 (3).

(*c*) Note that under s. 80 (9), the Criminal Evidence Act 1898, s. 1 (*d*) and the Matrimonial Causes Act 1965, s. 43 (1), will cease to have effect. As a result, a spouse will be compellable to disclose any communications made during the period of the marriage, and to give evidence proving that marital intercourse did or did not take place between spouses during any stage of the marriage.

NOTE: Section 80 (3) effectively overrules *Hoskyn* v. *Metropolitan Police Commissioner* (1979) in which, somewhat surprisingly, the House of Lords decided that the wife of an accused person charged with a crime of inflicting injury upon her was a competent, *but not compellable*, witness for the Crown. "It was for the wife's own protection that the common law made an exception to its general rule by making the wife a competent witness in respect of any charge against her husband for a crime of violence against her. But if she does not want to avail herself of this protection, there is, in my view, no ground for holding that the common law forces it upon her": *per* Lord Salmon. In a vigorous dissenting judgment, Lord Edmund-Davies stated: "A wife who has once been subjected to a 'carve-up' may well have more reasons than one for being an unwilling witness against her husband. In such circumstances it may well prove a positive boon to her to be directed by the court that she has no alternative but to testify." He cited with approval the statement of Lord Goddard, C. J. in *R.* v. *Algar* (1954): "At common law one spouse could not give evidence against the other except in the case of offences against the person or liberty of the other party to the marriage. In such cases a spouse is both competent and compellable." The 1984 Act, s. 80 (3), seems to favour the essence of the dissent expressed by Lord Edmund-Davies.

12. Other cases. The following further exceptions should be noted:

(*a*) The Sovereign and foreign Sovereigns are competent, but not compellable. (This principle applies also to certain diplomatic officials.)

(*b*) A banker may not be compelled in proceedings to which he is not a party to attend to give evidence which may be proved by an order to provide copies (etc.) of his books: *see* the Bankers' Books Evidence Act 1879, s. 6.

(*c*) A judge of a superior court may not be compelled to give evidence of judicial proceedings which have taken place before him: *Florence* v. *Lawson* (1851).

Oath and affirmation

13. The general rule. In general, *evidence must be given on oath*. *See*, e.g., the Magistrates' Courts Act 1980, s. 98.

(*a*) The oath was, at one time, taken on the Gospel. *Omychund* v. *Barker* (1745) decided that witnesses could give evidence on oath appropriate to their religions.

(*b*) The Oaths Act 1888 allowed an oath to be administered in a fashion which the person taking it declared to be binding on him. The Oaths Act 1909 set out the words to be used. The Oaths Act 1888, as amended by the Administration of Justice Act 1977, s. 8 (1) allowed affirmation (*see* **15** below). The Oaths Act 1961 allows affirmation where a holy book, necessary for the swearing of an oath, is unavailable. *See* now the Oaths Act 1978 which has consolidated the rules.

(*c*) In some cases (*see* **16–19** below) unsworn evidence may be given.

14. Administration of the oath. In principle, the oath may be administered by any person who has authority to hear evidence. In practice, it is administered by the clerk of the court or some other court official.

15. Affirmation. Affirmation involves the making of a solemn declaration and excludes any reference to God. Under the Oaths Act 1978, s. 5 (1) "Any person who objects to being sworn shall be permitted to make his solemn affirmation instead of taking the oath."

(a) It should be noted that evidence given on affirmation is not "unsworn evidence", since an affirmation is the equivalent, in effect, of an oath: 1978 Act, s. 5 (4).

(b) It is generally a contempt of court for a witness to refuse to be sworn or to affirm: *Hennegal* v. *Evance* (1806). Modern statutory provisions (*see*, e.g., the Magistrates' Courts Act 1980, s. 97) commonly contain comparable provisions.

Unsworn evidence

16. General. The following cases are considered below:

(a) The unsworn evidence of children (*see* **17** below).
(b) The unsworn statement of an accused person (*see* **18** below).
(c) Persons producing documents (*see* **19** below).

17. Unsworn evidence of children. In criminal proceedings, the unsworn evidence of children of tender years is generally admissible where the court is satisfied that they "do not understand the nature of an oath, but are possessed of sufficient intelligence to justify the reception of evidence and to understand the duty of speaking the truth": Children and Young Persons Act 1933, s. 38 (1). *See also* 7:**34**.

(a) The judge will determine whether the child has the appropriate intelligence and understanding: *R.* v. *Surgenor* (1940).

(b) Evidence of this nature must be corroborated: Children and Young Persons Act 1933, s. 38 (1). *See* 7:**34**.

(c) The child can be cross-examined on evidence.

(d) In *R.* v. *Hayes* (1977) it was held that, in deciding whether a child should be sworn, the vital consideration is whether he has sufficient appreciation of the solemnity of the occasion and the added responsibility to tell the truth which is involved in the taking of an oath. *See R.* v. *Campbell* (1983); *R.* v. *Bellamy* (1986).

18. Unsworn statement of an accused person. Prior to the Criminal

Evidence Act 1898, there was a custom whereby the accused was allowed to make an unsworn statement from the dock. His right was specifically protected under the 1898 Act, s. 1 (*h*). The right was abolished by the Criminal Justice Act 1982, s. 72 (but the accused may, if not represented by counsel or solicitor, address the court or jury by way of mitigation without being sworn).

19. Persons producing documents. Persons who do no more than produce documents, following a *subpoena duces tecum*, need not be sworn where some other witness is able to identify those documents. *See Perry* v. *Gibson* (1834). *See* O. 38, r. 13 (1).

> NOTE: At any time during a trial the judge may, at his discretion, order a witness to leave the court until he is called and application for such an order may be made by either party: *Moore* v. *Lambeth C.C. Registrar* (1969); *Southey* v. *Nash* (1837). Refusal to leave when ordered is contempt, but this does not necessarily render the witness incompetent: *Cobbett* v. *Hudson* (1852).

Progress test 4

1. Define (*a*) competency, (*b*) compellability.   (**2**)
2. What is the general rule concerning competency of witnesses?   (**3**)
3. May an insane person be a competent witness?   (**5**)
4. May a child give evidence in a civil case?   (**6**)
5. Is the accused ever a competent witness for the prosecution? (**7**)
6. Under what circumstances may a spouse be competent to give evidence?   (**8**)
7. Is the spouse of an accused person competent to give evidence for a co-accused?   (**8**)
8. Can the spouse of accused be compelled to give evidence? (**11**)
9. In what circumstances may a person affirm rather than take an oath?   (**15**)
10. When is the unsworn evidence of a child admissible?   (**17**)
11. Outline the decision in *R.* v. *Hayes* (1977).   (**17**)

12. May an accused person make an unsworn statement from the dock? (18)

5

Witnesses (2): stages of examination

Preliminary matters

1. Matter to be discussed in this chapter. The following topics are discussed below:

(a) The general rules regarding hearings in open court (*see* **2** below).

(b) Evidence before the trial and at previous trials (*see* **3–5** below).

(c) The problem of "leading questions" (*see* **6** below).

(d) Matters such as the calling of witnesses, language in which evidence is to be given (*see* **7** below).

(e) The three stages of examination of witnesses: examination-in-chief (*see* **8–10** below); cross-examination (*see* **11–13** below); re-examination (*see* **14–15** below).

2. Some general rules relating to testimony by a witness. Testimony should generally be given *orally in open court*. Questions are put by counsel, although the judge may also ask questions in any form of any witness during the proceedings.

3. Exceptions to the general rule. The following exceptions should be noted:

(a) Evidence may be taken *before the trial* (*see* **4–5** below) and may be presented at the trial in the form of affidavits or depositions.

(b) *See* the Criminal Justice Act 1967, s. 9 and the Magistrates' Courts Act 1980, s. 102 (relating to proof by written statement in a criminal trial); the Civil Evidence Act 1968, s. 2 and the Civil Evidence Act 1972, s. 1 (relating to proof in civil proceedings by statements out of court).

(c) Matters relating to, for example, secret processes (*see Mellor* v. *Thompson* (1885)); sexual incapacity (Matrimonial Causes Act 1973, s. 48 (2)); certain types of criminal offences against children (*see* Children and Young Persons Act 1933, ss. 37, 39; Children and Young Persons Act 1963, s. 57); state secrets (Official Secrets Act 1920, s. 8 (4)). These matters are generally heard *in camera*.

4. Evidence given before trial. This may be considered under the following headings:

(a) *Civil cases.* The parties may agree that a case is to be tried, wholly or in part, upon *affidavit*, i.e. written statement sworn or affirmed before a commissioner for oaths in the name of the deponent: *see* O. 38, r. 2(3). Such affidavits may be ordered by the judge to be read at the trial. Further, orders may be issued for the examination on oath of a person by an examiner (usually a barrister of not less than three years' standing) appointed by the court: *see* O. 39, r. 1. (Attendance for examination may be enforced by writ of subpoena: O. 39, r. 4 (a).) Interrogatories administered to an opponent may be used by a party as proof of facts stated therein: *see* O. 26, r. 7.

(i) Affidavits may be used in evidence notwithstanding irregularity in form: O. 41, r. 4. They should contain only those facts which the deponent is able to prove from his own knowledge: O. 41, r. 5(1).

(ii) For the purpose of interlocutory proceedings an affidavit may contain statements of information or belief with sources and grounds: O. 41, r. 5 (1)(2). *See Lumley* v. *Osborne* (1901).

(b) *Criminal cases: committal proceedings.* Under the Magistrates' Courts Act 1980, s. 102, a written statement by a person is admissible in evidence in committal proceedings if: it purports to be signed by the person who made it; it contains a declaration by that person that, to the best of his knowledge, it is true; a copy is given to all parties to the proceedings (or their solicitors) before it is given in evidence; no party objects to its being tendered.

(c) *Criminal cases: children.* Where the attendance of a child in court might involve serious danger to his health (and a magistrate is satisfied by a doctor's evidence that this is so), the deposition of the child may be taken out of court. *See* the Children and Young Persons Act 1933, ss. 42, 43; and the Magistrates' Courts Act 1980, s. 103 (preliminary enquiry into a sexual offence).

(*d*) *Criminal cases: depositions to perpetuate testimony. See* the Magistrates' Courts Act 1980, s. 105; Criminal Law Amendment Act 1867, s. 6. Where a person who is willing to give evidence relating to an indictable offence is dangerously ill and unlikely to recover and a deposition cannot be taken in the usual way, it may be taken out of court by a magistrate and used later at the trial of the accused if it is established that the deponent is dead, or unable to travel to give evidence *and* that reasonable notice is given to the person against whom the deposition is to be read *and* that such person (or his counsel) had, or might have had, a full opportunity of cross-examining the deponent. (Note that depositions are admissible only if the Magistrates' Courts Rules 1981, r. 33, are followed.)

(*e*) *Criminal cases: trial on indictment.* Under the Magistrates' Courts Act 1980, s. 102, in an indictable case—for the definition of indictable offence, *see* the Criminal Law Act 1977, s. 64 (1)—prosecution witnesses must be examined on oath before a magistrate and in the presence of the accused. Their depositions are read over to them and signed by them and the magistrate. At the subsequent trial (*see* the Criminal Justice Act 1925, s. 13 (3)) if the deposition is made by a witness subject to a conditional order to attend the trial and he has not been required to attend, or the deponent is unable to travel, or is dead, and the accused (or his counsel) has had the opportunity of cross-examining deponent, the deposition may be read, without further proof, as evidence. (These cases are, however, comparatively rare, being vastly outnumbered by "paper" committal proceedings (*see* the Magistrates' Courts Act 1980, s. 6(2).) *See* Practice Direction (4 June, 1986)

5. Depositions in former trials. By virtue of the Civil Evidence Act 1968, s. 2, evidence given in previous proceedings (civil *or* criminal) is generally admissible in a civil trial, so as to prove the facts stated. *See also* O. 38. Testimony of this kind is admissible (at common law) in criminal proceedings *if* the former proceedings related to the same issues *and* involved the same (or substantially the same) parties, *and* the party against whom the evidence is to be given had an opportunity of cross-examination on the previous occasion, *and* the witness cannot be called at the later trial because, for example, he is ill or dead.

6. The problem of "leading questions". A leading question may be described as one put to a witness which suggests the desired answer, or puts the answer into his mouth, or, in the case of a disputed matter, permits only the reply, "Yes" or "No". In general, questions of this nature, which "prompt" one's witness, are not allowed (but *see (c)* below).

(*a*) *Examples of leading questions.* Assume that, in the *examination-in-chief* of witness (*see* 8 below) counsel (C) wishes to elicit the fact (which is in dispute) that the witness (W) had been approached by the prisoner (P) at noon on Wednesday, July 20th, in Leicester Square, London.

    (*i*) C: "Were you in Leicester Square at noon on Wednesday, July 20th?"

          W: "Yes, I was."

          C: "And did P approach you there?"

          W: "Yes, he did."

    (*ii*) C: "You were, were you not, in Leicester Square at noon at Wednesday, July 20th?"

          W: "Yes."

          C: "And you were approached there, were you not, by P?"

          W: "Yes."

These modes of examination are generally prohibited in examination-in-chief, since they are based on leading questions.

(*b*) *The following pattern of questioning*, designed to elicit the information required in (*a*) above, *avoids the use of leading questions* (as defined above):

          C: "Where were you at noon on Wednesday, July 20th?"

          W: "I was in Leicester Square, London."

          C: "What happened while you were there?"

          W: "A person approached me."

          C: "Who was that person?"

          W: "It was P."

(c) *Circumstances in which the use of leading questions is permitted.*
The use of leading questions is generally permitted: in cross-
examination (*see* 11 below); in relation to undisputed matter (e.g.
witness's name, address, occupation); in relation to the identity of
persons or things; in the questioning of a hostile witness (*see* 9 below);
where a witness is forgetful and matters are put merely to enable him
to recollect points. (Note that parties in a civil action may consent to a
witness being "led".) *See Nichols* v. *Dowding* (1815); *R.* v. *Watson*
(1817); *R.* v. *MacDonell* (1909); *Moor* v. *Moor* (1954).

7. Other matters. The following points in relation to testimony and
the examination of witnesses should be noted:

(a) *The language to be used.* Evidence should be given in English.
Note, however:

(i) Under the Welsh Language Act 1967, s. 1, the Welsh
language may be used in any legal proceedings in Wales or Mon-
mouthshire by any party or witness who desires to use it.

(ii) Where a witness does not understand English, the evidence
is translated to the court by a sworn interpreter. *See R.* v. *Lee Kun*
(1916); *Re Fuld* (1965).

(b) *Judge's power to call witnesses.* The judge has no right to call
witnesses in a *civil case* except with the consent of all parties: *see Re
Enoch* (1910). In a *criminal case* the judge himself may call any
witness: *see R.* v. *Wallwork* (1958). In *civil and criminal cases* the judge
may recall any witness for further examination: *R.* v. *McKenna*
(1956). Cross-examination of a recalled witness by counsel requires
the judge's permission: *Coulson* v. *Disborough* (1894).

The first stage of examination: examination-in-chief

8. The object of examination-in-chief. Examination-in-chief
(known also as "direct examination") has as its object *the placing of a
witness's story before the court so as to obtain testimony in support of the
version of the facts for which the party calling that witness is contending.*

(a) It is conducted by the party calling the witness, usually
through counsel or solicitor.

(b) It is based on strictly relevant facts only.

(c) It may *not* be based on leading questions (save in relation to the exceptions stated at **6** (c) above and in relation to matter already put in evidence by the other side).

(d) In general, a party cannot cross-examine or otherwise discredit his own witness: *see Ewer* v. *Ambrose* (1825). But *see* **9** below.

9. The "hostile witness". A witness is considered "hostile" when, in the opinion of the court, he shows that he is adverse to the party calling him and is unwilling to tell the truth. *See*, e.g., *R.* v. *Booth* (1982).

(a) "Hostile" is not the same as "unfavourable". Assume that D calls W_1 to prove some fact in question and that W_1 fails to do so. W_1 may be considered an "unfavourable" witness. Although a party may not generally discredit his own witness (*see* **8** (d) above), D is not prevented from calling W_2 and W_3 later to prove the fact in question although the effect of the testimony of W_2 and W_3 is to contradict that of W_1. (It should be noted that in a civil case, although D cannot generally put to W_1 any previous inconsistent statement made by him, he can, with leave of the judge, prove that previous statement under the Civil Evidence Act 1968, s. 2.) *See Greenough* v. *Eccles* (1859); *Price* v. *Manning* (1889).

(b) Where the judge rules that a witness shows animosity *and* is unwilling to answer frankly, i.e. that he is "hostile", the party calling him may be given leave to cross-examine him. The party may, in a civil case, prove previous inconsistent statements. The party may not, however, attack a witness's character directly, for example, by asking about bad character. *See* the Criminal Procedure Act 1865, s. 3; Civil Evidence Act 1968, s. 3; *R.* v. *Fraser and Warren* (1956). Application for a witness to be considered hostile must be made immediately it becomes obvious that he is showing unmistakable signs of hostility: *R.* v. *Pestano* (1981).

(c) *See R.* v. *Mann* (1972); *R.* v. *Thompson* (1976)—a judge has a discretion at common law to allow a hostile witness to be cross-examined even though the witness has not made a previous inconsistent statement because of having "stood mute of malice"; and the common law discretion was neither destroyed nor removed by the Criminal Procedure Act 1865, s. 3 ("a party producing a witness . . . may, in case the witness shall, in the opinion of the judge, prove adverse, contradict him by other evidence, or, by leave of the judge, prove that he has made at other times a statement inconsistent with his present testimony . . .'').

10. Refreshing a witness's memory. Under certain circumstances permission may be granted to a witness under examination to refer to some document so as to recall some matter. (It should be noted that, in general, he should not "read aloud" from the document, but should merely look at it before giving his evidence.) *See* 17:**12** (*a*). Note the important provision in relation to civil cases of the Civil Evidence Act 1968, s. 3 (2): "Nothing in this Act shall affect any of the rules of law relating to the circumstances in which, where a person called as a witness in any civil proceedings is cross-examined on a document used by him to refresh his memory, that document may be made evidence in those proceedings; and where a document or any part of a document is received in evidence in any such proceedings by virtue of any such rule of law, any statement made in that document or part by the person using the document to refresh his memory shall by virtue of this subsection be admissible as evidence of any fact stated therein of which direct oral evidence by him would be admissible."

(*a*) The document used may be some writing made or verified by the witness relating to, and contemporaneously with, the fact to which he is testifying. A note checked from a tape recording of a conversation originally heard by witness may be used: *R*. v. *Mills* (1962). *See R*. v. *Kelsey* (1982); *see also A.-G.'s Reference No. 3 of 1979* (1979).

(*b*) The document should have been made by witness himself, or by someone recording matter within witness's knowledge, e.g. a diary, ship's log. *See Anderson* v. *Whalley* (1852).

(*c*) The document should have been made while the matter recorded was fresh in witness's recollection: *see Anderson* v. *Whalley* (1852); *Jones* v. *Stroud* (1825). For expanded notes made from jottings, *see A.-G.'s Reference No. 3 of 1979* (1979).

(*d*) The original document should be available, unless lost or destroyed, in which case a copy can be used: *Burton* v. *Plummer* (1834).

(e) Opposing counsel may inspect the document on request and cross-examine on it: *Senat* v. *Senat* (1965). *See Owen* v. *Edwards* (1984); *R*. v. *Harman* (1984).

(f) In *R*. v. *Richardson* (1971) the Court of Appeal considered an argument that it was improper for a witness to look, *outside the court*, at a document which could not be used within the court because of lack of contemporaneity. The Court rejected the argument, citing with approval "some sage observations" from *Lau Pak Ngam* v. *The Queen* (1966): "Testimony in the witness-box becomes more a test of memory than of truthfulness if witnesses are deprived of the opportunity of checking their recollections beforehand by reference to statements or notes made at a time closer to the events in question . . . Refusal of access to statements would tend to create difficulties for honest witnesses but be likely to do little to hamper dishonest witnesses." *See also R*. v. *Westwell* (1976); *R*. v. *Tyagi* (1986). (In practice it is customary to notify the other side that one's witness has read over his statement before going into court to give evidence.)

The second stage of examination: cross-examination

11. The object of cross-examination. Cross-examination (known also as "cross-examination to the issue") has as its main object *the eliciting of information concerning facts in issue favourable to the party on whose behalf it is conducted and the testing of the accuracy of evidence given against that party*. "It is deemed indispensable to the proper administration of justice that every witness should be subject to the ordeal of cross-examination by the party against whom he is called, so that it may appear, if necessary, what were his powers of perception, his opportunities for observation, his attentiveness in observing, the strength of his recollection and his disposition to speak the truth": Taylor (*On Evidence*, Vol. I).

(a) In general, no evidence affecting a party is admissible against that party unless he has had the opportunity of testing its veracity in a cross-examination: *Allen* v. *Allen* (1894).

(b) It is not limited to matters proved in the examination-in-chief, but may relate to all facts in issue, or relevant (*see R*. v. *Banks* (1916)) and to those which, although considered otherwise irrelevant, may tend to impeach credit or credibility (by showing, e.g., previous contradictory statements, bias, reputation for untruthfulness).

(c) Leading questions are permitted, and must be answered: *Parkin* v. *Moon* (1836).

(d) The general rule is that a cross-examination should be directed to facts, not arguments: *see R.* v. *Hart* (1932).

(e) Failure to cross-examine a witness may amount to an allegation of accepting his version of some matter: *R.* v. *Hart* (1932).

(f) "It is a complete mistake to think that a document which is otherwise inadmissible can be made admissible evidence simply because it is put to the accused person in cross-examination": *R.* v. *Treacy* (1944).

(g) Any witness is liable to be cross-examined, except one called for the sole purpose of producing a document, and one not subjected to examination-in-chief because he has been called in error: *Wood* v. *Mackinson* (1840).

(h) The judge may disallow a question put in cross-examination which appears to him vexatious or irrelevant.

(i) For an example of the statutory exclusion of some questions in cross-examination, *see* the Interception of Communications Act 1985, s. 9.

12. Cross-examination as to credit and credibility. Cross-examination as to *credit* is generally designed to discredit a witness by showing, for example, that his character and background may be such that he ought not to be believed. It usually relates to the *character* of witness. Cross-examination as to *credibility* may be concerned with attitudes, physical or mental (memory, hearing, etc.) likely to affect the credibility of witness's testimony. *See Maxwell* v. *DPP* (1935); *Toohey* v. *Metropolitan Police Commissioner* (1965) (evidence of effect of witness's hysteria on his credibility held admissible).

(a) A witness (other than accused in a criminal case) may be asked questions in cross-examination designed to discredit him and relating, for example, to his integrity, veracity, etc. Where the questions relate *entirely* to witness's credit, the witness's answer is generally to be taken as final, so that no further evidence can be recalled to rebut that answer: *see Harris* v. *Tippett* (1811); *A.-G.* v. *Hitchcock* (1847); *R.* v. *Mendy* (1976).

(*b*) There are exceptional cases, relating to a witness's credit only, where evidence *may* be adduced to contradict witness's denials:

(*i*) *Previous inconsistent statements. See* the Criminal Procedure Act 1865, s. 5. Witness upon cross-examination may be asked whether he has made former, inconsistent (formal or informal) statements. *See R.* v. *Hart* (1957). Under the Civil Evidence Act 1968, s. 3 (1), in a civil case, a previous statement, once proved, may be evidence of any fact stated therein of which direct oral evidence by the witness would be admissible.

(*ii*) *Reputation for untruthfulness.* Independent evidence may be brought to show that the other party's witness has a reputation for untruthfulness and is unworthy of credit on oath: *see R.* v. *Brown* (1867); *R.* v. *Longman and Richardson* (1969).

(*iii*) *Unsoundness of mind or other relevant disability.* Medical evidence affecting reliability may be called. *See Toohey* v. *Metropolitan Police Commissioner* (1965); *R.* v. *Eades* (1972).

(*iv*) *Bias.* Independent evidence of the witness's bias relating to parties may be independently proved: *see R.* v. *Shaw* (1888).

NOTE: On the question of evidence relating to previous convictions, *see* 15:3–11. Note also that a defendant's legal aid application should not be used against him for purposes of cross-examination as to credit: *R.* v. *Stubbs* (1982).

13. Restoring a witness's credit. Following an attack on witness's credit, that credit may be restored in one of the following ways:

(*a*) by cross-examining the attacking witness as to his hostility;

(*b*) by bringing general evidence establishing that the attacked witness is, in fact, worthy of credit;

(*c*) by bringing general evidence establishing that the attacking witness is not, in fact, worthy of credit.

The third stage of examination: re-examination

14. The object of the re-examination. Re-examination of a witness by the party calling him (the right to which arises wherever there has been cross-examination) has as its object *the demonstration of the real meaning of the evidence arising in cross-examination e.g. by the explanation of ambiguous terms used in the cross-examination, motives for conduct admitted in cross-examination.* (The re-examination may attempt the reinstatement of that part of witness's testimony apparently shaken by cross-examination.) *See Dicas* v. *Lord Brougham* (1833).

15. Restrictions on re-examination. The following should be noted:

(*a*) Re-examination is confined to matter arising out of the cross-examination and no new matter may be introduced without leave of the judge: *Prince* v. *Samo* (1838).

(*b*) Leading questions may not be asked (except where permitted in relation to the same matter in examination-in-chief: *see* 8 (*c*) above).

Progress test 5

1. Under what circumstances may evidence taken before the trial be given in civil proceedings? (**4**)

2. What is meant by "deposition to perpetuate testimony" in a criminal case? (**4**)

3. May evidence given in former proceedings be admissible in a civil trial? (**5**)

4. What are "leading questions"? (**6**)

5. Give examples of leading questions. (**6**)

6. When are leading questions permitted? (**6**)

7. What is the extent of a judge's power to call witnesses? (**7**)

8. What is the object of examination-in-chief? (**8**)

9. When is a witness considered "hostile"? (**9**)

10. May a hostile witness be cross-examined? (**9**)

11. Under what conditions may a witness refresh his memory? (**10**)

12. What is the object of cross-examination? (**11**)

13. Explain "cross-examination as to credit and credibility". (**12**)

14. Following an attack on witness's credit, how may that credit be restored? (**13**)

15. What is the object of re-examination and what are the restrictions applicable? (**14, 15**)

Part two
Proof (1)

6
The burden of proof

Preliminary matters

1. Matters to be covered in Part two. In this Part we consider some problems concerning proof: each relates, in essence, to what is meant by "proof" in the law of evidence.

(*a*) In this chapter we examine the *burden of proof* (*see* **3–24** below).

(*b*) In Chap. 7 we consider the problems arising from the varying *standards of proof* and from *corroboration*.

(*c*) In Chap. 8 we discuss *documentary evidence*.

2. The concept of "proof" in the law of evidence. The term "proof" as used in the law of evidence must be differentiated clearly from "proof" in its usual, scientific context. Scientific proof involves a pattern of sequential, logical arguments resulting in the establishing of the validity of some proposition. Proof in the law of evidence is no more than the aggregation of facts and circumstances that convince a tribunal of the truth of some allegation, or, put in another way, it is *those methods by which the existence or non-existence of facts is established to the satisfaction of the court.* It is important to note that this differs from the concept of scientific proof, and that logical structure—considered essential to scientific proof—is *not* an aspect of proof in the law of evidence.

3. The concept of burden of proof—onus probandi. *See* **5** below. In general, the burden, or onus, of proof is the *obligation of proving* *facts* arising during a hearing. The prosecution alleges, for example, that A stole B's coat; there is then a *burden of proof*, relating to the Theft Act 1968 and its precise application to A, resting on the prosecution. X brings an action for defamation against Y; there is then a *burden of proof* on X relating to publication and damage suffered (unless any of these facts be admitted by Y). It should be noted that there is a duty on a trial judge, when summing up, to give a *clear direction* on the burden and standard of proof: *see*, e.g., *R*. v. *Zarrabi* (1985).

4. Matters to be covered below. Problems relating to the burden of proof are set out as follows:

(*a*) The essence of *burden of proof* (*see* **5–12** below).

(*b*) The incidence of the burden in *civil* cases (*see* **13–16** below).

(*c*) The incidence of the burden in *criminal* cases (*see* **17–19** below).

(*d*) Situations in which the *legal burden* of proof is on the defence (*see* **20–22** below).

(*e*) Situations in which the *evidential burden* of proof is on the defence (*see* **23–24** below).

The essence of burden of proof

5. The nature of burden of proof. The "main facts" or "facts in issue" (*see* 2:4) must be proved and the obligation of proving those and other relevant facts rests on the parties propounding them. The "incidence" of the burden (i.e. its "resting place") is not always immediately obvious. The general rules (e.g. "he who asserts must prove") are subject to a number of exceptions, some of which are set out below.

6. Differences in meaning attached to the phrase "burden of proof". "Burden of proof" may be used in relation to the following concepts which should be noted very carefully:

(*a*) general burden (*see* **7** below);

(*b*) specific burden (*see* **8** below);

(*c*) evidential burden (*see* **9** below).

7. The "general burden". Known also as the "persuasive burden", the "burden of establishing the case", the "legal burden", the "burden of proof on the pleadings" and the "fixed burden of proof".

(a) It is used to refer to the general obligation on a party to prove his case by proving the facts in issue.

(b) It is, essentially, that burden resting on the party who will certainly fail on the issue, wholly or in part, if, after all the evidence has been considered, there remains with the jury any significant doubt.

8. The "specific burden". This expression is used by some writers to refer to the specific obligation on a party to prove some individual issue or some fact relevant to that issue. General and specific burdens comprise the "legal burden of proof", according to other writers.

9. The "evidential burden". Known also as the "particular burden" or the "burden of adducing evidence".

(a) It refers to the obligation on a party of adducing appropriate evidence in support of some fact in dispute, so as to justify some finding of fact in favour of that party.

(b) A failure by a party to discharge the evidential burden brings the risk (but not always the certainty, however) of that party's failing on the issue, wholly or in part.

(c) Successful discharge of the evidential obligation may "shift" a similar burden so that it rests on the other party (*see* **11–12** below). *See*, e.g., *R*. v. *Immigration Appeal Tribunal, ex p. Bhatia* (1985).

(d) The appropriate standard of proof (*see* Chap. 7) is to be taken into account in determining whether or not the evidential burden has been discharged.

10. Examples of the burdens. The following examples should be noted:

(a) *P sues D for negligence.* The *general burden* of establishing negligence (i.e. a breach of D's legal duty to take care, resulting in damage, undesired by D, to P) rests on P. The *specific burden* (i.e. of proving specific acts on D's part allegedly amounting to negligence) rests on P. The *evidential burden* (i.e. of introducing evidence which supports each specific act alleged by P) rests on P. If D should allege contributory negligence by P, the *specific and evidential burdens* in relation to that allegation will rest on D.

(b) *P is prosecuted for the murder of Q*. The *general burden* of establishing P's guilt is on the prosecution (*see* **17** below). The *specific burden* (i.e. of proving that P unlawfully killed Q with malice aforethought, etc.) rests on the prosecution. The *evidential burden* (i.e. of adducing evidence of P's malice aforethought) rests on the prosecution. Assume that P pleads insanity; in that case the *specific burden* of proving insanity will rest on P (*see* **21** below).

11. The "shifting of the burden". This phrase indicates the moving, during the trial, of the burden of proof from one side to another, when one party has discharged his obligation of proof. The following examples illustrate the shifting of the burden:

(a) *The fact in issue is whether or not A is legitimate*. B, who wishes to establish this fact, adduces evidence which results in the presumption of A's legitimacy (*see* **10:24**). B's opponent, C, whose case rests on his denial of A's legitimacy, must now discharge his evidential burden by establishing, e.g., that A's presumed parents had been, in fact, judicially separated for twelve months before A's birth (which may destroy the presumption of legitimacy): *see Hetherington* v. *Hetherington* (1887). In a sense, the burden of proof here has shifted from B to C. *See* **10:3**.

(b) *P claims damages for negligence* from D, whose vessel has collided with P's ship. P establishes that his ship was at anchor and that there were normal weather conditions. D must show that the collision resulted from inevitable accident: *The Merchant Prince* (1892). In a sense, the legal burden has shifted and the burden of disproving negligence has fallen on D.

(c) *The operation of the rule contained in the maxim res ipsa loquitur* gives rise to an apparent shifting of the burden. *See* **10:27**. *See Lloyde* v. *W. Midlands Gas Board* (1971). P, who alleges negligence on D's part, must show that D was responsible for those acts said to constitute negligence. Since the working of the principle embodied in the maxim depends on an absence of explanation how the accident complained of occurred and on the assumption that it could not have occurred without negligence, D has the burden of showing that he used all reasonable care in the circumstances or that the manner of the accident precluded negligence on his part. *See Moore* v. *Fox & Sons* (1956); *The Kite* (1933) ("What the defendants have to do here is not to prove that their negligence did not cause this accident. What they have to do is to give a reasonable explanation which, if it be accepted, is an explanation showing that it happened without their negligence. They need not even go so far as that, because, if they give a reasonable explanation which is equally consistent with the accident happening without their negligence, they have again shifted the burden of proof back to the plaintiffs to show, as they have always to show from the beginning, that it was the negligence of the defendants that caused the accident": *per* Langton, J.) The following points relating to *res ipsa loquitur* should be noted:

(*i*) "There must be reasonable evidence of negligence, but where the thing is shown to be under the management of the defendant or his servants, and the accident is such as in the ordinary course of things does not happen if those who have the management use proper care, it affords reasonable evidence, in the absence of explanation by the defendant, that the absence arose from want of care": *per* Erle, C. J. in *Scott* v. *London and St. Katherine Docks Co.* (1865) (in which bags of sugar had fallen from a warehouse on to a passer-by).

(*ii*) Where *res ipsa loquitur* has been invoked as a principle, the plaintiff is entitled to have his case left to be decided by the jury and, in that event, if the defendant gives no evidence a verdict for the plaintiff should stand.

12. The "shifting of the burden": a caution. The doctrine of "shifting of the burden" has been criticised as being based on a fundamental misconception. Thus, in **11** (*a*) above, it is argued that what shifts is *not* the obligation; B has an obligation to prove one set of facts (relating to A's *legitimacy*); C has a subsequent obligation to prove a *different* set of facts (relating to A's *illegitimacy*). The specific burden on B differs from that on C. *See* **10:3.** Similarly, in **11** (*b*) above, the burden of proof on P is not *precisely* that resting on D. To that extent, the burden has not shifted; the plaintiff, it has been said, "lays down his load while the defendant picks up another load."

NOTE: *See* also 10:3 and, for further examples of the shifting of the burden, the Bills of Exchange Act 1882, s. 30 (2), *Stupple* v. *Royal Insurance Co.* (1971), in relation to the Civil Evidence Act 1968, s. 11 (2), as effectively shifting the legal burden of proof; and *Hunter* v. *Chief Constable of West Midlands* (1982).

The incidence of the burden in civil cases

13. The general burden of proof: the general rule. The rule is that the general burden of proof rests upon the person who asserts the affirmative of an issue.

(*a*) The rule is often stated in the form of the maxim *ei qui affirmat non ei qui negat incumbit probatio* ("the burden of proof lies upon he who affirms, not upon the person who denies").

(*b*) "It is an ancient rule founded on considerations of good sense and it should not be departed from without strong reasons": *per* Viscount Maugham in *Joseph Constantine Steamship Line Ltd.* v. *Imperial Smelting Co. Ltd.* (1942).

(*c*) The plaintiff must prove all the facts which constitute essential elements in his cause of action, i.e. he must prove all the facts in his statement of claim.

(*d*) The plaintiff must prove all those positive allegations necessary to rebut a defence.

(*e*) The defendant must prove any particular defences raised by him.

(*f*) The general burden of proof does not usually shift from the party on whom it was placed as a result of the substantive law or the pleadings: *Pickup* v. *Thames & Mersey Marine Insurance Co.* (1878).

14. The problem of a negative allegation. Assume that P asserts a negative.

(*a*) P asserts that D "did *not* repair the house in accordance with the terms of the covenant." This is, in essence, although not in strict form, a positive averment ("D allowed the house to fall into disrepair contrary to. . . .") couched in the form of a negative, and the legal burden would be carried by P. "It is not so much the form of the issue which ought to be considered, as the substance and effect of it . . . The plaintiff here says, 'You did not repair'; he might have said, 'You let the house become dilapidated,' . . .": *per* Lord Abinger in *Soward* v. *Leggatt* (1836).

(*b*) "If the assertion of a negative is an essential part of the plaintiff's case, the proof of the assertion still rests upon the plaintiff. The terms 'negative' and 'affirmative' are after all relative and not absolute": *per* Bowen, L. J. in *Abrath* v. *N.E. Railway* (1886). Assume that in an action for malicious prosecution, P alleges that D instituted proceedings against him with no reasonable or probable cause (i.e. a negative allegation). The burden is upon P to prove the fact of the prosecution and, prima facie, the want of reasonable and probable cause by D. The burden might then shift to D to show such cause. (Note here the "distribution of particular issues" among P and D; the general burden rests on P.)

15. The particular and evidential burden of proof: the general rule. This burden is usually on the party who bears the general burden. It may be stated more fully, thus:

(*a*) *Prior to the giving of any evidence*, the particular and evidential burden rests on the party asserting the affirmative of an issue, who would fail if no evidence at all were to be adduced.

(*b*) *Following the giving of any evidence*, the particular and evidential burden will rest on the party who would fail if no more evidence on either side were to be given. (This burden may, therefore, shift throughout the trial.)

16. Burden of proof where admissibility of evidence is in issue. The general rule is that in such a case the burden of proving the fact of admissibility rests on the party alleging this fact. Thus, where a party is attempting to prove a declaration of a deceased person, he has to prove *all* the conditions relating to the admissibility of evidence of that nature.

The incidence of the burden in criminal cases

17. The general burden of proof: the general rule. Given the presumption of innocence (*see* 10:**16**) and the rule that "he who asserts must prove", the general burden of proving the guilt of the accused rests on the prosecution. The prosecution must prove the commission of the offence, any requisite intent and the identity of the offender.

(*a*) The burden of proof generally rests on the prosecution even where it involves proof of a negative, e.g. absence of consent on a charge of assault: *R.* v. *Horn* (1912).

(*b*) Some of the few exceptional cases where the general burden lies on the accused are considered at **20–22** below.

18. The specific and evidential burdens. The general rule is that the burden of proving each and every separate issue (as ascertained by consideration of the substantive law) will rest on the prosecution. Note *Woolmington* v. *DPP* (1935).

(*a*) *The facts.* W was charged with murdering his wife. He claimed that he had shot her accidentally while threatening to shoot himself. He was convicted after a summing-up which contained the following statement by Swift, J.: "If the Crown satisfy you that this woman died at the prisoner's hands, then he has to show that there are circumstances to be found in the evidence which has been given from the witness box in this case which alleviate the crime, so that it is only manslaughter, or which excuse the homicide altogether by showing that it was a pure accident."

(*b*) *In the Court of Appeal. W's conviction was upheld.*

(*c*) *In the House of Lords. W's appeal was allowed* and his conviction quashed. "Throughout the web of English criminal law one golden thread is always to be seen, that *it is the duty of the prosecution to prove the prisoner's guilt* subject to what I have already said as to the defence of insanity and subject also to any statutory exception. If, at the end of and on the whole of the case, there is a *reasonable doubt*, created by the evidence given by either the prosecution or the prisoner, as to whether the prisoner killed the deceased with a malicious intention, the prosecution has not made out the case and the prisoner is entitled to an acquittal. *No matter what the charge or where the trial, the principle that the prosecution must prove the guilt of the prisoner is part of the common law of England and no attempt to whittle it down can be entertained* . . . If the jury are either satisfied with (the accused's) explanation or, upon a review of all the evidence, are left in reasonable doubt whether, even if his explanation be not accepted, the act was unintentional or provoked, the prisoner is entitled to be acquitted": *per* Viscount Sankey.

NOTE: *See* also *R.* v. *Bone* (1968), in which a *general direction* as to burden of proof was held insufficient; and *Yayasena* v. *The Queen* (1970)—discharge of the evidential burden requires "such evidence as, if believed and if left uncontradicted and unexplained, could be accepted by the jury as proof": *per* Lord Devlin.

19. Exceptional cases where the burden of proof may rest on the accused. As an exception to the general rule stated above, there are some few cases in which the burden of proof may fall on the defence. They are considered at **20–24 below**.

Exceptional situations in which the legal burden of proof is on the defence

20. Proof of special plea in bar. Proof relating to special plea in bar, such as *autrefois acquit* or *autrefois convict* (*see* 11:**18**), is on the accused.

21. Proof of insanity. The burden of proof of insanity, where such an issue is raised by the defence, is on the accused. *See* the Criminal Procedure (Insanity) Act 1964, s. 6; *R.* v. *Robertson* (1968) (where the burden of proof was on the prosecution under s. 4).

(*a*) "The jurors ought to be told in all cases that every man is presumed to be sane . . . until the contrary be proved to their satisfaction": *R.* v. *M'Naghten* (1843).

(*b*) The judge may rule that the accused has not discharged the burden if, in his view, there is insufficient evidence to justify a finding of insanity: *R.* v. *Windle* (1952).

(*c*) The burden of proving a preliminary issue of accused's unfitness to plead, if raised by the defence, is on the accused: *R.* v. *Podola* (1960). Similarly, in the case of a plea of diminished responsibility raised by defence, the burden is on the accused: *R*. v. *Dunbar* (1958).

22. Express statutory provision. The following examples should be noted.

(*a*) Prevention of Corruption Act 1916, s. 2, by which a gift to an official is deemed to have been given and received corruptly unless the contrary shall be proved. *See R*. v. *Evans-Jones and Jenkins* (1923); *R*. v. *Carr-Briant* (1943).

(*b*) Bills of Exchange Act 1882, s. 30 (2): ". . . If in an action on a bill it is admitted or proved that the acceptance, issue, or subsequent negotiation of the bill is affected with fraud, duress, or force and fear, or illegality, the burden of proof is shifted, unless and until the holder proves that, subsequent to the alleged fraud or illegality, value has in good faith been given for the bill."

(*c*) Homicide Act 1957, s. 2 (2): "On a charge of murder, it shall be for the defence to prove that the person charged is by virtue of this section [relating to diminished responsibility] not liable to be convicted of murder."

(*d*) Magistrates' Courts Act 1980, s. 101: "Where the defendant to an information or complaint relies for his defence on any exception, exemption, proviso, excuse or qualification, whether or not it accompanies the description of the offence or matter of complaint in the enactment creating the offence or on which the complaint is founded, the burden of proving the exception, exemption, proviso, excuse or qualification shall be on him; and this notwithstanding that the information or complaint contains an allegation negativing the exception, exemption, proviso, excuse or qualification."

(*e*) *R*. v. *Edwards* (1975) is of interest in this context.

(*i*) E was charged on indictment with selling intoxicating liquor without holding a licence, contrary to the Licensing Act 1964, s. 160 (1). The prosecution proved that E had sold intoxicating liquor, but brought forward no evidence to show that he had *not* got a licence. E was convicted and his appeal was dismissed. The Court of Appeal held that where an enactment makes the performing of a particular act an offence, subject to a proviso in favour of a particular person, or particular circumstances, whether or not the matter is peculiarly within the knowledge of the accused, there is no need for the prosecution to prove a prima facie case of lack of excuse or special circumstances. The persuasive burden of proof shifts to the defendant. This is an exception to the fundamental rule that the Crown must establish every element of the offence charged.

(*ii*) *Per* Lawton, L. J.: "In our judgment this line of authority (cited here) established that over the centuries the common law, as a result of experience and the need to ensure that justice is done both to the community and to defendants has evolved an exception to the fundamental rule of our criminal law that the prosecution must prove every element of the offence charged. This exception, like so much else in the common law, was hammered out on the anvil of pleading. It is limited to offences arising under enactments which prohibit the doing of an act save in specified circumstances or by persons of specified classes or with specified qualifications or with the licence or permission of specified authorities. Whenever the prosecution seeks to rely on this exception, the court must construe the enactment under which the charge was laid. If the true construction is that the enactment prohibits the doing of acts, subject to provisos, exceptions and the like, then the prosecution can rely on the exception."

(*f*) *See* also Prevention of Crime Act 1953, s. 1 (1); and the Misuse of Drugs Act 1971, s. 28 (2) (*see R*. v. *Champ* (1982)—the burden of proving that the defendant did not know that a plant she was cultivating was cannabis rested on her).

Exceptional situations in which the evidential burden of proof is on the defence

23. Principal situations in this category. Exceptional cases arise principally where there is an initial burden on the prosecution of proving some negative averment or disproving some possible defence. In such types of case a burden rests on the defence of adducing some evidence in support of any possible defences if such evidence has not emerged during the prosecution's case (although the burden of disproving them rests on the prosecution). "It would be quite unreasonable to allow the defence to submit, at the end of the prosecution's case, that the Crown had not proved affirmatively and beyond reasonable doubt that the accused was at the time of the crime, sober or not sleep-walking or not in a trance or blackout": *per* Devlin, J. in *Hill* v. *Baxter* (1958).

24. Legal and evidential burdens in criminal cases. *Per* Lord Simon in *DPP* v. *Morgan* (1976): "In the criminal law the probative burden of every issue lies on the prosecution (except for the single common law exception of insanity and on some statutory exceptions). But the prosecution may adduce evidence sufficient, at a certain stage in the trial, to discharge provisionally the probative burden and thus call for some explanation on behalf of the accused (generally by evidence; though forensic analysis discounting the prosecution's case sometimes suffices): the evidential burden has shifted, though the probative burden remains on the prosecution. Again, the accused may raise a case fit for the consideration of the jury on a fresh issue. For example, although the prosecution may have provisionally discharged the onus of proving an assault, the accused may raise an issue of self-defence in a form fit for the consideration of the jury: if so, the evidential burden of disproving it will shift to the prosecution, which has, of course also (once the defence is raised in a form fit for the consideration of the jury) the probative burden of disproving it. In this way *the evidential burden of proof will often shift backwards and forwards during a trial, the probative burden remaining throughout on the prosecution.*" *See* also *R.* v. *Newcastle-upon-Tyne Justices, ex p. Hindle* (1984); and *R.* v. *Hunt* (1986).

Progress test 6

1. What is meant by "proof" in the law of evidence? **(2)**
2. Explain the term "burden of proof". **(3)**
3. In what different senses may the phrase "burden of proof" be used? **(6)**
4. Explain the term "evidential burden". **(9)**
5. X sues Y for negligence. Upon whom rests (*a*) the general burden; (*b*) the evidential burden? **(10)**
6. Does the burden of proof ever shift during a trial? **(11–12)**
7. "The burden of proof is on the person who affirms, not the

person who denies." Comment. **(13)**

8. If the plaintiff asserts a negative, on whom does proof of the assertion rest? **(14)**

9. In a civil case where the admissibility of evidence is in issue, on whom does the burden of proving that fact fall? **(16)**

10. Upon whom is the legal burden of proof when the issue of insanity is raised in a trial for murder? **(21)**

11. Comment on the Magistrates' Courts Act 1980, s. 101, in relation to the burden of proof. **(22)**

7

The standard of proof and corroboration

Preliminary matters

1. The problem of standards of proof. Given a solution to the problems of the incidence of burden of proof, that is, on whom it rests and in what circumstances (*see* Chap. 6), a further question arises: *what is the necessary standard ("quantum", "level", "extent", "degree") of proof in the case of the legal burden?* For example:

(*a*) X is charged with the theft of Y's money. What standard of proof is needed to convince the court of X's guilt?

(*b*) H petitions for divorce on the ground of adultery by his wife, W. What standard of proof is appropriate in these circumstances?

These and similar questions are discussed in the *first part* of this chapter.

2. The problem of corroboration of evidence. Corroboration in the law of evidence involves the concept of *confirmation* of some fact by independent evidence. Consider the following problems:

(*a*) C, a child, gives sworn evidence in a trial. Must that evidence be corroborated?

(*b*) A_1 and A_2 are accomplices. Can the evidence of A_2 be admitted so as to corroborate that of A_1?

(*c*) Can X be convicted of an offence under the Perjury Act 1911, solely upon Y's evidence?

These and similar questions are discussed in the *second part* of this chapter.

3. Matters to be discussed. The following specific matters are discussed below:

(*a*) Different standards of proof relating to the legal burden of proof (*see* **4–6** below).

(*b*) Standard of proof required in criminal cases (*see* **7–8** below).

(*c*) Standard of proof required in civil cases (*see* **9–10** below).

(*d*) Standard of proof required in some special cases (*see* **11–15** below).

(*e*) Essential features of corroboration (*see* **16–20** below).

(*f*) Rules relating to corroboration (*see* **21–26** below).

(*g*) Corroboration as a matter of law (*see* **27–34** below).

(*h*) Corroboration as a matter of practice (*see* **35–41** below).

(*i*) Identification evidence (*see* **42–44** below).

Different standards of proof relating to the legal burden

4. General rules. Different rules apply to criminal and civil cases. In general, the traditional rules are that in *criminal cases* the standard of proof is *proof beyond reasonable doubt*; in *civil cases* the standard of proof is *proof on a preponderance of probabilities*. "The difference between the criminal standard of proof and the civil standard of proof is no mere matter of words: it is a matter of critical substance. No matter how grave the fact which has to be found in a civil case, the mind has only to be reasonably satisfied and has not, with respect to any matter in issue in such a proceeding, to attain that degree of certainty which is indispensable to the support of a conviction upon a criminal charge": *Rejfek* v. *McElroy* (1965).

5. No "absolute" standards. Within the standards stated at **4** above there are varying degrees of proof which will tend to differ in relation to the seriousness of the facts to be proved. *Per* Denning, L. J. in *Bater* v. *Bater* (1951): "The difference of opinion which has been evoked about the standard of proof in recent years may well turn out to be more a matter of words than anything else. It is of course true that by our law a higher standard of proof is required in criminal cases than in civil cases. But this is subject to the qualification that there is no absolute standard in either case. In criminal cases the charge must be proved beyond reasonable doubt, but there may be degrees of proof within that standard. . . . A civil court, when considering a charge of fraud will naturally require for itself a higher degree of probability than that which it would require when asking if negligence is established. It does not adopt so high a degree as a criminal court, even when it is considering a charge of a criminal nature; but still it does require a degree of probability which is commensurate with the occasion."

6. Continuing discussion relating to the nature of the standards. It will be seen below that there has been a continuing argument relating to the nature of standards of proof. The following areas of controversy should be noted:

(*a*) The phrase "beyond reasonable doubt" (*see* **8** below).

(*b*) The standard of proof required in criminal cases where the burden is on the defence and in civil cases where a criminal offence is alleged (*see* **12–13** below).

(*c*) The precise nature of the standard of proof required in matrimonial cases (*see* **14–15** below).

(*d*) Whether there exists a "third standard" of proof. Some writers point to the need for "convincing proof" that an instrument did not represent the parties' common intention, in a case of claim for rectification of contract (*see Josceleyne* v. *Nissen* (1970)). *See* also *Roberts & Co.* v. *Leicestershire C.C.* (1961) (rectification following unilateral mistake).

Standard of proof in criminal cases

7. Statement of the rule. In a criminal case the proper standard of proof is *proof beyond reasonable doubt*. *See R.* v. *Winsor* (1865); *Woolmington* v. *DPP* (1935) (*see* **6:18**).

(*a*) "The degree is well settled. It need not reach certainty, but it must carry a high degree of probability. *Proof beyond a reasonable doubt does not mean proof beyond the shadow of a doubt*. The law would fail to protect the community if it admitted fanciful possibilities to deflect the course of justice. If the evidence is so strong against a man as to leave only a remote possibility in his favour, which can be dismissed with the sentence 'of course it is possible but not in the least probable', the case is proved beyond reasonable doubt, but nothing short of that will suffice": *per* Denning, J. in *Miller* v. *Minister of Pensions* (1947).

(b) "What is a reasonable doubt . . . varies in practice according to the nature of the case and the punishment which may be awarded": *per* Lord Oaksey in *Preston-Jones* v. *Preston-Jones* (1951).

(c) In practice, therefore, it must be made clear to the jury that even though they may believe the accused to be probably guilty, they have to acquit should the evidence have led to their having any reasonable doubt on the matter.

(d) No precise formula is essential: it suffices that the judge's direction is in accordance with the appropriate principle, stated by Lord Diplock in *Walters* v. *R.* (1969): "If the jury are made to understand that they have to be satisfied and must not return a verdict against the defendant unless they feel sure, and that the onus is all the time on the prosecution and not on the defence, then whether the judge uses one form of language or another is neither here nor there." *See*, however, *R.* v. *Gourley* (1981)—rejection by the Court of Appeal of a judge's direction that the standard of proof required was "where you can say that you are satisfied—anything less will not do." In *R.* v. *Sweeney* (1983) the Court of Appeal rejected the phrase, "you must be satisfied so that you are reasonably sure"—use of "reasonably" sufficed to vitiate the direction. *See* also *R.* v. *Holland and Smith* (1983). Note also *McGreevey* v. *DPP* (1973)—no special direction on the standard of proof was called for even where the Crown's case rested on circumstantial evidence.

8. Problems in interpretation of "beyond reasonable doubt". These may be illustrated by the following statements:

(a) "Once a judge begins to use the words 'reasonable doubt' and to try to explain what is a reasonable doubt and what is not, he is much more likely to confuse the jury than if he tells them in plain language, 'It is the duty of the prosecution to satisfy you of the prisoner's guilt'.": *per* Lord Goddard in *R.* v. *Kritz* (1950).

(b) "If the jury is told that it is their duty to regard the evidence and see that it satisfies them so that they can feel sure when they return a verdict of guilty, that is much better than using the expression 'reasonable doubt' and I hope in future that this will be done": *per* Lord Goddard in *R.* v. *Summers* (1952).

(*c*) "Let us leave out of account, if we can, any expression such as 'giving the prisoner the benefit of the doubt'. It is not a question of giving the benefit of a doubt; *if the jury are left with any degree of doubt whether the prisoner is guilty, then the case has not been proved*": *per* Lord Goddard in *R.* v. *Onufrejczyk* (1955).

(*d*) "One would be on safe ground if one said in a criminal case to the jury: 'you must be satisfied beyond reasonable doubt', and one could also say, 'you, the jury, must be completely satisfied', or better still, 'you must feel sure of the prisoner's guilt'." *per* Lord Goddard in *R.* v. *Hepworth and Fearnley* (1955).

(*e*) "A reasonable doubt is a doubt which the particular jury entertain in the circumstances. Jury men themselves set the standard of what is reasonable in the circumstances . . . A reasonable doubt which a jury may entertain is not to be confined to a 'rational doubt', or a 'doubt founded on reason' ": *per* Barwick, C. J. in *Green* v. *The Queen* (1971).

(*f*) "Too close a judicial self analysis is not helpful in deciding the issue. When a judge begins to doubt whether or not he has reasonable doubt it obscures rather than clarifies his difficult task": *per* Lord Pearce in *Blyth* v. *Blyth* (1966). *See R.* v. *Yap Chuan Ching* (1976).

Standard of proof in civil cases

9. Statement of the rule. In a *civil case* the proper standard of proof is *proof on a preponderance of probabilities.* See *Newis* v. *Lark* (1571); *Bonnington Castings Co. Ltd.* v. *Wardlaw* (1956).

(*a*) "That degree is well settled. It must carry a reasonable degree of probability, not so high as is required in a criminal case. If the evidence is such that the tribunal can say: 'we think it more probable than not', the burden is discharged, but if the probabilities are equal it is not": *per* Denning, J. in *Miller* v. *Minister of Pensions* (1947).

(*b*) In practice the standard appears to require that the party upon whom the legal burden of proof rests will be entitled to a verdict in his favour if he has established by his evidence *some preponderance of probability in his favour*, i.e. if he has convinced the court that his version of the facts is more likely than that presented by the opposing party.

10. "Probability". What is "probable" may turn on the gravity of that which is alleged. "The very elements of gravity become a part of the whole range of circumstances which have to be weighed in the scale when deciding as to the balance of probabilities": *per* Morris, L. J. in *Hornal* v. *Neuberger Products* (1957). "In proportion as the offence is grave, so ought the proof to be clear": *per* Lord Denning in *Blyth* v. *Blyth* (1966).

Standard of proof in special cases

11. The problems. Difficulties concerning standard of proof have arisen, in particular, in the following circumstances:

(*a*) In criminal cases where burden of proof is on the accused (*see* **12** below).

(*b*) In civil cases in which a criminal offence is alleged (*see* **13** below).

(*c*) In matrimonial cases (*see* **14–15** below).

12. Criminal cases where burden of proof is on accused. In such cases the standard is the civil standard, i.e. proof on a preponderance of probability.

(*a*) In *R.* v. *Carr-Briant* (1943) X was charged under the Prevention of Corruption Act 1916, by which a person who was seeking a government contract and paid money to a government official was deemed to have given or paid that money corruptly. X was convicted after a summing-up in which the trial judge stated that X had to satisfy the jury beyond reasonable doubt that he had not acted corruptly. X's conviction was *quashed* by the Court of Appeal. "In our judgement in any case where, either by statute or at common law, some matter is presumed against an accused person 'unless the contrary is proved,' the jury should be directed that it is for them to decide whether the contrary is proved, that the burden of proof required is less than that required at the hands of the prosecution in proving the case beyond a reasonable doubt, and that the burden may be discharged by evidence satisfying the jury of the probability of that which the accused is called upon to establish": *per* Humphreys, J.

(*b*) Where insanity, unfitness to plead or diminished responsibility are pleaded *by the accused*, the civil standard of proof only is required: *see Sodeman* v. *R.* (1936); *R.* v. *Dunbar* (1958); *R.* v. *Podola* (1960).

(*c*) Where *the prosecution* raises the issue of unfitness to plead, the burden of proof must be satisfied beyond reasonable doubt: *see R.* v. *Podola* (1960); *R.* v. *Robertson* (1968).

13. Civil cases in which a criminal offence is alleged. The rule seems to be that no more than *proof on a preponderance of probabilities* is needed: *Hornal* v. *Neuberger Products* (1957).

(*a*) In *Hornal* v. *Neuberger Products* (1957) P had claimed damages for breach of warranty, or, in the alternative, for fraud. A director of the defendant company had falsely stated that a lathe sold to P had been re-conditioned by a named firm. The county court judge had been satisfied on a balance of probabilities that the alleged false statement had been made; he also stated, however, that he would *not* have been satisfied if the criminal standard of proof had been applied. The Court of Appeal held that the judge had applied the *correct* standard. "It would bring the law into contempt if a judge were to say that on the issue of warranty he finds that the statement was made, and on the issue of fraud he finds that it was not made": *per* Lord Denning.

(*b*) See *Re Dellow's W.T.* (1964) in which, in a case relating to mutual wills where a testator had been feloniously killed by the beneficiary, and the question arose as to the standard of proof in civil cases needed to establish a felonious killing, it was held that the gravity of the issue merely became *part of all the circumstances to be considered by the court* in deciding whether the burden of proof had been discharged.

(*c*) Note also exceptional cases such as *Judd* v. *Minister of Pensions* (1966) where, on a claim before a Pensions Appeal Tribunal by a member of H.M. Forces to a pension under Royal Warrant 1949, art. 4, which could be dismissed by the Minister only if he is satisfied "beyond reasonable doubt" that the disability was not due to or aggravated by war service, it was held that the standard of proof was the same as that resting upon the prosecution in a *criminal* trial. (Note that, in general, tribunal proceedings demand that cases be established on a balance of probabilities.)

14. In matrimonial cases: the background. The development of the law of evidence in relation to matters of this nature may be epitomised by reference to three important cases:

(a) *Ginesi* v. *Ginesi* (1948). In this case, relating to an application for discharge of a matrimonial order, it was stated that "adultery was regarded by the ecclesiastical courts as a quasi-criminal offence, and it must be proved with the same strictness as is required in a criminal case": *per* Tucker, L. J.

(b) *Preston-Jones* v. *Preston-Jones* (1951). In this case, relating to a petition for divorce on the ground of adultery, medical evidence was given showing that it was most improbable that the child to which H's wife had given birth was H's. It was held that, because of "the gravity and public importance" of the issues involved in cases of this nature, proof "beyond reasonable doubt" was necessary.

(c) *Blyth* v. *Blyth* (1966). In this case, relating to condonation in proceedings for divorce, the House of Lords allowed an appeal against an affirmation by the Court of Appeal of the dismissal of a petition because a requirement that the court should be satisfied that the adultery had not been condoned meant "satisfied beyond reasonable doubt". The House of Lords held that condonation need not be disproved "beyond reasonable doubt". *Per* Lord Denning: "So far as the grounds for divorce are concerned, the case, like any civil case, may be proved by a preponderance of probability, but the degree of probability depends on the subject-matter. In proportion as the offence is grave, so ought the proof to be clear."

15. In matrimonial cases: the present position. It would appear that *the "preponderance of probabilities" test should be applied in matrimonial cases*; *see dicta* of Edmund-Davies, L. J. in *Bastable* v. *Bastable* (1968) (in which it was stated, *obiter*, that the standard of proof required to satisfy the court that adultery had been committed was higher than the ordinary balance of probabilities required in normal civil litigation). Note also the Matrimonial Causes Act 1973, s. 1 (1), under which there is a burden on a petitioner for divorce to establish one of the factual situations listed as proof of the "irretrievable breakdown" of the marriage, and the standard of proof required is the balance of probabilities.

NOTE: *See R.* v. *Marlow Justices, ex p. O'Sullivan* (1983), in which the civil standard of proof (balance of probabilities) was applied to forfeiture of recognisance proceedings under the Magistrates' Courts Act 1980, s. 115.

Corroboration: the essential features

16. The essence of corroboration. Corroboration is, essentially, *independent, admissible and confirmatory evidence tending to support or confirm that an item of principal evidence is true.* It has no technical legal meaning. "Perhaps the best synonym is 'support' ": *DPP* v. *Hester* (1973). *See R.* v. *Beck* (1982)—corroboration must be independent evidence which confirms in a material particular not only the evidence that the crime was committed but, additionally, that the accused committed it. *See* also *R.* v. *Stainton* (1983).

17. Examples of corroboration. Corroboration, which is *not* limited to the evidence of another witness, may be perceived in the following examples:

(*a*) C_1, a child, gives *unsworn evidence* of having seen X in a named place on a certain date. C_2, another child, gives *sworn evidence* later that, in the company of C_1, he, too, saw X at the same place on the same date. The evidence of C_2 is corroborative of that given by C_1. *See DPP* v. *Hester* (1973); Children and Young Persons Act 1933, s. 38 (1).

(*b*) On A's trial for subornation of perjury, a letter which could be construed as subornation, is admitted as evidence and suffices as corroboration of other evidence to that effect. *See R.* v. *Threlfall* (1914).

(*c*) X was accused of having attempted the miscarriage of Y. Y's evidence was corroborated by evidence of X's silence in the face of an accusation by Y's father: "I have here the things you gave my daughter so as to produce abortion". *See R.* v. *Cramp* (1880); *R.* v. *Keeling* (1942).

(*d*) The Court of Appeal held that evidence of the refusal of accused to give a sample of his hair to be compared with hairs found at the scene of a robbery was evidence amounting to corroboration of the evidence of an accomplice: *R.* v. *Smith* (1985).

18. The general principle relating to corroboration. *In general, corroboration is not required*, so that evidence of one witness may suffice. As exceptions, however, corroboration may be required by law or as a matter of practice and in such cases the sole evidence of a single witness will not normally suffice. (". . . The power of lying is unlimited, the causes of lying and delusion are numerous, and many of them are unknown, and the means of detection are limited": Stephen.)

19. Importance of the distinction between corroboration required by law and as a matter of practice. The distinction is vital for the following reasons:

(*a*) In the case of corroboration *required by law*, i.e. by statute, the court *cannot act* on uncorroborated evidence.

(*b*) In the case of corroboration required merely *as a matter of practice*, the court *can act* upon uncorroborated evidence (after appropriate warning has been given to the jury: *see* **35** below).

20. Matters discussed below. The following topics are discussed in the remainder of this chapter:

(*a*) The rules relating to corroboration in the law of evidence (*see* **21–26** below).

(*b*) Corroboration required as a matter of law (*see* **27–34** below).

(*c*) Corroboration required as a matter of procedure (*see* **35–41** below).

The rules relating to corroboration

21. The content of corroboration. Corroboration must consist of admissible evidence. Irrelevant evidence will not cease to be inadmissible simply because it seems corroborative.

22. No prescribed form. In general, corroboration need not involve the testimony of a second witness (*see* **17** above). In a few cases, however, some of which are mentioned at **27** below, statute may necessitate the evidence of *two or more* credible witnesses.

23. There can be no self-corroboration. Corroboration "must be extraneous to the witness who is to be corroborated": *per* Lord Hewart in *R.* v. *Whitehead* (1929). *See* also *R.* v. *Lillyman* (1896).

(*a*) In the case of a complaint by a person alleging a sexual offence, which is made soon after the alleged offence, that complaint may be admitted to establish consistency; it is incapable of constituting corroboration of that person's testimony. *See* **38** below.

(*b*) *See* the Civil Evidence Act 1968, s. 6 (4) (*a*): ". . . a statement which is admissible in evidence by virtue of s. 2 or s. 3 of this Act shall not be capable of corroborating evidence given by the maker of the statement." *See* **17:24**.

(*c*) Corroboration can only be afforded to or by a witness who is otherwise to be believed. "If a witness's testimony falls of its own inanition, the question of his needing, or being capable of giving, corroboration does not arise" *per* Lord Hailsham in *DPP* v. *Kilbourne* (1973). "The essence of corroborative evidence is that one creditworthy witness confirms what another creditworthy witness has said": *per* Lord Morris in *DPP* v. *Hester* (1973). (On the matter of *lies* amounting to corroboration of the evidence of a prosecution witness, *see R.* v. *Lucas* (1981), *R.* v. *West* (1984).)

24. Corroboration must implicate the accused. In criminal cases, corroboration must confirm, in some material particular, not only that the crime has been committed, but also that the accused has committed it. "Evidence in corroboration must be independent testimony which affects the accused by connecting or tending to connect him with the crime. . . . It is sufficient if there is confirmation as to a material circumstance of the crime and the identity of the prisoner. . . . The corroboration need not be direct evidence that the accused committed the crime; it is sufficient if it is merely circumstantial evidence of his connection with the crime": *per* Lord Reading in *R.* v. *Baskerville* (1916). *See* also: *R.* v. *Knight* (1966) (evidence of Y's distressed condition soon after X was seen with Y may constitute corroboration of evidence identifying X as the assailant of Y); *R.* v. *Longstaff* (1977) (failure to direct jury that corroboration must implicate accused).

25. Corroboration may be constituted by the conduct of the person against whom it will operate. Thus, the accused's running away (*see R.* v. *Knight* (1966)) or giving a false alibi when questioned (*see Credland* v. *Knowles* (1951)) or similar conduct on his part (*see DPP* v. *Kilbourne* (1973)) might corroborate evidence against him. *See* also the Police and Criminal Evidence Act 1984, s. 62 (10) (at 20:**19** (*a*)) concerning corroboration resulting from the refusal of a person to provide an "intimate sample".

26. Judge and jury in relation to corroboration. The following points should be noted:

(*a*) Whether evidence is corroboration is a question of fact for the jury to determine.

(*b*) The judge may indicate that some evidence is *capable* of constituting corroboration; it is a misdirection, however, if he should seek to direct the jury as a matter of law that it *does* constitute corroboration: *R.* v. *Tragen* (1956).

(*c*) The judge must explain what is meant by corroboration, i.e. that it is constituted by independent evidence of some material fact implicating the accused and tending to confirm his guilt: *see R.* v. *Clynes* (1960). He need not use the word "corroboration": *see R.* v. *O'Reilly* (1967). He must *identify* for the jury the evidence which they are entitled to treat as corroboration: *R.* v. *Cullinane* (1984). *See R.* v. *Lucas* (1981).

(*d*) Where no corroborative evidence has been adduced, the judge must explain this to the jury: *R.* v. *Anslow* (1962). He must warn the jury that any evidence which is *likely* to be treated as corroboration by them when in law it cannot be treated as such, must not be considered as corroboration: *R.* v. *Goddard* (1962).

(*e*) Where the judge gives a misdirection relating to some piece of evidence as capable of constituting corroboration, the resulting conviction can be quashed: *R*. v. *Price* (1969).

Corroboration as a matter of law

27. General. There are some few exceptional cases in which statutory provisions preclude the court's acting on a single witness's evidence unless there is corroboration. These cases are set out at 28–34 below. In these cases an absence of corroborative evidence will be fatal to the prosecution or the claim.

28. Perjury Act 1911, s. 13. In the case of an indictment for perjury or subornation of perjury or other offence under the 1911 Act: "a person shall not be liable to be convicted of any offence against this Act or of any offence declared . . . to be perjury . . . solely upon the evidence of one witness as to the falsifying of any statement alleged to be false."

(*a*) Such corroboration may be, for example, by a second witness or admission by accused (*see R*. v. *Hook* (1858)).

(*b*) Inconsistent statements made by accused are not, in themselves, sufficient corroboration.

29. Treason. A conviction for high treason requires (unless the accused confesses) at least two witnesses. *See* the Treason Act 1795, s. 1.

30. Personation at an election. At least two witnesses are needed on a charge of personation at an election: Representation of the People Act 1983, s. 168 (5).

31. Procuration of women or girls. A charge of procuration for purposes of prostitution or unlawful sexual intercourse (*see* the Sexual Offences Act 1956, ss. 2, 3, 4, 22, 23) requires at least two witnesses, unless the witness is corroborated in some material particular by some evidence which implicated the accused.

32. Affiliation proceedings. Under the Affiliation Proceedings Act

1957, s. 4, if the case depends on the evidence of the complainant mother, she must be corroborated in some material particular by some other evidence to the satisfaction of the magistrates (or the Crown Court) before an affiliation order may be made against the putative father. If the case is proved without relying on the mother's evidence, corroboration is no longer required.

(*a*) Evidence of acts of familiarity between the parties might amount to corroboration: *see Moore* v. *Hewitt* (1947).

(*b*) Evidence of mere opportunity for sexual intercourse will not suffice: *Burbury* v. *Jackson* (1917).

(*c*) Letters from the defendant to the mother may constitute corroboration: *see Jeffery* v. *Johnson* (1952).

33. Driving a motor vehicle at a speed greater than the maximum allowed. *See* the Road Traffic Regulation Act 1984, s. 89 (2), by which a person accused of driving above the maximum speed shall not be convicted solely on the evidence of one witness to the effect that *in his opinion* accused was driving at a speed exceeding the limit.

34. The unsworn evidence of a child. *See* 4:17. A child of tender years who understands the duty of telling the truth, but does not understand the nature of an oath, may give *unsworn* evidence in a criminal trial: Children and Young Persons Act 1933, s. 38. But under that same section the accused cannot be convicted unless that evidence is corroborated by some other material evidence which implicates him. For evidence of children in committal proceedings for sexual offences, *see* the Magistrates' Courts Act 1980, s. 103.

(*a*) The *unsworn evidence* of a child *can be corroborated* by the *sworn evidence* of another child (and vice versa): *DPP* v. *Hester* (1973).

(*b*) The *unsworn evidence* of a child *cannot be corroborated* by the *unsworn evidence* of another child: *DPP* v. *Hester* (1973). *See* also *R.* v. *Campbell* (1956).

(*c*) As a general rule the precautions usually adopted for children of tender years should be adopted with *any* witness under 14: *R.* v. *Khan* (1981).

Corroboration as a matter of practice

35. General. There are some exceptional circumstances in which, although lack of corroboration is not *always* fatal, the judge has the duty of warning the jury of the fact that there is an absence of corroboration *and* of the danger in acting upon uncorroborated evidence. These are set out at **36–41** below. Note, however, that where a warning *has* been given, a judge (alone) and jury *are entitled* to act on evidence which has *not* been corroborated.

36. Claims against the estate of a deceased person. "The statement of a living man is not to be disbelieved because there is no corroboration, but we must take into account the necessary absence through death of one of the parties to the transaction, and in considering the statement of the survivor it is natural to look for corroboration in support of it; but if the evidence given by the living man does bring conviction to the tribunal which has to try the question, then there is no rule of law which prevents that being acted upon. . . .": *per* Hannen, J. in *Re Hodgson* (1885).

37. Sworn evidence of children. *See* **34** above. The sworn evidence of children need not be corroborated as a matter of law. The jury should be warned, however, of the *risk* of acting on the uncorroborated evidence of children. *See R.* v. *Dossi* (1918); *R.* v. *Cleal* (1942); *R.* v. *Campbell* (1956); *R.* v. *Sawyer* (1959); *DPP* v. *Hester* (1973); *R.* v. *Buck* (1981).

38. Sexual offences. *See* **31** above for corroboration as essential as a *matter of law* in the case of some offences under the Sexual Offences Act 1956. In other sexual cases, corroboration has come to be regarded as a *matter of practice*. *See* **13:22**.

 (*a*) It has been suggested that for all practical purposes the rule has become a rule of law: *see R.* v. *Trigg* (1963). *See* also *R.* v. *O'Reilly* (1967).

 (*b*) The evidence will amount to corroboration only if it supports complainant's allegation in some material particular *and* if it clearly implicates accused.

 (*c*) Evidence of a complaint made by the victim of a sexual offence soon after the offence is admissible but does *not* amount to corroboration (since it is, in effect, not independent corroboration). *See R.* v. *Goddard* (1962).

39. Matrimonial cases. That testimony alleging a matrimonial offence should be corroborated was a rule of practice, not of law. The concept of a matrimonial "offence" has disappeared from English law after reforms in the law of divorce and domestic proceedings before magistrates.

40. Accomplices (1): *Davies* v. *DPP*(1954). The House of Lords considered a case in which X, a witness for the prosecution, and the accused, Y, had been involved in a fight between rival gangs, during which Z was stabbed to death. X had been acquitted previously of the murder of Z, for which murder Y was being tried. There was no proof that X knew before the stabbing incident that Y possessed a knife; the trial judge did not treat X as an accomplice to Z's murder. It was held by the Court of Appeal and the House of Lords that X was *not* an accomplice. Y's appeal against conviction was dismissed. Lord Simonds, L.C. formulated three propositions:

(*a*) "In a criminal trial where a person who is an accomplice gives evidence on behalf of the prosecution, it is the duty of the judge to warn the jury that, although they may convict upon his evidence, it is dangerous to do so unless it is corroborated."

(*b*) "This rule, although a rule of practice, now has the force of a rule of law."

(*c*) "Where the judge fails to warn the jury in accordance with this rule, the conviction will be quashed, even if in fact there be ample corroboration of the evidence of the accomplice, unless the appellate court can apply the proviso to [s. 2 (1) of the Criminal Appeal Act 1968]."

The term "accomplices" was considered by Lord Simonds as comprising three categories (which "would be inconvenient for any authority other than the legislature to disturb"): persons who are *participes criminis* in respect of the actual crime charged ("the natural and primary meaning of the term 'accomplice' "); receivers of stolen goods giving evidence at the trial of those alleged to have stolen the goods; parties to other crimes alleged to have been committed by accused of which similar fact evidence (*see* 14:3) would be considered admissible.

41. Accomplices (2): other points. The following matters should be noted.

(*a*) "The rule, it will be observed, applies only to witnesses for the prosecution": *per* Lord Simonds, L.C., in relation to the term "accomplices". It may be that this is unduly restrictive. Excluded would be, for example, a *particeps criminis* who is a co-accused giving evidence against the accused person. *See R.* v. *Prater* (1960), in which P, W and others were charged with conspiracy to defraud. W gave evidence on his own behalf which implicated P. No warning concerning corroboration was given and P was convicted. The Court of Criminal Appeal stated that it was "desirable", but not essential, to give a warning in such a case. Also excluded from operation of the rule would be an *agent provocateur* (*see*, e.g., *R.* v. *Bickley* (1909)) and the child victim of a sexual assault (*see R.* v. *Pitts* (1912)). Note *R.* v. *Bagley* (1980) in which the Court of Appeal held that there was no rule of law that when a co-defendant gave evidence in his own defence against another defendant a full warning against uncorroborated evidence should be given. It was for the judge to decide what warning, if any, was proper. *See* also *R.* v. *Knowlden* (1983); *R.* v. *Smith* (1985).

(*b*) In *DPP* v. *Kilbourne* (1973) the accused was convicted on counts relating to several sexual offences against a group of four boys, all of whom gave sworn evidence. Because the evidence of one group of boys was admitted in relation to the charges concerning the other group, it was held by the House of Lords that it was not material that each boy was technically an accomplice in relation to the offence committed by accused against him, so that the evidence of each boy was capable of corroborating that of the others.

(*c*) When evidence against a defendant is given by possible accomplices, it is not sufficient for the judge merely to direct the jury as to the need for corroboration; he must indicate those parts of the evidence which can properly be regarded as corroboration: *R.* v. *Charles* (1976). *See* also *R.* v. *Reeves* (1978).

(*d*) If evidence alleged by the prosecution to be corroborative is said by the defence to be the result of conspiracy (i.e., collusion between witnesses), then unless the judge exercises his discretion to exclude it, the issue must be decided by the jury: *R.* v. *Johannsen* (1977).

(*e*) The words used by a judge who considers the usual form of warning inappropriate in a particular case must be such that the risks and dangers are explained in plain and simple language; thus, "You need to consider his evidence with a great deal of care indeed" was *not* strong enough to amount to a warning: *R.* v. *Vincent and Taylor* (1983).

NOTE: On the matter of the uncorroborated evidence of patients detained in a secure hospital under the Mental Health Act 1983, *see R.* v. *Spencer* (1986). In this case the Court of Appeal stated that the categories of evidence requiring a full corroboration warning to the jury are closed, and that so far as the evidence of mental patients was concerned, a judge was not obliged to give a full corroboration warning; his direction that such evidence was to be approached "with great caution" was adequate. (*R.* v. *Bagshaw* (1984) was overruled.) (The House of Lords upheld the judgement.)

A note on identification evidence in criminal proceedings

42. Evidence of identification and corroboration. In general, corroboration is *not required* in a case turning on evidence of identification of the accused. In *Arthurs* v. *A.-G. for N. Ireland* (1971) the House of Lords had stated that a summing-up need *not* contain any general warning on the basis of identification evidence, at any rate where the accused was someone known to the identifying witness. *See* also *R.* v. *Long* (1973). Note, however, a comment of the Criminal Law Revision Committee (11th Report, 1976) that mistaken identification is "by far the greatest cause of actual or possible wrong convictions."

43. Guide-lines in criminal cases. In *R.* v. *Turnbull* (1977) the Court of Appeal convened a full court of five judges to consider several appeals against conviction where the cases against appellants were based wholly or substantially on identification evidence. (Some general similarities may be evident in the resulting guide-lines and the rationale of rules of corroboration.) Guide-lines were formulated in the court's judgment, delivered by Lord Widgery, C.J.

(*a*) When summing up in a case involving disputed identity, the judge must warn the jury of the special need for caution before convicting the accused in reliance on the correctness of the identification(s). He should instruct the jury as to the reason for the need for such a warning and should make reference to the possibility that a mistaken witness can be a convincing one. Provided this is done in clear terms the judge need not use any particular form of words.

(*b*) The judge should direct the jury to examine closely the circumstances in which the identification by each witness came to be made. He should remind the jury of any specific weaknesses which had appeared in the identification evidence.

(*c*) The judge should leave identification evidence to the jury only where the quality of such evidence is good.

(*d*) Where the quality of the identifying evidence is poor ("as, for example, when it depends solely on a fleeting glance or on a longer observation made in difficult conditions"), the judge should withdraw the case from the jury and direct an acquittal unless there is other evidence which goes to support the correctness of the identification. ("This may be corroboration in the sense lawyers use that term, but it need not be so if its effect is to make the jury sure that there has been no mistaken identification.")

(*e*) The judge should identify to the jury the evidence which he adjudges is capable of supporting the evidence of identification.

(*f*) Care should be taken by the judge when directing the jury about the support for an identification which may be derived from the fact that they have rejected an alibi. (Note that an "alibi" is set up by the accused when he alleges that, at the time of the commission of the offence with which he is charged, he was "elsewhere".) The jury should be reminded that proving the accused has told lies about where he was at the material time does not by itself prove that he was where the identifying witness says he was.

44. Case law following *R*. v. *Turnbull*. The following decisions of the Court of Appeal should be noted.

(*a*) *R.* v. *Keane* (1977). In *R*. v. *Turnbull* (1977), the court stated that "a failure to follow these guide-lines is likely to result in a conviction being quashed and will do so if in the judgment of this court on all the evidence the verdict is either unsatisfactory or unsafe." In *R*. v. *Keane*, the appellant had been convicted of causing grievous bodily harm with intent; the trial had turned on identity. The trial judge's summing-up had *not* complied with the guide-lines in *R*. v. *Turnbull* and the conviction was quashed. *Per* Scarman, L.J.: "It would be wrong to interpret or apply *Turnbull* inflexibly. It imposes no rigid pattern, establishes no catechism, which a judge in his summing-up must answer if a verdict of guilty is to stand. But it does formulate a basic principle and sound practice . . . Unfortunately the summing-up of this case falls short of the requirements of sound practice."

(*b*) *R*. v. *Hunjan* (1979). A conviction for possessing and supplying a controlled drug contrary to the Misuse of Drugs Act 1971, s. 4, was quashed because the *Turnbull* warnings were not given, or in so far as they were given were not given adequately.

(*c*) *R*. v. *Weeder* (1980). A trial judge had not erred in directing the jury that one identifying witness could support identification by another.

(*d*) *R*. v. *Curry and Keeble* (1983). The *Turnbull* direction was intended to deal only with cases of "fleeting encounters".

(*e*) *R*. v. *Nelson and McLeod* (1983). There is no need for a jury to be given the *Turnbull* warning where there had been a continued assault punctuated by two short gaps during which time the assailants had retreated and the victim had identified them shortly after, even if identification is in issue.

(*f*) *R*. v. *Tyson* (1985). The warning about the special need for caution before convicting in reliance upon identification evidence was considered necessary even where the opportunities for observation were good and witness was convinced that he had identified defendant correctly.

Progress test 7

1. What is the proper standard of proof in criminal cases?   (**7**)

2. Outline some of the problems that have arisen in the interpretation of the phrase "beyond reasonable doubt".   (**8**)

3. What is the proper standard of proof in civil cases?   (**9**)

4. What is the required standard of proof where the burden of proof is on accused?   (**12**)

5. Comment on the decision in *R*. v. *Carr-Briant* (1943).   (**12**)

6. What is the proper standard of proof where the prosecution raises the issue of unfitness to plead?   (**12**)

7. Comment on the decision in *Hornal* v. *Neuberger Products* (1957).   (**13**)

8. What is the importance of the decision in *Blyth* v. *Blyth* (1966)?   (**14**)

9. What is meant by "corroboration"?   (**16, 17**)

10. State the general principle relating to corroboration.   (**18**)

11. Is "self-corroboration" recognised?   (**23**)

12. Explain the statement: "Corroboration must implicate the accused."   (**24**)

13. Outline some of the duties of judge and jury in relation to corroboration.   (**26**)

14. Comment on the Perjury Act 1911, s. 13, as it relates to corroboration.   (**28**)

15. When is corroboration needed in affiliation proceedings?   (**32**)

16. Enumerate some of the cases in which corroboration is required as a matter of practice.   (**36–39**)

17. Comment on *Davies* v. *DPP* (1954) and *R*. v. *Prater* (1960).   (**40, 41**)

18. Outline the guide-lines set out in *R*. v. *Turnbull* (1977).   (**43**)

8
Documentary evidence

Preliminary matters

1. The nature of documentary evidence: a reminder. *See* 2:**17** (*b*) and 2:**19**. Documentary evidence is evidence of some fact brought to the knowledge of the court resulting from an inspection of some document produced to the court. Such evidence may be adduced, for example, where a party is relying on the contents of a lease so as to prove some fact in issue (*see* 2:**4**). Two matters of proof may generally arise, each of which may involve some of the problems discussed in this chapter:

(*a*) The party must prove the *contents* of the document (e.g. by producing the document itself where that is possible) (*see* **7** below).

(*b*) The party must prove the *validity or due execution* of that document (*see* **18** below).

2. An added problem: the admissibility of extrinsic evidence. Assume that a party wishes to contradict the terms of a transaction contained in a document. May he bring forward *extrinsic evidence*, i.e. of terms *other than those mentioned* in the document? May he give evidence of the *meaning of terms* used in the document itself? These problems are discussed at **22–30** below.

3. What is a "document"? In general, a document may be said to be any permanent record of a fact made with the intention of recording that fact or transmitting it. *See*, e.g., *H.* v. *Schering Chemicals* (1983).

(*a*) This general definition would include, e.g. paper on which words are written, stamped or typed.

(*b*) The Civil Evidence Act 1968, s. 10 (1), gives an extended definition, whereby "document" includes, in addition to a document in writing, any map, plan, graph or drawing; any photograph; any disc, tape, sound track or other device in which sounds or other data (not being visual images) are embodied so as to be capable (with or without the aid of some other equipment) of being reproduced therefrom; and any film (including microfilm), negative, tape or other device in which one or more visual images are embodied so as to be capable of being reproduced therefrom. *See Grant* v. *Southwestern and Country Properties* (1974)—tape recording of information held to be a "document" which could be produced for inspection.

4. Documents, "private" and "public". For purposes of the law of evidence, documents may be classified as either *private* or *public*.

(*a*) *Private documents.* These include wills, deeds, etc.

(*b*) *Public documents.* These are documents made for the purpose of the public using them and being able to refer to them: *Sturla* v. *Freccia* (1880). They include, e.g. statutes, court records, registers of births, marriages and deaths. *See* 18:17.

5. Matters to be discussed. The following matters are discussed below:

(*a*) Proving the contents of a document (*see* **6–9** below).

(*b*) Principal exceptions to the rule relating to proof of contents (*see* **10–17** below).

(*c*) Proof of execution of private documents (*see* **18–21** below).

(*d*) Extrinsic evidence in relation to documents (*see* **22–23** below).

(*e*) Extrinsic evidence as a substitute for documents (*see* **24–25** below).

(*f*) Extrinsic evidence in variation or contradiction of a document (*see* **26–27** below).

(*g*) Extrinsic evidence as an aid to interpretation (*see* **28–30** below).

Proving the contents of a document

6. General. Given a party's reliance on the contents of some document so as to prove a fact, that party must generally prove contents *and* due execution. The nature of the proof required may depend on whether the document is private or public (*see* **4** above).

7. The general rule. In general, the party relying on the contents of a document must give evidence usually involving the production of the original document, which is *primary evidence* of its contents: *see Macdonell* v. *Evans* (1852). Examples of the rule in operation are as follows:

(*a*) *Macdonell* v. *Evans* (1852). In an action on a bill of exchange, a witness called by P was asked in cross-examination by D's counsel, who produced a letter purporting to have been written by witness: "Did you not write that letter as an answer to a letter which charged you with forgery?" P's counsel objected on the ground that this was an attempt to get in evidence of the other letter's contents without production of the document itself. The objection was *upheld*. "If the contents of an absent document may be repeated under pretence of testing the credit or the memory of a witness, it will always be in the power of parties to evade the rule which requires the best evidence to be produced, viz, the instrument itself": *per* Cresswell, J.

(*b*) *R.* v. *Stevenson and Hulse* (1971). The prosecution sought to adduce evidence consisting of tape recordings of the defendants' voices. The defence claimed that these recordings were not original, and this issue was tried in the jury's absence. It was held that as it was not shown that the recordings were original, they were *not admissible* in evidence.

NOTE: The following limitations to the rule should be noted: (1) it applies only where the words in a document are relied on *directly* (*see R.* v. *Holy Trinity, Hull* (1827));
(2) it does not prohibit a reference to a document's *terms* for purposes of identifying it (*see Boyle* v. *Wiseman* (1855)).

8. Kinds of primary evidence of contents. Three kinds of primary evidence may be considered: the original document; a copy of some document which must be enrolled; parties' admissions.

(a) *Original document.* This is, obviously, the best primary evidence of contents. In relation to the question: "Which of a number of documents may be said to be the 'original'?", the following points should be noted:

(i) Where an agreement is drawn up in two identical documents and *each* is executed by *both parties*, both documents are treated as "duplicate originals": *Forbes* v. *Samuel* (1913).

(ii) The top and carbon copies of an *unsigned document* are treated as originals. But if a document has been *signed* and sent off, an unsigned carbon is treated as a copy.

(iii) In the case of a deed and counterpart, each executed by only one party, they are not treated as duplicate originals. Each will be treated as a *separate* original.

(iv) See also *Colling* v. *Treweek* (1827); *R.* v. *Regan* (1887).

(b) *Copy of document which must be enrolled.* Some private documents, e.g. a probate, must be filed in a public office. In such a case the copy issued by the public office may be treated as the original and may be received as primary evidence. *See Re Harrison* (1885); *Re Battie-Wrightson* (1920).

(c) *Parties' admissions.* Where a party admits (orally, in writing, or by conduct) the contents of a document, those admissions are primary evidence against him. In such a case the opposing party need not produce the original. *See Slatterie* v. *Pooley* (1840); *Price* v. *Woodhouse* (1849).

9. Kinds of secondary evidence which can be given in relation to a document's contents. It will be recalled (*see* 2:22 (b)) that secondary ("inferior") evidence is that which, in itself, suggests the existence of other, more original, evidence. Thus, an example of "substitutionary" evidence of this nature is the testimony of a witness who has read a document in question; that testimony is secondary evidence of the document's contents.

(a) Secondary evidence of the contents of *private* documents is not generally admissible if primary evidence is available: *Jones* v. *Tarleton* (1842).

(b) There are, in general, no degrees of such secondary evidence (but note, as an exception, the case of *public* documents—*see* **15** below—and the fact that bankers' books are usually proved by examined copies—*see* **16** below), so that although a party may have a *copy* of a document, he may give *oral evidence* of it: *Doe d. Gilbert* v. *Ross* (1840).

(*c*) Secondary evidence may take the following forms, for example:

(*i*) *Examined copies*, i.e. sworn as to accuracy by a witness who has checked with the original. See *Rolf* v. *Dart* (1809).

(*ii*) *Certified copies*, i.e. copies signed and certified by an officer having charge of the original. *See* the Evidence Act 1851, s. 14.

(*iii*) *Office copies*, i.e. copies of judicial documents made by the officer having charge of the original. *See* O. 38, r. 10 (1).

(*iv*) *Government Printer's copies*, i.e. copies of statutes, etc.

(*v*) *Printed or lithographed copies*—which are secondary evidence of the original.

(*vi*) *Drafts, abstracts, etc.*

(*vii*) *Copies of copies.* See *Everingham* v. *Roundell* (1838); *R.* v. *Collins* (1960).

(*viii*) *Oral evidence of contents*.

Principal exceptions to the general rule relating to proof of contents

10. General. There are seven principal sets of circumstances constituting very wide exceptions to the general rule formulated at **7** above. Should one of these exceptions apply, then secondary evidence of a document may be given (and it should be recalled—*see* **9** (*b*) above—that generally there are no degrees of secondary evidence). The exceptions arise as follows:

(*a*) Where, in civil proceedings, a party fails to comply with a notice to produce (*see* **11** below).

(*b*) Where the original is in possession of a third party who justifiably refuses to produce it (*see* **12** below).

(*c*) Where the original has been lost or destroyed (*see* **13** below).

(*d*) Where production of the original is impossible or very inconvenient (*see* **14** below).

(*e*) Where the original is a public document (*see* **15** below).

(*f*) Where the Bankers' Books Evidence Act 1879, ss. 3–5, applies (*see* **16** below).

(*g*) Where the Civil Evidence Act 1968, ss. 2, 4, 5, applies (*see* **17** below).

11. Party in civil proceedings failing to comply with notice to produce. In this case the party serving notice may put a copy in evidence.

(*a*) A notice to produce does not generally compel production. Where a party wishes to compel production a *subpoena duces tecum* (i.e. "attend and bring the document in question with you") should be served on the opponent (but *not* in a *criminal* case).

(*b*) Notice to produce may be served *during* a trial if the original is in court: *Dwyer* v. *Collins* (1852).

(*c*) Notice to produce is *not required* where the document in question is itself a notice (e.g. notice to quit) or where notice to produce is otherwise excused (e.g. where an opponent admits the loss of a document: *see R.* v. *Haworth* (1830)) or where, from the very nature of the case, the opponent must have known that he was required to produce the original (e.g. certificate of insurance in a trial relating to driving without being insured).

(*d*) *See* O. 24; O. 27.

12. Original in possession of third party who, with justification, refuses to produce it. The third party may be out of the jurisdiction, or he may hold the document as trustee or solicitor for another: *see Mills* v. *Oddy* (1834).

(*a*) The principle will not apply where the third party has been served with a *subpoena duces tecum* and unlawfully fails to obey (in which case he may be committed for contempt).

(*b*) *See R.* v. *Inhabitants of Llanfaethly* (1853).

13. Original has been lost or destroyed. In such a case adequate proof of loss or destruction must be given before production is excused and it must be shown that a proper search has been made. *See Brewster* v. *Sewell* (1820).

14. Production of original is physically impossible or very inconvenient. Examples: an inscription on a wall, or document in the custody of a foreign court. *See Mortimer* v. *M'Callan* (1840); *Owner* v. *Bee Hive Spinning Ltd.* (1914).

15. Original is a public document. *See* **4** (*b*) above. Public documents may be proved by secondary evidence, but the appropriate form of proof is necessary. (*See*, e.g., the Child Abduction and Custody Act 1985, s. 22.) Note the following:

(*a*) *Public Acts of Parliament:* judicial notice is taken of these Acts (*see* **9:22** (*a*)).

(*b*) *Private Acts of Parliament, Orders in Council, Statutory Instruments:* proved by production of a Queen's Printer's copy.

(*c*) *Bye-laws:* proved by a printed copy endorsed by the clerk to a local authority.

(*d*) *Treaties, other acts of state:* proved by an examined copy.

(*e*) *Judgments of Supreme Court:* proved by production of a copy.

(*f*) *Convictions:* proved by a certified copy of the court record, signed by the clerk or other person having custody of it. *See*, e.g., the Police and Criminal Evidence Act 1984, s. 73 (1) (at **15:23**).

16. Bankers' books. *See* **18:22**. An examined copy of an entry in a bankers' book kept in the ordinary course of business, where the book is in the custody of the bank, is received as prima facie evidence of that entry: Bankers' Books Evidence Act 1879.

(*a*) The Act applies to civil *and* criminal cases. The provisions of the Act do not extend, however, to investigations to establish whether or not there is a case against a person: *R.* v. *Nottingham City Justices, ex p. Lynn* (1984). *See* also *Bonalumi* v. *Home Department* (1985).

(*b*) Section 7 of the Act allows a party to legal proceedings to apply for an order to inspect and take copies. *See* O. 38, r. 13.

(*c*) Copy letters concerning bank accounts are *not* "bankers' books" within the Act: *R.* v. *Dadson* (1983). "Bankers' books" include records of customers' transactions and details of cheques recorded on microfilm: *Barker* v. *Wilson* (1980).

17. Civil Evidence Act 1968, ss. 2, 4, 5. "Where in any civil proceedings a statement contained in a document is proposed to be given in evidence by virtue of sections 2, 4 or 5 of this Act, it may, subject to any rules of court, be proved by the production of the document or (whether or not that document is still in existence) by the production of a copy of that document, or of the material part thereof, authenticated in such a manner as the court may approve": s. 6 (1).

Proof of execution of private documents

18. General. In the case of a *public* document, mere production of an appropriately certified or sealed copy is sufficient proof of execution: *see* Evidence Act 1845, s. 1; Evidence Act 1851, s. 14. But in the case of a *private* document, the court requires to be satisfied of its having been duly executed. Due execution may be proved by:

(*a*) proof of handwriting (*see* **19** below);

(*b*) proof of attestation, where that is legally necessary for a document (*see* **20** below);

(*c*) proof by presumption (*see* **21** below).

19. Proof of handwriting. See 15:32 (*b*). In the case of an unattested document, or of an attested document which does not legally require attestation, handwriting and signature may be proved by the following methods:

(*a*) The evidence of the writer.

(*b*) The evidence of a witness who saw the document signed.

(*c*) The evidence of a witness "who has seen the party write on some other occasion, or he has corresponded with him and transactions have taken place between them, upon the faith that letters purporting to have been written or signed by them have been so written or signed": *Doe d. Mudd* v. *Suckermore* (1837).

(*d*) By comparison. "Comparison of a disputed writing with any writing proved to the satisfaction of the judge to be genuine shall be permitted to be made by witnesses; and such writings, and the evidence of witnesses respecting the same, may be submitted to the court and jury as evidence of the genuineness or otherwise of the writing in dispute": Criminal Procedure Act 1865, s. 8. (Note that this Act applies to civil *and* criminal proceedings.) The comparison may be made by judge, jury (*see* s. 8 above) or by an ordinary witness who may, but need not, be an expert. *See R.* v. *Silverlock* (1894). ("Is he skilled? Has he an adequate knowledge? Looking at the matter practically, if a witness is not skilled the judge will tell the jury to disregard his evidence": *per* Lord Russell); *R.* v. *Smith* (1909). (For comments on expert witnesses, *see* 15:34–35.)

(*e*) Admissions of the party against whom the document has been tendered.

NOTE: A jury should not be asked to compare handwriting without an expert's assistance: *R.* v. *O'Sullivan* (1969). The standard of proof to be applied by a judge in deciding whether writing is genuine, for the purposes of the Criminal Procedure Act 1865, was said to be the *civil* standard of proof: *R.* v. *Angeli* (1978). In *R.* v. *Ewing* (1983), however, the Court of Appeal held that the standard should have been "beyond reasonable doubt".

20. Proof of attestation. By "attestation" is meant the signing of a document by one who is not a party to it, but who is a witness to the signature of another. (Thus, the Wills Act 1837, s. 9 (as substituted by the Administration of Justice Act 1982, s. 17), requires, in the case of wills and codicils, the attestation of two witnesses present at the same time; no specific form of attestation is necessary.)

(*a*) In the case of proof of execution of a will, one of the attesting witnesses must be called to prove attestation: *Forster* v. *Forster* (1864).

(*b*) Where the absence of all attesting witnesses is explained, other evidence may be admissible.

(*c*) Where an attesting witness is dead or beyond the jurisdiction or cannot be discovered, secondary evidence of execution can be given by proof of his handwriting (but only if evidence of execution cannot be obtained by any other evidence): *Clarke* v. *Clarke* (1879).

(*d*) In the case of a document other than a will or codicil, which is required to be attested by law, proof of execution may be offered as if no attesting witness is alive: Evidence Act 1938, s. 3.

(*e*) An attesting witness may be cross-examined by the party calling him: *Jones* v. *Jones* (1908).

21. Proof by presumption. For presumptions, *see* Chap. 10. The relevant presumptions are as follows:

(*a*) *Documents not less than twenty years old.* Under the Evidence Act 1938, s. 4, there is a presumption that, in the case of civil or criminal proceedings, a document not less than twenty years old has been validly executed.

(*i*) The document must be produced from "proper custody", i.e. it must be produced from a place in which it might naturally and reasonably be expected to be found: *see Doe* v. *Fowler* (1850); *Hubbard* v. *Lees* (1866).

(*ii*) The document must be otherwise free from any suspicion.

(*b*) *Date of execution and alterations.* The following presumptions apply:

(*i*) A document is presumed to have been executed on the date stated thereon: *Anderson* v. *Weston* (1840).

(*ii*) Alterations or erasures in a *deed* are presumed to have been made *before* execution; in a *will*, *after* execution: *Doe d. Tatum* v. *Catomore* (1851). (Note that no alteration in a will has any effect unless executed with the formalities of a will: Wills Act 1837, s. 21.)

(*c*) *Parties to a conveyance.* "The persons expressed to be parties to any conveyance shall, until the contrary is proved, be presumed to be of full age at the date thereof": Law of Property Act 1925, s. 15.

Extrinsic evidence in relation to documents

22. The general problem. Assume that a transaction has been recorded in a document. Can extrinsic evidence (i.e. any evidence—oral or documentary—other than the document itself) be used so as to vary or contradict, or effectively substitute for, that document? Consider the following problems:

(*a*) X agrees in writing to let a house to Y, together with items of furniture therein. Y wishes to give evidence of X's having agreed orally to send in extra furniture. Is Y's evidence admissible? (*See Angell* v. *Duke* (1875).) *See* **26** below.

(*b*) T devises property to "George Gord, the son of Gord". There are two persons of that very description. Is evidence of T's declarations of intention admissible to show which person he had in mind? (*See Doe d. Gord* v. *Needs* (1836).) *See* **30** (*c*) (*ii*) below.

(*c*) A leases land to B, reserving all sporting rights. Is B allowed to give evidence in proof of a prior oral agreement by which A promised to keep down rabbits on the land if B would take the lease? (*See Morgan* v. *Griffith* (1871).) *See* **27** (*g*) below.

23. The general rule stated. The general rule is that extrinsic evidence is *not admissible* "to contradict, vary, add to or subtract from the terms of a written contract or the terms in which the parties have deliberately agreed to record any part of their contract": *per* Lord Morris in *Bank of Australasia* v. *Palmer* (1897).

(*a*) Note that extrinsic evidence is often known as "parol evidence"; in practice it is not only oral evidence, however, but may include, e.g. documents.

(*b*) The exceptions to the general rule are considered at **25, 27, 30** below.

Extrinsic evidence as substitute for a document

24. The general rule. Should there be embodied in a document the terms agreed on by the parties, that writing will form an exclusive record of the transaction, so that *no evidence except the document itself* (or, where appropriate, secondary evidence of contents) may be given to prove those terms.

NOTE: (1) Evidence of identification of parties and things to which the document in question refers may be received: *see Charrington* v. *Wooder* (1914).
(2) The rule binds parties to the transaction and any third party wishing to prove terms embodied in the document: *Augustien* v. *Challis* (1847).

25. Exceptions to the rule. The following should be noted:

(*a*) Extrinsic evidence is allowed to show an apparent connection between two or more documents in which the transaction is recorded *if* one document refers to the other(s): *Long* v. *Miller* (1879).

(*b*) Where statute requires contractual terms to be contained in a written memorandum and the court will accept in lieu part-performance of the contract, extrinsic evidence of the contract may be admitted: *Chapronière* v. *Lambert* (1917).

(*c*) Where, by law, all the terms of a contract must be evidenced in writing, extrinsic evidence may be admitted to prove the existence of terms other than those contained in a memorandum: *Beckett* v. *Nurse* (1948).

(*d*) Where the *fact* of the transaction rather than its *terms* must be proved, extrinsic evidence may be given even though the transaction is recorded in a document: *Alderson* v. *Clay* (1816).

(*e*) Where the writing is intended as a mere record of the transaction, extrinsic evidence may be given as to the terms of the transaction: *Allen* v. *Pink* (1838).

Extrinsic evidence in variation or contradiction of a document

26. The general rule. Following the reduction to the form of a document of some transaction, extrinsic evidence will *not* be admitted to contradict, vary, add to or subtract from the terms of that document: *Bank of Australasia* v. *Palmer* (1897). Thus, in *Angell* v. *Duke* (1875) (*see* 22 (*a*) above), Y's evidence was held *inadmissible* because the oral agreement had been superseded by the written agreement. *See also Newman* v. *Gattie* (1907).

27. Exceptions to the rule. The following should be noted:

(*a*) Extrinsic evidence may be admissible to contradict a public document (but not a judicial record): *Kemp* v. *Elisha* (1918).

(*b*) Extrinsic evidence may be admitted where a party's capacity in which he has examined a document is equivocal: *Young* v. *Schuler* (1883). Such evidence may be given to show, e.g. that a party executed a document as agent for his undisclosed principal.

(*c*) Extrinsic evidence of the legality or illegality of consideration is admissible: *Woods* v. *Wise* (1955).

(*d*) Extrinsic evidence of the true nature of a transaction, whatever its apparent nature, may be given, e.g. to show that what seems in a will to be a beneficial gift is a secret trust: *Re Boyes* (1884).

(*e*) Where a contract not required by law to be in written form purports to be embodied in a document which is held by the court to be not intended as an expression of the entire agreement, extrinsic evidence may be given of agreed, omitted terms which are not inconsistent with the documentary terms. See *Angell* v. *Duke* (1875) (at **22** (*a*) above); *Brown* v. *Byrne* (1854).

(*f*) Extrinsic evidence may be admitted to show that a document is invalid because of circumstances such as duress, undue influence, mistake, which attended its making: *Murray* v. *Parker* (1854).

(*g*) Extrinsic evidence is admissible to prove some prior or contemporaneous collateral agreement or warranty which is consistent with the document: *Heilbut Symons & Co.* v. *Buckleton* (1913). Thus, in *Morgan* v. *Griffith* (1871) (*see* **22** (*c*) above), B's evidence was admissible.

(*h*) Extrinsic evidence may be admissible to show a subsequent variation or discharge of a written agreement. Where the original agreement, must by law, be in writing, evidence of verbal discharge (but *not* verbal variation) is admissible: *see Morris* v. *Baron & Co.* (1918); *Goss* v. *Nugent* (1833).

Extrinsic evidence as an aid to interpretation

28. The problem. Consider the following cases, which illustrate aspects of the general problem arising when extrinsic evidence is considered in relation to ambiguity or inaccuracy in a document.

(*a*) *Baylis* v. *A.-G.* (1741). X leaves a legacy to "Mr.—". Is extrinsic evidence admissible to fill in the blank? *See* **30** (*b*) (*i*) below.

(*b*) *Dashwood* v. *Magniac* (1891). T devised land to Y "with a power to cut timber for repairs of the estate." Is extrinsic evidence admissible to show what trees, according to local usage, were recognised in the term "timber"? *See* **30** (*d*) (*iii*) below.

29. The general rule. In interpreting and construing a document, extrinsic evidence is *not generally admissible* to ascertain the intentions of the writer of the document, so as to affect interpretation or construction. "Interpretation" refers to the ascertaining of the meaning of words used in a document; "construction" refers to the application of rules of law to an understanding of the document after its language has been made clear. (The terms are often used synonymously.)

Note that, under the Administration of Justice Act 1982, s. 21, extrinsic evidence, including evidence of a testator's intention, may be admitted to assist in the *interpretation of a will* in so far as any part of it is meaningless or ambiguous.

30. Examples of the general rule. The following should be noted:

(*a*) Where it is obvious from the words of the document in their context or from the surrounding facts that an apparent, primary meaning of the words cannot have been intended by the writer, extrinsic evidence of surrounding circumstances *may be given* to show that those words were used in a secondary sense, always provided that the secondary sense is such that it can be supported by the words.

(*i*) Evidence of the writer's direct declaration of intention *cannot* be given.

(*ii*) In *Re Jeans* (1895) T left property to his "children" and evidence was held admissible to show that T, who had no children of his own and had four stepdaughters who called him "father", had those stepdaughters in mind when he used the term "children".

(*iii*) In *N.S.P.C.C.* v. *Scottish N.S.P.C.C.* (1915) T left a legacy to the "National Society for the Prevention of Cruelty to Children." There was an English society of that name and extrinsic evidence was *not admissible* to show that T intended the legacy to go to the Scottish N.S.P.C.C.

(*iv*) Note the so-called "armchair principle". "You may place yourself, so to speak, in (the testator's) armchair, and consider the circumstances by which he was surrounded when he made his will to assist you in arriving at his intention": *per* James, L. J. in *Boyes* v. *Cook* (1880).

(*b*) Extrinsic evidence can be used to fill in a *partial* (but not a total) blank or to make clear terms which assume clarity only when other circumstances are explained.

(*i*) In *Hunt* v. *Hort* (1791) T left a legacy to "Lady —" and extrinsic evidence was *not admissible* to fill in this total blank.

(*ii*) *See* also *Baylis* v. *A.-G.* (1741) (at **28** (*a*) above, where extrinsic evidence was *not admissible*); *Rossiter* v. *Miller* (1878).

(*c*) Extrinsic evidence is admissible to explain an equivocation or a *latent ambiguity* (i.e. an ambiguity which does not appear on the face of the document, as contrasted with a *patent ambiguity*, which is apparent on the face of the document). "(If the testator's intention) establishes that the description in the will may apply to each of two or more persons, then a latent ambiguity is exposed, and rather than the devise should fail altogether for uncertainty, the law allows the ambiguity which is exposed by the parol evidence to be cleared up and removed by similar evidence, provided such parol evidence is sufficient to enable the court to ascertain the sense in which the testator employed that particular expression upon which the ambiguity arises": *per* Bovil, C. J. in *Grant* v. *Grant* (1870). *See Mayer* v. *Hurr* (1985)—extrinsic evidence admissible to discover the true meaning of an ambiguous conveyance.

(*i*) In *Raffles* v. *Wichelhaus* (1864) a contract referred to merchandise arriving "ex *Peerless* from Bombay", and extrinsic evidence *was admitted* to show that there were two ships of that name arriving from Bombay, and to show what was in the mind of the parties.

(*ii*) In *Doe d. Gord* v. *Needs* (1836) T devised property to "George Gord, son of Gord", and extrinsic evidence of T's intentions *was admitted* to show which of two persons of that description he had in mind.

(*iii*) *See* also *Re Hubbuck* (1905); *Re Jackson* (1933).

(*d*) Extrinsic evidence may be allowed to make clear customs, trade usages, codes, symbols, foreign languages, etc. in a document.

(*i*) In *Smith* v. *Wilson* (1832) extrinsic evidence of local usage *was admitted* to show that "thousand rabbits" meant "twelve hundred rabbits."

(*ii*) In *Jolly* v. *Young* (1800) extrinsic evidence *was allowed* to show a trade usage by which "month" in a charterparty meant a calendar, not a lunar, month.

(*iii*) *See* also *Dashwood* v. *Magniac* (1891) (at **28** (*b*) above, where extrinsic evidence of local usage *was admitted*); *L.C.C.* v. *S. Metropolitan Gas Co.* (1904).

(*e*) Extrinsic, circumstantial (not direct) evidence may be admissible to show what the writer of a document had described incorrectly. *See Doe d. Hiscocks* v. *Hiscocks* (1839); *Re Alcock* (1945).

NOTE: *See* 19:22–23, 25 for evidence from documentary records and computer records used in *criminal proceedings*.

Progress test 8

1. Give examples of *public* and *private* documents. (4)
2. How does the "original document rule" apply to documentary evidence? (7)
3. Comment on the decision in *Macdonnell* v. *Evans* (1852). (7)
4. Where a party admits the contents of a document, does this constitute primary evidence against him? (8)
5. Enumerate some of the forms of secondary evidence in relation to documentary evidence. (9)
6. Outline the principal exceptions to the general rule concerning the necessity for primary evidence of a document's contents. (10)
7. Consider the case of a party in civil proceedings failing to comply with a notice to produce. (11)
8. Consider the case of an original document which is destroyed or lost. (13)
9. What is the appropriate form of proof (in the case of secondary evidence) of (a) a statute; (b) a bye-law; (c) a conviction? (15)
10. How may handwriting be proved? (19)
11. How is attestation proved? (20)
12. Explain "proof by presumption". (21)
13. State the general rule in relation to the admissibility of extrinsic evidence. (23)
14. When is extrinsic evidence admitted to show an apparent connection between documents recording a transaction? (25)
15. Is extrinsic evidence admissible (a) to contradict a public document; (b) to show the true nature of a transaction? (27)
16. Is extrinsic evidence admissible to identify the person a testator had in mind when he left a legacy to "Lord —"? (30)
17. Outline the decisions in *Re Jeans* (1895); *Raffles* v. *Wichelhaus* (1864); *Smith* v. *Wilson* (1832). (30)

Part three

Proof (2)

9

Matters of which proof is not required (1): formal admissions and judicial notice

Preliminary matters

1. Matters to be covered in Part three. In this Part we consider some further problems concerning *proof*: each relates to matters arising out of the general rule that all facts have to be proved by sufficient evidence (*see* 1:3 (*b*)).

(*a*) In this and the following chapter we consider those facts which, generally, *need not be proved by evidence*.

(*b*) In Chapters 11 and 12, we consider those facts of which, generally, proof *will not be allowed*.

(*c*) In Chapters 13–15, we consider the matters of which, generally, proof *is allowed*.

2. Essence of "matters of which proof is not required". This phrase must *not* be taken to mean "matters of which proof is *not allowed*" (*see* e.g. the doctrine of estoppel at 11:3). It refers to matters *which do not require any affirmative proof*. Three of these matters are discussed in this and the following chapter:

(*a*) *Facts admitted in civil or criminal cases:* these need not be proved (*see* 3–13 below).

(*b*) *Facts of which the courts take judicial notice:* proof of these facts need not be adduced (*see* 14–29 below).

(*c*) *Facts which may, or must, be presumed in favour of some party:* proof of these facts by that party is not generally necessary (*see* Chap. 10).

Formal admissions: the general position

3. The general rule. No evidence will be required of any matter which is formally admitted. *See Ellis* v. *Allen* (1914); *Urquhart* v. *Butterfield* (1887). (Note that, in general, an "admission" refers to *some facts*, whereas a "confession" (*see* Chap. 20) admits the *entire charge*.)

4. Formal and informal admissions. *Formal* judicial admissions only are in consideration here; they must be distinguished clearly from *informal* admissions (which may be admitted as an exception to the general rule against hearsay: *see* 18:3). The *formal* admission is *generally conclusive* for purposes of the trial and the facts admitted cease, effectively, to be in issue. The *informal* admission is *not conclusive*; it is merely admissible evidence to be weighed by the court.

Formal admissions in criminal proceedings

5. The position before 1967. Formal admissions were not generally received in criminal proceedings, except in the case of a plea of guilty. *See A.-G.* v. *Bertrand* (1867); *R.* v. *Riley* (1896). It should be noted that a plea of guilty is an admission of the offence only; it does not, in itself, amount to an admission of the truth of the depositions. (Note also that, *following conviction*, defendant may make admissions of other offences he wishes to be taken into consideration.)

6. The position following the Criminal Justice Act 1967. Under the Criminal Justice Act 1967, s. 10, formal admissions by or on behalf of prosecution or defendant may be made in criminal cases before (with counsel's approval) or at the trial. *See* 20:4.

   (*a*) The admissions by a party of a fact are, as against that party, conclusive evidence of the fact admitted: s. 10 (1).

   (*b*) If made other than in court, the admission must be in writing: s. 10 (2) (*b*).

   (*c*) The admission is treated as available also for the purposes of subsequent criminal proceedings (including appeal) relating to the matter in question: s. 10 (3).

(d) The admission may be withdrawn by leave of the court: s. 10 (4).

Formal admissions in civil proceedings

7. The general position. Formal admissions may be made in the modes indicated at **8–13** below. It should be noted that counsel may, generally, make any admission on behalf of, and binding on, his client which, having honestly exercised his judgment, he thinks proper, but he has no authority on any matters collateral to the suit: *Swinfen* v. *Chelmsford* (1860).

8. Stages of the proceedings at which formal admissions may be made. This procedure is governed by the Rules of the Supreme Court. It relates to: pleadings (*see* **9** below); answer to notice (*see* **10** below); answer to interrogatories (*see* **11** below); correspondence (*see* **12** below); the trial (*see* **13** below).

9. Pleadings. Formal admissions may be made by the pleadings. Such admissions may be:

(a) *express*, as where defendant admits (". . . defendant admits that he did sign the agreement . . ."), or

(b) *implied*, as where defendant fails to deny an allegation (since a fact alleged in a pleading and not specifically denied is generally taken to be admitted: *see* O. 18, r. 13).

10. Notice to admit. A notice under O. 27, rr. 1–5, calls on a party to admit documents or facts mentioned therein. Resulting admissions may be amended or withdrawn on terms: r. 2.

11. Answer to interrogatories. A party may, by leave of the court, deliver written interrogatories to the other party prior to the trial; they must be answered by affidavit. Answers thus elicited may be used at the trial against the party who has given them. *See* O. 26.

12. Correspondence. Letters written by counsel or a solicitor arising out of their authority to act on behalf of the client may contain certain matter amounting to formal admissions and these will bind the client (*see* 7 above). *See* O. 27, r. 1; *Ellis* v. *Allen* (1914).

13. At the trial. The party or his counsel or solicitor may admit facts during the course of the trial. Note that where admissions of fact have been made, the plaintiff may apply, at any stage, for such judgment as he may be entitled to: O. 27, r. 3.

Judicial notice: the general concept

14. The idea of judicial notice. There are circumstances in which the court may accept a fact without the necessity of accepting evidence of it, the fact being so notorious—and the term is used here not in its pejorative sense, but in the sense of "widely or commonly known"—that there is no necessity to consider formal evidence as to its existence and nature. "Judges are entitled and bound to take judicial notice of that which is the common knowledge of the great majority of mankind and of the great majority of men of business": *per* Brett, J. in *R.* v. *Aspinall* (1876).

15. Definition of judicial notice (or "judicial cognisance"). "Judicial notice refers to facts which a judge can be called upon to receive and to act upon either from his general knowledge of them, or from enquiries to be made by himself for his own information from sources to which it is proper for him to refer": *per* Lord Sumner in *Commonwealth Shipping Representative* v. *P. & O. Branch Services* (1923).

16. Aspects of the doctrine. The following points should be noted:

(*a*) Judicial knowledge applies in both criminal and civil proceedings, and to judge and jury.

(*b*) Judges are allowed a wide discretion; they may notice facts which they cannot be required to notice.

(*c*) Judicial notice is generally conclusive.

(*d*) "Only if no person can raise a question" should judicial notice be taken: *R.* v. *Luffe* (1807).

17. Reasons for the existence of the doctrine. The following reasons have been suggested:

(a) *The saving of time.* It might be impossible to conduct a trial if every fact not admitted had to be proved by evidence which could be difficult to obtain, or if notorious facts which could be proved with relative ease required long, formal proof.

(b) *Desire for uniformity.* Judicial notice of facts may assist in creating a pattern of uniformity of decision. It should be noted, however, that judicial notice will not necessarily create precedent: *see* e.g. *Duff Development Co.* v. *Government of Kelantan* (1924).

18. Classification of facts judicially noted. There is no one, authoritative classification; that given below is derived from the standard texts and is used here for convenience only:

(a) Matters of common and certain knowledge (*see* **19–20** below).

(b) Law, procedure and custom (*see* **21–22** below).

(c) Constitutional, political and administrative matters (*see* **23–24** below).

(d) Official seals, signatures, gazettes (*see* **25–26** below).

Matters of common and certain knowledge

19. The general rule. It is unnecessary to call evidence of matters of common knowledge which are so notorious (*see* **14** above) that proof is, clearly, not required, and in such a case the judge is required to recognise their existence and to direct the jury to assume them (and should he not do so, the jury would be entitled to take notice without direction).

20. Examples of the rule. The following examples should be noted:

(a) *Human affairs.* Judicial notice has been taken of the following: that the value of money has fallen since 1189 (*Bryant* v. *Foot* (1868)); that the streets of London are full of traffic (*Dennis* v. *White & Co.* (1916)); that it is impossible to predict fortunes by referring to the stars (*Penny* v. *Hanson* (1887)); that a flick knife is an offensive weapon (*R.* v. *Simpson* (1983)).

(b) *Human nature.* Judicial notice has been taken of the fact that the mischievous nature of children makes them unusually vulnerable to danger (*British Railways Board* v. *Herrington* (1972)).

(*c*) *The course of nature, e.g. calendars, time.* Judicial notice has been taken of the following: that certain days of the week occur on dates marked in the calendar (*Pearson* v. *Shaw* (1844)); that a fortnight is an impossible period for human gestation (*R.* v. *Luffe* (1807)).

(*d*) *Other notorious facts.* Judicial notice has been taken of standards of weights and measures; of the coinage of the realm; of the rules of the road; of the meaning of common words.

Matters relating to law, procedure and custom

21. The general rule. It is not generally necessary to call evidence of English law, of the contents of statutes and various customs.

22. Examples of the rule. The following examples should be noted:

(*a*) *English law and statutes.* A judge will take judicial notice of the English common law and of the contents of statutes (which, since the Interpretation Act 1889, s. 9 (now repealed and replaced by the Interpretation Act 1978, s. 3), includes both public general Acts and private Acts passed since 1850) and the procedure of Parliament. *See Stockdale* v. *Hansard* (1839).

(*i*) "English law" refers to all branches of the law, but excludes foreign law, Scots law (save in the House of Lords) and Commonwealth law.

(*ii*) Foreign law (*see* 3:7) must be proved as a fact, to be decided by the judge (not the jury). Under the Civil Evidence Act 1972, s. 4 (1), evidence of foreign law may be given by any suitably qualified person whether or not he has acted or is entitled to act as a legal practitioner in the country concerned. *See* also the County Courts Act 1984, s. 68.

(*iii*) Under the European Communities Act 1972, s. 3 (1): "For the purposes of all legal proceedings any question as to the meaning or effect of any of the Treaties, or as to the validity, meaning or effect of any Community instrument, shall be treated as a question of law and, if not referred to the European Court, be for determination as such in accordance with the principles laid down by and any relevant decision of the European Court."

(*iv*) Judges are bound to recognise and give effect to all equitable estates, titles and rights and all equitable duties and liabilities: Supreme Court Act 1981, s. 49.

(*v*) Should the judge not bear in mind a law in question, he may refer to, or be referred to, it so as to refresh his memory. But this does not amount to "proving the law".

(*b*) *Customs.* Local and general customs, professional customs (e.g. the banker's lien: *see Brandao* v. *Barnett* (1846)) may be judicially noticed when they have been judicially ascertained and established.

(*i*) Market overt and the practices of conveyancers are among the customs to have been judicially noticed. *See Re Rosher* (1884).

(*ii*) It seems necessary to prove a general custom at least once. *See Edelstein* v. *Schuler* (1902).

(*iii*) Particular customs will not be judicially noticed, but will require separate proof: *Moult* v. *Halliday* (1898).

Constitutional, political and administrative matters

23. The general rule. The court will take judicial notice of all public, constitutional and administrative matters relating to the government of the country. *See Duff Development Co.* v. *Government of Kelantan* (1924).

24. Examples of the rule. The following examples should be noted:

(*a*) *Sovereign and principal officers of state.* Judicial notice is taken of the accession and demise of British monarchs and of the past and present heads of government departments, and of judges of the Supreme Court. *See Whaley* v. *Carlisle* (1866).

(*b*) *Political and allied matters.* Judicial notice is taken of matters relating to: the sovereign status of a foreign government; a state of war (*see R.* v. *Bottrill* (1947)) (but not generally relating to the date of a particular military operation—*see Jabbour* v. *Custodian of Israeli Absentee Property* (1954)); the extent of territorial waters.

(*i*) Information relating to these matters is supplied by a Secretary of State.

(*ii*) The information thus supplied cannot be questioned: *Duff*

Development Co. v. *Government of Kelantan* (1924). "It is settled law that it is for the court to take judicial cognisance of the status of any foreign government. If there can be any doubt on the matter the practice is for the court to receive information from the appropriate department of H.M. Government, and the information so received is conclusive": *per* Viscount Finlay.

(*c*) *Administrative matters relating to state and county divisions.* The extent of British jurisdiction, administrative divisions of the U.K. are judicially noticed. The report of a Secretary of State on these matters will be conclusive evidence: *The Fagernes* (1927).

Official seals, signatures, gazettes

25. The general rule. The court will judicially notice matters relating to the official gazettes and to the various seals.

26. Examples of the rule. The following should be noted:

(*a*) *Gazettes.* The official gazettes (e.g. of London) are judicially noticed on production. The entire gazette, not cuttings, must be produced: *R.* v. *Lowe* (1883).

(*b*) *Seals and signatures.* Royal and Duchy seals, seals of the Courts, of the Central Office, of the district registries, signatures of the judges of superior courts, are judicially noticed.

Some problems relating to judicial notice

27. General. The following problems are among those arising from the operation of the principle of judicial notice:

(*a*) What is the dividing line between judicial notice and evidence? (*See* **28** below.)

(*b*) How far does personal knowledge enter into judicial notice? (*See* **29** below.)

28. Judicial notice and evidence. In some cases, judicial notice is taken without any inquiry, e.g. the case of a notorious fact. Where matters are not clear, the judge may refresh his memory—by consulting appropriate books or by listening to experts: *see Kerr* v.

Kennedy (1942). Does this involve the *reception of evidence?*

(*a*) In *McQuaker* v. *Goddard* (1940) P had been bitten by a camel while visiting D's zoological gardens. The question was (for purposes of the law concerning liability for animals) whether the camel was a wild or domestic animal. The trial judge had consulted works of reference and heard witnesses on the habits of the camel. The Court of Appeal held that the judge had *not* been taking evidence, as such. The witnesses had done no more than help the judge in "forming his view as to what the ordinary course of nature in this regard in fact is, a matter of which he is supposed to have complete knowledge": *per* Clauson, L. J. *See* also *Turner* v. *Coates* (1917).

(*b*) In the case of a judge consulting assessors, "all that happens is that the court is equipping itself for its task by taking judicial notice of all such things as it ought to know in order to do its work properly": *per* Lord Denning in *Baldwin & Francis Ltd.* v. *Patent Appeal Tribunal* (1959).

29. Personal knowledge. In general, judge or jury may not act on mere personal knowledge of the facts: *Palmer* v. *Crone* (1927). The rule applies to *particular facts*; it will not exclude, for example, a judge's drawing on his *general knowledge* in taking judicial notice: *see R.* v. *Field* (1895) (concerning a magistrate's knowledge of a matter in question); *Ingram* v. *Percival* (1969); *Wetherall* v. *Harrison* (1976); *Chesson* v. *Jordan* (1981).

Progress test 9

1. Distinguish formal and informal admissions. (**4**)
2. What is the position today concerning formal admissions in criminal proceedings? (**6**)
3. Outline the position concerning the modes in which formal admissions may be made in civil proceedings. (**7–13**)
4. Define "judicial notice". (**15**)
5. Does the principle of judicial notice apply to (*a*) judge *and* jury; (*b*) civil *and* criminal proceedings? (**16**)
6. What is the rationale of judicial notice? (**17**)

7. Illustrate the application of the principle of judicial notice to matters relating to (*a*) the course of nature; (*b*) the coinage of the realm. (**20**)

8. Is it necessary to call evidence in a matter relating to (*a*) the interpretation of the common law; (*b*) foreign law; (*c*) private Acts of Parliament? (**22**)

9. Is judicial notice taken of (*a*) general customs; (*b*) particular customs? (**22**)

10. Will judicial notice be taken of parliamentary procedure? (**22**)

11. Consider a case in which information is sought by the court relating to the status of a newly-independent Commonwealth state. (**24**)

12. "The dividing line between judicial notice and proof is very thin." Comment. (**28**)

13. May a judge act on his general knowledge in taking judicial notice? (**29**)

10

Matters of which proof is not required (2): presumptions

Preliminary matters

1. Nature of a presumption. Following consideration, in the previous chapter, of formal admissions and judicial notice, the third aspect of matters of which proof is not required is considered here—presumptions. It is important to differentiate the meaning attached to the term in ordinary usage and in the law of evidence. A "presumption" is, in non-legal language, some belief dictated by probability, or a reason lending probability to some belief. In the law of evidence it has a more restricted, technical meaning. At any time during its proceedings the court *may* (but need not) draw inferences from the evidence which has been adduced. *A party may be entitled to rely on some recognised inferences from which the court may presume, provisionally or conclusively, further matter in favour of that party. Inferences of this nature are known in the law of evidence as presumptions.* (By "inferences" is meant here the processes of moving from a statement considered to be true to another which follows from the truth of the former.)

2. Definition and examples of presumptions. A presumption is *an assumption which must or may be made and maintained until evidence to the contrary is given.* Note Wills' definition: "a presumption is a probable consequence drawn from facts (either certain, or proved by direct testimony) as to the truth of a fact alleged but of which there is no direct proof." Black writes of a presumption as: "an inference affirmative or disaffirmative of the truth or falsehood of any proposition or fact drawn by a process of probable reasoning in the absence of actual certainty of its truth or falsehood, or until such certainty can be ascertained." Some preliminary examples are as follows:

(a) That official acts are presumed to have been properly and regularly performed: *Berryman* v. *Wise* (1791).

(b) That no child under 10 years of age can be guilty of an offence: *see* the Children and Young Persons Act 1933, s. 50.

(c) That "any article commonly used for human consumption shall, if sold or offered, exposed or kept for sale, be presumed, until the contrary is proved, to have been sold or, as the case may be, to have been or to be intended for sale, for human consumption": Food Act 1984, s. 98 (a).

3. Presumptions and the burden of proof. "Although the word 'presumption' is used with different shades of meaning in different branches of law, its use always relates in some way to the burden of proof. The implication is that a particular conclusion is likely to be drawn by the court in the absence of good reason for reaching a different one": Cross. The operation of a presumption may affect the burden of proof (*see* 6:5).

(a) Should a presumption operate in favour of a party on whom rests the burden of proving some fact, he may avoid that burden without adducing evidence in proof of that fact.

(b) The burden of proof may also shift (*see* 6:11) from one party (in whose favour the presumption is raised) to the opposing party. Assume, for example, that a fact in issue is X's legitimacy, which X maintains. It is for X to prove the fact of his legitimacy. If X is able to show that he was conceived in lawful wedlock, the presumption of legitimacy (*see* 24 below) emerges in his favour. The burden of proof then shifts to his opponent to prove X's illegitimacy. *See* 6:11 (a).

4. Controversy relating to the use of the term "presumption". In the case of a presumption of law (*see* 8 below), e.g. that a child under ten cannot commit a crime, no evidence in rebuttal is allowed; the presumption is effectively irrebuttable. It has been suggested, therefore, that "presumptions" of this nature are not, in fact, presumptions; rather are they substantive rules of law masquerading in the guise of presumptions. The term "presumption" ought, it has been argued, to be applied only to those presumptions which are rebuttable.

5. The problem of conflicting presumptions. It is possible that one presumption may rebut another presumption, so that each is effectively cancelled out. In such a case they are dealt with as conflicting evidence would ordinarily be dealt with, that is, they are left to the jury. *See R.* v. *Willshire* (1881); *Monckton* v. *Tarr* (1930) ("These two presumptions, one on one side and one on the other, being considered of equal weight . . . we get rid of presumptions altogether": *per* Romer, L. J.).

6. Matters to be discussed below. The following matters relating to presumptions are discussed in this chapter:

   (*a*) Classification of presumptions (*see* **7–10** below).
   (*b*) Irrebuttable presumptions of law (*see* **11–14** below).
   (*c*) Rebuttable presumptions of law (*see* **15–30** below).
   (*d*) Rebuttable presumptions of fact (*see* **31–35** below).

Classification of presumptions

7. General. There is no "authoritative" classification of the large number of presumptions in the law of evidence. There is a "standard" classification which is adopted in this chapter; it does not derive, however, from statute. Other classifications considered include the novel proposals of Lord Denning which were produced as a consequence of his belief that existing classifications were "unscientific". (*See* **9** below.)

8. The "standard" classification. This is based on three categories of presumptions:

   (*a*) *Irrebuttable presumptions of law* (*praesumptiones juris et de jure*) (presumptions drawn by the law and in an obligatory manner). These are *inferences which the law will not allow to be contradicted by the calling of evidence.* Thus, no evidence would be admissible which was calculated to show that a child aged six had a "guilty intention". In effect, presumptions of this nature are no more than rules of the substantive law.

(*b*) *Rebuttable presumptions of law (praesumptiones juris sed non de jure)*. These very important presumptions are *conclusive until disproved by evidence to the contrary*.

(*c*) *Rebuttable presumptions of fact (praesumptiones hominis vel facti)*. These are *inferences which the court may, but need not, draw from the facts before it*.

This classification forms the basis of the discussion at **11–35** below.

9. Lord Denning's proposals for classification. Lord Denning has suggested a three-fold classification (*see* 61 L.Q.R. 379):

(*a*) *Provisional presumptions*. These are presumptions of fact which *may* be inferred. They cast a provisional burden of adducing evidence on the person against whom they operate. Failure to discharge that burden is not always fatal.

(*b*) *Conclusive presumptions*. These are irrebuttable presumptions of law, on proof of which "the court must draw a particular inference, whether true or not".

(*c*) *Compelling presumptions*. These are conclusions which must be drawn, as a matter of law, on proof of the basic facts "unless the other side proves the contrary or proves some other fact which the law recognises as sufficient to rebut the inference", e.g. the presumption of legitimacy (*see* **24** below). "Whereas provisional presumptions gives rise to provisional burdens within a single issue, a compelling presumption gives rise to a separate issue on which the legal burden is on the other side."

10. Other classifications. Other classifications draw attention to various, assumed basic differences in the nature of presumptions, e.g.:

(*a*) *Direct and inferential*. *Direct* presumptions arise without proof of basic facts; *inferential* presumptions depend on the proof of basic facts.

(*b*) *Presumptions of fact and presumptions of law*.

(c) *Conclusive and rebuttable presumptions.*

Irrebuttable presumptions of law

11. General. Known also as "conclusive" presumptions, these are, in effect, rules of substantive law couched in terms of adjective rules, rather than rules of evidence. They necessitate the drawing of conclusions; they do not allow for rebutting evidence. Examples of these "absolute inferences" are given at **14–16** below.

12. Presumptions concerning children. Under the Children and Young Persons Act 1933, s. 50, no child under ten years of age can be guilty of an offence; and no rebutting evidence is admissible. *See* also the Children and Young Persons Act 1969, s. 4 (1) (not yet in force).

There is, however, no comparable presumption in the *civil* law that a boy under 14 years of age cannot father a child (*see L.* v. *K.* (1985)).

13. Statutory provisions. There are occasional statutory provisions which establish conclusive (or irrebuttable) presumptions, but their use and frequency has tended to diminish. For an example *see* the Bankruptcy Act 1914, s. 137 (2) (repealed); *see* also the Animal Health Act 1981, s. 79 (1), for the *implied* irrebuttable presumption that documents are properly executed.

14. Ignorantia juris neminem excusat ("ignorance of the law is no excuse"). Every man is taken to be cognisant of the law "otherwise there is no knowing of the extent to which the excuse of ignorance might be carried": *R.* v. *Bailey* (1800). No rebutting evidence is admissible.

Rebuttable presumptions of law

15. General. These are the most important of the presumptions and are known also as "inconclusive" presumptions. Presumed facts under this heading *must be found until evidence to the contrary disproves them.*

(*a*) Most of these presumptions (*see* presumption of legitimacy at 24 below) depend on proof of some basic fact.

(*b*) Once the basic fact has been established, the appropriate conclusion *must* be drawn if there is no evidence to the contrary.

(*c*) In effect, presumptions of this kind afford only prima facie evidence (*see* 2:28 (*b*)) of the facts presumed.

The presumption of innocence

16. Statement of the presumption. An accused person is generally presumed innocent until the prosecution has proved the case against him beyond reasonable doubt: *Woolmington* v. *D.P.P.* (1935). *See* 6:18. The rule applies also to civil disputes: *Joseph Constantine Steamship Line Ltd.* v. *Imperial Smelting Co. Ltd.* (1942).

17. Further points. The following points should be noted:

(*a*) The presumption arises without proof of other facts.

(*b*) It may also be applicable to an allegation of criminality in a civil case: *see Williams* v. *E. India Co.* (1802).

(*c*) There is an added presumption of innocence in the specific case of a child aged between 10–14. The presumption is that he is *doli incapax* (i.e. incapable of crime), but he can be shown capable of discriminating between good and evil, so that the presumption may be rebutted by proof of "mischievous discretion", i.e. a knowledge that he was doing wrong. *Malitia supplet aetatem* ("malice supplements age"). *See R.* v. *Owen* (1830); *R.* v. *B.* (1979)—evidence of previous convictions can be adduced by the prosecution to rebut the presumption of *doli incapax*; *J. M.* v. *Runeckles* (1984)—to rebut the presumption of *doli incapax* the prosecution must prove that the child knew that what it had done was seriously wrong, not merely naughty or mischievous.

The presumption of sanity

18. Statement of the presumption. Every person is presumed sane until the contrary be proved.

19. Further points. The following points should be noted:

(a) In a *criminal case* the jury must be told that the presumption holds until the contrary be proved: *see R.* v. *M'Naghten* (1843).

(b) It has been suggested that the presumption of sanity may arise also in some civil cases, for example, those relating to wills where the sanity of the testator is in dispute. Thus, if a will is shown to have been duly executed and attested and—on the face of it—appears to be rational, there is a presumption of the testator's sanity. Testamentary capacity is presumed until the contrary has been shown. See *Sutton* v. *Sadler* (1857).

The presumption of marriage

20. Statement of the presumption. The presumption is two-fold:

(a) Where there is evidence of a marriage ceremony the presumption is raised that the parties were thereby validly married. *See Piers* v. *Piers* (1849)—although there was no evidence of a special licence needed for a marriage in a private house having been obtained, the marriage was presumed valid.

(b) Where there is evidence of a ceremony of marriage having been followed by cohabitation of the parties, the validity of the marriage will be presumed, in the absence of decisive evidence to the contrary: *Russell* v. *A.-G.* (1949).

NOTE: There is also a presumption that a marriage is monogamous: *Cheni* v. *Cheni* (1965).

21. Further points. The following points should be noted:

(a) In *Tweny* v. *Tweny* (1946) it was stated that a marriage "remains a valid marriage until some evidence is adduced that the marriage was, in fact, a nullity".

(b) In *Re Taplin* (1937) it was shown that X had lived with Y as his wife for nearly twenty years in Rockhampton. Their children's birth certificates made reference to a marriage in Victoria, but there was no record of the marriage of X and Y in Victoria. It was held that the parties must be presumed validly married, since the presumption of validity of marriage could be rebutted only by very cogent evidence. *See* also *Elliott* v. *Totnes Union* (1892).

(c) "Where a man and woman are proved to have lived together as man and wife, the law will presume, unless the contrary be clearly proved, that they were living together in consequence of a valid marriage and not in a state of concubinage": *Sastry Velaider Aronegary* v. *Sembeculty Vaigalie* (1881).

(*d*) "The presumption in favour of a marriage duly celebrated casts upon those who deny it the burden of producing reasonable evidence of the fact which renders the marriage void": *per* Dixon, J. in *Axon* v. *Axon* (1937).

The presumption of death

22. Statement of the presumption. In general, in the absence of acceptable evidence that a person was alive at some time during a continuing period of seven years or more, then if it can be shown:

(*a*) that there are persons who would be likely to have heard of him during that period of time, *and*

(*b*) that those persons have not heard of him, *and*

(*c*) that all appropriate enquiries have been made,

there arises a presumption that the person has died during that period: *Chard* v. *Chard* (1956).

23. Further points. The following points should be noted:

(*a*) There is no presumption as to the date of death.

(*b*) There arises no presumption that the person in question died at any particular time: *Re Phene's Trusts* (1870). *See* also *Chipchase* v. *Chipchase* (1939).

(*c*) There is no presumption that a person who has been heard of less than seven years ago is still alive.

(*d*) Under the Law of Property Act 1925, s. 184: "In all cases where, after the commencement of this Act, two or more persons have died in circumstances rendering it uncertain which of them survived the other or others, such deaths shall (subject to any order of the court), for all purposes affecting the title to property, be presumed to have occurred in order of seniority, and accordingly the younger shall be deemed to have survived the elder." The operation of the section will not be excluded unless there is clear evidence that one person did survive the other: *Re Bate* (1947). *See* also *Hickman*

v. *Peacey* (1945); *In re Rowland* (1963).

(*e*) Under the proviso to the Offences against the Person Act 1861, s. 57 (relating to bigamy), nothing in the section shall apply to a person marrying a second time whose spouse has been continually absent from that person for the space of seven years last past and has not been known by the person to have been living at that time.

    (*i*) This does not in itself raise a presumption of death.

    (*ii*) *See R.* v. *Curgerwen* (1865); *R.* v. *Kay* (1887).

(*f*) Under the Matrimonial Causes Act 1973, s. 19 (1): "any married person who alleges that reasonable grounds exist for supposing that the other party is dead may (subject to certain rules, now superseded by the Domicile and Matrimonial Proceedings Act 1973) present a petition to the court to have it presumed that the other party is dead and to have the marriage dissolved, and the court may, if satisfied that such reasonable grounds exist, grant a decree of presumption of death and dissolution of the marriage . . ." *See Gallacher* v. *Gallacher* (1964).

(*g*) Where the presumption of a person's death emerges before the issue of proceedings in his name, those proceedings are a nullity: *Kamouh* v. *B.A.C.* (1982).

The presumption of legitimacy

24. Statement of the rule. A child born to parents married to each other is presumed to be their legitimate child. *See Gardner* v. *Gardner* (1877). Equally, a child is presumed legitimate if conceived at a time when the parents were married to each other: *Re Leman's W.T.* (1946). See *The Banbury Peerage Case* (1811).

25. Further points. The following points should be noted:

(*a*) At common law the presumption might be rebutted by evidence that was "strong, distinct, satisfactory and conclusive": *see Morris* v. *Davies* (1837); *The Aylesford Peerage Case* (1885).

(*b*) The presumption could be rebutted by, for example, the husband showing that he could not have had intercourse with his wife at the relevant time (e.g. because he was abroad), or that he is sterile.

(c) Where a couple are living apart under the terms of a decree of judicial separation the court will draw the inference that the couple in question have not had intercourse during the time in question. See *Ettenfield* v. *Ettenfield* (1940). (Even where intercourse did take place during the time in question it might be possible, e.g. by blood tests, to establish that the husband was not the father of the child.)

(d) ". . . The presumption of legitimacy now merely determines the onus of proof. Once evidence has been led it must be weighed without using the presumption as a make-weight in the scale for legitimacy. So even weak evidence against legitimacy must prevail if there is not other evidence to counterbalance it. The presumption will only come in at that stage in the very rare case of the evidence being so evenly balanced that the court is unable to reach a decision on it. I cannot recollect ever having seen or heard of a case of any kind where the court could not reach a decision on the evidence before it": *per* Lord Reid in *S.* v. *McC.* (1972). See also *T. (H.)* v. *T. (E.)* (1971).

(e) "Any presumption of law as to the legitimacy or illegitimacy of any person may in any civil proceedings be rebutted by evidence which shows that it is more probable than not that that person is illegitimate or legitimate, as the case may be, and it shall not be necessary to prove that fact beyond reasonable doubt in order to rebut the presumption": Family Law Reform Act 1969, s. 26.

(f) "Our courts in my view apply exactly the same weight of presumption in favour of a foreign marriage as of an English one, and the nationality of any later marriage brought into question is quite immaterial": *per* Sir Jocelyn Simon in *Mahadervan* v. *Mahadervan* (1964).

(g) See also the Civil Evidence Act 1968, s. 16 (4); and the Matrimonial Causes Act 1973, s. 48 (1).

Other rebuttable presumptions of law

26. **Omnia praesumuntur rite et solemniter esse acta (all things are presumed to be done correctly and solemnly).** The so-called "presumption of legality". Where official acts are in question, there is a rebuttable presumption that all necessary conditions have been complied with. The presumption should be applied in a *criminal*

case very carefully: *Scott* v. *Baker* (1969). *See Eaglehill* v. *J. Needham Ltd.* (1973); *Campbell* v. *Wallsend Slipway Co.* (1977) where a person acting in a public capacity (as a health and safety inspector) was presumed to have been properly appointed. For rebuttal of the presumption, *see Woollett* v. *Minister of Agriculture and Fisheries* (1955).

27. Res ipsa loquitur (the thing speaks for itself). *See* 6:11 (*c*). In some actions for injury, the mere fact of an accident occurring will raise the inference of defendant's negligence so that a prima facie case exists. "There is, in the circumstances of the particular case, some evidence which, viewed not as a matter of conjecture, but of reasonable argument, makes it more probable that there was some negligence, upon the facts as shown and undisputed, than that the occurrence took place without negligence": *per* Kennedy, L. J. in *Russell* v. *L. & S.W. Railway* (1908).

(*a*) "You may presume negligence from the mere fact that it happens": *Ballard* v. *N. British Railway* (1923).

(*b*) *See Byrne* v. *Boadle* (1863); *Mahon* v. *Osborne* (1939); *Ward* v. *Tesco* (1976)—plaintiff slipped on yoghurt spilt on floor of defendant's shop.

28. Possession. Where the question relates to which of several occupiers is in legal possession, there is a presumption that the one with legal title is the legal possessor: *Ramsay* v. *Margrett* (1894).

29. Lawful origin. Where asserted rights have been exercised without interruption for such a period of time that they might be taken fairly to have had a lawful origin, there is a presumption of such lawful origin: *Johnson* v. *Barnes* (1873). ("I do not think we should be justified in giving this effect to the documents, if the result would be to set aside a right which has been so long exercised in fact . . . It appears to me . . . that we are bound in accordance with one of the best established principles of law, to presume a legal origin, if one were possible, in favour of a long and uninterrupted enjoyment of a right": *per* Kelly, C.B.)

30. Documents. For presumptions relating to written documents not less than twenty years old, *see* 8:21 (*a*). For presumptions relating to date of execution of and alterations in documents, *see* 8:21 (*b*). Note, also, the presumptions in the Law of Property Act 1925, s. 15, that parties to a conveyance are presumed to be of full age and, under s. 45 (6), that recitals and descriptions of facts in deeds are to be taken as "sufficient evidence of the truth of such facts", except so far as they may be proved to be inaccurate.

Rebuttable presumptions of fact

31. General. Known also as "provisional presumptions", these are *inferences which may be drawn (but there is no compulsion as to this)* on the basis of common sense and experience. They have been further divided into:

(*a*) *strong presumptions*, which shift the burden of proof; and

(*b*) *slight presumptions*, which do not shift the burden of proof. Examples are given at **32–34** below.

32. Intention. There is a presumption that a person intends the natural consequences of his acts. Note, however, that "a court or jury in determining whether a person has committed an offence:

(*a*) shall not be bound in law to infer that he intended or foresaw a result of his actions by reason only of its being a natural and probable consequence of those actions; but

(*b*) shall decide whether he did intend or foresee that result by reference to all the evidence, drawing such inferences from the evidence as appear proper in the circumstances": Criminal Justice Act 1967, s. 8.

33. Continuance. The court may, in general, infer from the existence of some state of affairs in the past that it continues. *See A.-G.* v. *Bradlaugh* (1885); *R.* v. *Lumley* (1869)—presumption of the continuance of human life; *Re Forster's Settlement* (1942); *Coles* v. *Underwood* (1984).

34. Guilty knowledge. Where X is found in possession of property recently stolen, the jury may be directed that they may infer X's guilty knowledge if he offers no explanation of his possession of the property, or if they are satisfied that an explanation he offers is not true. X will be convicted only where the jury is satisfied beyond reasonable doubt that he had such guilty knowledge. *See* the Theft Act 1968, s. 27 (3); *R.* v. *Hepworth and Fearnley* (1955); *R.* v. *Smith* (1983); *R.* v. *Bradley* (1980)—s. 27 (3) does not allow evidence to be given of another offence (of "handling" stolen property) prior to the offence being charged. *See* also the Criminal Justice Act 1967, s. 8 (at **32** above).

35. Main differences between presumptions of law and presumptions of fact. It should be noted that, in general, a presumption of *law* is drawn by the *judge* and a presumption of *fact* by the *jury*. Further, a presumption of *law* will almost always alter the burden of proof; a presumption of *fact* may occasionally do so. Note, in particular:

(*a*) A presumption of *law* is a conclusion prescribed by law; a presumption of *fact* derives its strength, essentially, from logic.

(*b*) A presumption of *law must be drawn* when particular facts are established and there is an absence of proof to the contrary; a presumption of *fact may be drawn* if the court so wishes.

Progress test 10

1. Define "presumption". (**2**)
2. In what ways can the operation of a presumption affect the incidence of the burden of proof? (**3**)
3. Explain the problem of "conflicting presumptions". (**5**)
4. State the "orthodox" classification of presumptions. (**8**)
5. State Lord Denning's proposals for the classification of presumptions. (**9**)
6. State any two irrebuttable presumptions of law. (**12–14**)
7. Consider the operation of the presumption of innocence in relation to an offence of stealing alleged to have been committed by a child who is shown to be aged ten. (**17**)
8. What is meant by the "presumption of marriage"? (**20**)
9. In what circumstances will the presumption of death operate? (**22**)

10. How does the presumption of legitimacy operate? (24–25)

11. What is meant by a "rebuttable presumption of fact"? (31)

12. Comment on the presumption of guilty knowledge where X is found in possession of property recently stolen. (34)

11

Matters of which proof is not allowed (1): estoppels

Preliminary matters

1. General. Chapters 9 and 10 dealt with matters of which proof is generally *not required*; in this and the following chapter we consider matters of which proof *will not be allowed*. The rules of exclusion illustrated here operate so as to *exclude facts* (as contrasted with *hearsay—see* Part 4—which operates so as to exclude a particular *mode of proof of facts*). Some of the matters to be discussed may be exemplified by the following cases:

(*a*) A sues B for infringement of a patent. A obtains judgment on the ground that the patent was valid. At a later date A sues B for a further infringement of that patent. B is *estopped* from denying the validity of the patent in question: *Shoe Machinery Co.* v. *Cutlam* (1896).

(*b*) In an action for negligence relating to a submarine disaster, documents concerning the construction of the vessel which were in the possession of defendant were not allowed to be produced: *Duncan* v. *Cammell Laird & Co. Ltd.* (1942).

2. Matters to be discussed. The following matters concerning circumstances in which proof is not allowed are considered in this chapter and the next:

(*a*) *Estoppel* (*see* 1 (*a*) above): *see* **3–29** below.
(*b*) *Privilege* (*see* 1 (*b*) above): *see* Chap. 12.

3. Estoppel: definition and examples. Estoppel is an exclusionary rule of evidence, the application of which may result in a party's being prohibited from asserting or denying some fact. The following cases illustrate this rule in the law of evidence. Note that, in each case, the effect of the rule is *to render some relevant facts inadmissible as evidence*.

(a) *Greenwood* v. *Martins Bank Ltd.* (1933). A husband failed to inform the bank that his wife was forging his signature on cheques. The House of Lords held that the husband's failure estopped him from setting up the forgeries in a subsequent action by the bank to recover sums paid to the wife and debited to his account with the bank.

(b) *Dixon* v. *Kennaway* (1900). A company authorised the issue of a certificate stating that X was the registered holder of shares. It was later estopped from alleging, in an action, that X was not entitled to those shares.

(c) *Hill* v. *Hill* (1954). W's petition for divorce on grounds of cruelty alleged acts of violence by H, but the petition was dismissed on the ground that the acts were trivial. H later petitioned for divorce on the grounds of W's desertion. W pleaded that she had just cause for leaving H and attempted to show this by proof of the very same acts of violence. It was held that W was estopped by the previous finding that these acts were trivial from advancing them as just cause for leaving H.

4. Types of estoppel. Estoppels arise on three grounds:

(a) by record (*see* **9–19** below);

(b) by deed (*see* **20–22** below);

(c) by conduct (*see* **23–29** below).

5. The general conditions applying to estoppels. The following points should be noted:

(a) An estoppel must be expressly pleaded: *Vooght* v. *Winch* (1819).

(b) Estoppels must be mutual, that is, they must bind both parties to the litigation.

(*c*) An action cannot be founded on an estoppel: *Combe* v. *Combe* (1951). *See* O. 18, r. 8. *See* **28** (*e*) below.

(*d*) An estoppel must be certain and unambiguous, "clear and unqualified": *Freeman* v. *Cooke* (1848); *Canadian and Dominion Sugar Co. Ltd.* v. *Canadian National Steamships Ltd.* (1947).

(*e*) Estoppel binds only parties to the litigation; it does *not* bind the court (*see* **17** below).

(*f*) An estoppel will be overruled by a positive rule of law: *Leslie Ltd.* v. *Sheill* (1914); nor can it be set up "in the face of a statute": *see Kok Hoong* v. *Leong Cheong Kweng Ltd.* (1964).

6. Estoppel: a mere rule of substantive law. It has been argued that estoppel is not a rule of evidence, but rather a mode of substantive law (*see* comments of Lord Wright in *Canadian and Dominion Sugar Co. Ltd.* v. *Canadian National Steamships Ltd.* (1947): "Estoppel is often described as a rule of evidence, as indeed it may be so described. But the whole concept is more correctly viewed as a substantive rule of law . . ."), since it can have the effect of a rule of substantive law where a party is prohibited from asserting or denying a fact in issue; in that case it effectively creates a right against the person estopped and prevents his ignoring that right.

7. Estoppel: a mere rule of procedure. It has been argued, also, that estoppel is not a rule of evidence, but rather a mere rule of procedure or pleading. Thus, an estoppel must be expressly pleaded; failure to plead an estoppel may effectively waive its benefit.

8. Estoppel: an exclusionary rule of evidence. Estoppel may, in fact, be waived; hence it has the character of evidence and is distinguished from a rule of the substantive law. Further, it cannot be used as a cause of action, but as a defence only. Nor does the fact that estoppel has to be expressly pleaded transform it into a rule of pleading; it has been pointed out, for example, that the Limitation Acts (e.g. the Limitation Act 1980) have to be pleaded, but it cannot be argued that, therefore, they constitute mere rules of pleading. Estoppel is—it would seem—an *exclusionary rule of evidence*, but often it has the *effect* of a rule of substantive law.

Estoppel by record

9. How estoppel by record arises. Estoppel by record, known also as "judgment estoppel" and *estoppel per rem judicatam* has been stated in the following manner by Spencer-Bower, and referred to in *Carl-Zeiss-Stiftung* v. *Rayner and Keeler Ltd. (No. 2)*(1967): "Where a final judicial decision has been pronounced by either an English, or (with certain exceptions) a foreign, judicial tribunal of competent jurisdiction over the parties to, and the subject-matter of, the litigation, any party or privy to such litigation, as against any other party or privy thereto, and, in the case of a decision *in rem*, any person whatsoever, as against any other person, is estopped in any subsequent litigation from disputing or questioning such decision on the merits, whether it be used as the foundation of an action, or relied upon as a bar to any claim, indictment or complaint, or to any affirmative defence, case, or allegation, if, but not unless, the party interested raises the point of estoppel at the proper time and in the proper manner."

(*a*) In essence, therefore, it arises where a person is estopped from raising some allegation previously decided against him by a court of competent jurisdiction. *See Re May* (1885).

(*b*) The matter which the party is estopped from raising is known as *res judicata*.

(*c*) The basic principle has been expressed in the maxim *res judicata pro veritate accipitur* (a matter adjudged is taken for truth, i.e. a judicial decision is considered conclusive until it has been reversed and its truth may not be contradicted). *See Sambasivam* v. *Public Prosecutor of Malaya* (1950).

(*d*) "The doctrine . . . is one founded on considerations of justice and good sense. If an issue has been distinctly raised and decided in an action, in which the parties are represented, it is unjust and unreasonable to permit the same issue to be litigated afresh between the same parties or persons claiming under them": *per* Lord Maugham in *New Brunswick Rail Co.* v. *British and French Trust Corporation Ltd.* (1939).

(*e*) The doctrine has been considered as an essential product of the adversary system, which is typical of procedure in an English trial (*see* 1:1 (*a*)). "Estoppel merely means that, under the rules of the adversary system of procedure upon which the common law of England is based, a party is not allowed, in certain circumstances, to prove in litigation particular facts or matters which, if proved, would assist him to succeed as plaintiff or defendant in an action": *per* Lord Diplock in *Thoday* v. *Thoday* (1964).

(*f*) *Res judicata* cannot be founded on dismissal of an action for want of prosecution: *Pople* v. *Evans* (1968). *See* the Prosecution of Offences Act 1985, s. 22 (4), for a new rule: a criminal case struck out for delay acts as an *acquittal* for all purposes.

10. Underlying principles. The principles upon which estoppel by record is based are embodied in the following maxims:

(*a*) *Interest reipublicae est ut sit finis litium.* "It is in the public interest that there should be an end to litigation."

(*b*) *Nemo debet bis vexari pro eadem causa.* "No person should be in jeopardy twice on the same cause."

11. Types of judicial decision. Two separate types of judicial decision are relevant in this context:

(*a*) *Judgments in rem*, finally determining parties' status and conclusive upon "the world at large". *See* **12** below.

(*b*) *Judgments in personam*, determining interests, rights and liabilities of the litigants. *See* **13** below.

12. Judgments in rem. These are judicial decisions which declare, define or, in some other way, determine the jural relations of a person (i.e. his status) to the world in general. *See Minna Craig Steamship Co.* v. *Chartered Mercantile Bank of India, London and China* (1897). A judgment *in rem* operates so as to estop any person from disputing its basis.

(*a*) Examples: a declaration of legitimacy; declaration as to the validity of a marriage; grant of probate; receiving order made against a debtor.

(*b*) The decision following criminal proceedings may be considered as conclusive *in rem* in relation to the fact of acquittal or
conviction.

(*c*) The judgments of this nature are, in effect, conclusive
evidence for or against *all* persons of *all* those matters actually
decided and of *all* the matters necessarily implied by the judgments:
Hoystead v. *Commissioner of Taxation* (1926).

(*d*) Judgments obtained by fraud do not raise an estoppel.
("Fraud is an extrinsic, collateral act which vitiates the most solemn
proceedings of the courts of justice": *per* De Grey, C. J. in *Duchess of
Kingston's Case* (1776).)

(*e*) *See* also *Geyer* v. *Aguilar* (1798); *Wakefield Corporation* v.
Cooke (1904).

13. Judgments in personam. These are judicial decisions, known
also as judgments *inter partes*, which do not operate so as to affect
status.

(*a*) A decision *inter partes* operates as an estoppel, in favour of,
and against, parties and privies only, not third persons or strangers,
as to the very facts in issue. "Privies have been described as those
who are privy to the party in estate or interest. Before a person can
be privy to a party there must be community or privity of interest
between them": *per* Lord Reid in *Carl-Zeiss-Stiftung* v. *Rayner and
Keeler Ltd.* (*No. 2*) (1967). Privity may be (*see* 18:8):

    (*i*) *in law*, e.g. testator and executor;

    (*ii*) *in blood*, e.g. ancestor and heir;

    (*iii*) *in estate*, e.g. lessee and assignee of lease.

(*b*) "It is unquestionably not the general rule of law that a
judgment obtained by A against B is conclusive in an action by B
against C. On the contrary, the rule of law is otherwise . . . a
judgment *inter partes* is conclusive only between the parties and
those claiming under them": *per* Mellish, L. J. in *Gray* v. *Lewis*
(1873).

(*c*) Identity of parties involved in the original judgment and in the
issue before the court is essential if the doctrine is to operate. In
Townsend v. *Bishop* (1939), X, the owner of a car, brought an action
against Y, the owner of a lorry, arising from damage to his car caused

by an accident in which Z (X's son) had been driving the car. The court held that the accident had been caused by Z's negligence. In a later action for personal injuries brought by Z against Y, it was held that Z was not estopped by the earlier judgment from denying his negligence.

(*d*) A person who sues in one capacity will not be estopped in a future action by or against him in a different capacity even though both actions arise on the one incident: *Marginson* v. *Blackburn B.C.* (1939).

14. Issue estoppel. *Issue estoppel* is contrasted with *action estoppel* ("If one party brings an action against another for a particular cause and judgment is given on it, there is a strict rule of law that he cannot bring another action against the same party for the same cause": *per* Lord Denning in *Fidelitas Shipping* v. *V/O Exportchleb* (1966)). Issue estoppel was considered in *Mills* v. *Cooper* (1967): "A party to civil proceedings is not entitled to make, as against the other party, an assertion, whether of fact or of the legal consequences of facts, the correctness of which is an essential element in his previous cause of action or defence in previous civil proceedings between the same parties or their predecessors in title, and was found by a court of competent jurisdiction in such previous civil proceedings to be incorrect, unless further material which is relevant to the correctness or incorrectness of the assertion by that party in the previous proceedings has since become available to him": *per* Diplock, J.

(*a*) "The requirements of issue estoppel still remain:

   (*i*) that the same question has been decided;

   (*ii*) that the judicial decision which is said to create the estoppel was final; and

   (*iii*) that the parties to the judicial decision or their privies were the same persons as the parties to the proceedings in which the estoppel is raised": *per* Lord Guest in *Carl-Zeiss-Stiftung* v. *Rayner and Keeler Ltd.* (1967).

(*b*) " 'Issue estoppel' is not a rule of evidence . . . [it] is a particular application of the general rule of public policy that there should be finality in litigation": *per* Diplock, L. J. in *Mills* v. *Cooper* (1967).

(*c*) The judge will determine, by reference to the pleadings in the former action or the wording of the judgment, any question of identity of issues: *Thoday* v. *Thoday* (1964).

(*d*) The test is generally to inquire whether both issues could be supported by the same evidence: *Brunsden* v. *Humphrey* (1884).

(*i*) If a certain fact has been put in issue in the former case and has been decided between the parties, it cannot be re-opened by the parties or their privies: *Priestman* v. *Thomas* (1884).

(*ii*) *See also Marriot* v. *Hampton* (1797); *Conquer* v. *Boot* (1928).

15. Examples relating to issue estoppel. The following cases should be noted:

(*a*) *Priestman* v. *Thomas* (1884). P attempted to have a grant of probate set aside in the Probate Division on the ground of its having been forged. D was estopped from denying this, since it had been held in previous proceedings between P and D in the Chancery Division, that the will had been forged.

(*b*) *Wood* v. *Luscombe* (1966). L and W, each driving a motor cycle, collided and in an action by L against W, both were found equally to blame. Later, a pillion passenger involved in the accident brought an action against L; L brought in W as a third party and claimed contribution under the Law Reform (Married Women and Tortfeasors) Act 1935. W was estopped from denying that he and L were equally to blame for the collision, because the issue of blame had been determined by the judgment in the original action.

16. Judgments in criminal cases and estoppels in civil cases. The general rule is that judgments in criminal cases will *not* give rise to estoppels in civil cases (and vice versa). Note, however, the Civil Evidence Act 1968, s. 13 (1): "In an action for libel or slander in which the question whether a person did or did not commit a criminal offence is relevant to an issue arising in the action, proof that, at the time when that issue falls to be determined, that person stands convicted of that offence shall be conclusive evidence that he committed that offence; and his conviction thereof shall be admissible in evidence accordingly." The result of this section is that P, plaintiff in an action for, say, libel, will be estopped from denying the truth of defendant's allegation that he, P, is guilty of some criminal offence for which he has been convicted.

17. The question of matrimonial proceedings: estoppel does not bind the court. "Once an issue of a matrimonial offence has been litigated between the parties and decided by a competent court, neither party can claim as of right to reopen the issue and litigate it all over again if the other party objects . . . But the divorce court has the right, and indeed the duty in a proper case, to reopen the issue or to allow either party to reopen it, despite the objection of the other party (that is what is meant by saying that estoppels do not bind the divorce court)": *per* Denning, L. J. in *Thompson* v. *Thompson* (1957).

(*a*) Under the Matrimonial Causes Act 1973, s. 4, the court's jurisdiction will not be excluded where a petitioner has been granted a magistrates' maintenance order or judicial separation upon the same or substantially the same facts which are proved on a petition for divorce. The court will treat the order or decree as proof of the reasons for which it was granted, *but* it will, nevertheless, receive evidence from petitioner before pronouncing a decree of divorce.

(*b*) See *Winnan* v. *Winnan* (1949); *Hayward* v. *Hayward* (1961).

18. Action estoppel in criminal cases. Action estoppel in criminal proceedings arises from a plea of *autrefois acquit* or *autrefois convict*.

(*a*) *Autrefois acquit* ("formerly acquitted") is a plea in bar that accused has been acquitted previously of the same offence. "The test to establish the plea is (1) that defendant had been previously acquitted of the same offence, or (2) that he could have been convicted at the previous trial of the offence with which he is subsequently charged, or that the two offences are substantially the same": *Re Wilson* (1948). *See* also *Halsted* v. *Clark* (1944); *R.* v. *Thomas* (1950). It will *not* suffice that the charge in the case arises out of the same incident as the charge in the former case. *See* also **9** (*f*) above.

(*b*) *Autrefois convict* ("formerly convicted") is a plea in bar that accused has been previously tried and convicted for the same offence. The offence with which he is charged must be the same, or practically the same, offence as that with which he was previously charged. *See Connelly* v. *D.P.P.* (1964); *Iremonger* v. *Vissenga* (1976).

19. Issue estoppel in criminal proceedings. "Issue estoppel can be said to exist where there is a judicial establishment of a proposition of law or fact between parties to earlier litigation and when the same question arises in later litigation between the same parties. In the latter litigation the established proposition is treated as conclusive between the same parties": *R.* v. *Hogan* (1974). In *DPP* v. *Humphrys* (1977) the House of Lords held that *issue estoppel was not part of the criminal law of England.* "The doctrine would . . . be inappropriate, artificial, unnecessary and unfair": *per* Lord Salmon. (*See*, however, *R.* v. *Hay* (1983); *R.* v. *Doosti* (1986).)

Estoppel by deed

20. How estoppel by deed arises. Estoppel by deed arises usually on the rule that no person who is party to a deed or instrument under seal may dispute or deny its contents. "A party who executes a deed is estopped in a court of law from saying that the facts stated in the deed are not truly stated": *per* Bayley, J. in *Baker* v. *Dewey* (1823). The estoppel operates as between the parties and their privies (*see* 13 (*a*) above): *Bowman* v. *Taylor* (1834).

21. Underlying principle. "Estoppel by deed is a rule of evidence founded on the principle that a solemn and unambiguous statement or engagement in a deed must be taken as binding between parties and privies and therefore as not admitting any contradictory proof": *per* Lord Russell in *Greer* v. *Kettle* (1938).

22. Further points relating to estoppel by deed. The following points should be noted:

(*a*) Estoppel by deed may extend to a statement made in a recital in that deed: *Bowman* v. *Taylor* (1834).

(*b*) A recital in a deed may operate as an estoppel of one party only; a recital introduced by mistake will *not* operate as an estoppel: *Greer* v. *Kettle* (1938). The intention of the parties will depend on the construction of that document.

(*c*) Estoppel will operate only in respect of matters material to the transaction and intended to be binding.

(*d*) The doctrine applies only in actions on the deed: *Carpenter* v. *Buller* (1841).

(*e*) Operation of the doctrine requires a clear and unambiguous statement in the deed: *District Bank* v. *Webb* (1958).

(*f*) A party may set up the plea of fraud, mistake, etc. which would have allowed him the right of rescinding the deed: *Greer* v. *Kettle* (1938).

(*g*) A receipt for money in a deed will not create an estoppel; but in the absence of proof that payment was not made, the receipt may suffice as evidence that payment was made: *see* the Law of Property Act 1925, s. 68.

Estoppel by conduct

23. How estoppel by conduct arises. Estoppel by conduct, known also as "estoppel *in pais*", arises thus: "Where one by his words or conduct wilfully causes another to believe in the existence of a certain state of things, and induces him to act on that belief, or to alter his own previous position, the former is concluded from averring against the latter a different state of things existing at that time": *Pickard* v. *Sears* (1837).

24. Underlying principle. "The principle on which estoppel *in pais* is founded is that the law should not permit an unjust departure by a party from an assumption of fact which he has caused another party to adopt or accept for the purpose of their legal relationship": *per* Dixon, J. in *Grundt* v. *Great Boulder Proprietary Gold Mine Ltd.* (1937).

25. Types of estoppel by conduct. The following types of estoppel by conduct are considered below:

(*a*) Estoppel *by agreement* (*see* 26 below).
(*b*) Estoppel *by representation* (*see* 27 below).

26. Estoppel by agreement. Where X and Y enter an agreement based on the existence of a certain state of affairs, both X and Y and those claiming through them will be estopped from denying that this state of affairs exists. Thus, a landlord who has granted a lease will be estopped from alleging his want of title.

27. Estoppel by representation. The following statements of principle should be noted carefully:

(a) "The essential factors giving rise to an estoppel are, I think: a representation or conduct amounting to a representation intended to induce a course of conduct on the part of the person to whom the representation was made; an act or omission resulting from the representation, whether actual or by conduct, by the person to whom the representation was made; detriment to such person as a consequence of the act or omission where silence cannot amount to a representation, but, where there is a duty to disclose, deliberate silence may become significant and amount to a representation. The existence of a duty on the part of a customer of a bank to disclose to the bank his knowledge of such a forgery as the one in question [*see* 3 (*a*) above] was rightly admitted": *per* Lord Tomlin in *Greenwood* v. *Martins Bank* (1933).

(b) "If a man, whatever his real meaning may be, so conducts himself that a reasonable man would take his conduct to mean a certain representation of facts, and that it was a true representation, and that the latter was intended to act upon it in a particular way, and he with such belief does act in that way to his damage, the first is estopped from denying that the facts were as represented": *per* Brett, J. in *Carr* v. *London and N.W. Rail Co.* (1875).

28. Further points on estoppel by representation. The following points should be noted:

(a) In the case of agency by estoppel, where X represents Y as being his agent, X is then estopped from denying that Y acted with his authority: *Drew* v. *Nunn* (1879).

(b) By the Partnership Act 1890, s. 14 (1), where X represents himself as a partner in a firm, he is liable to anyone who has given credit to the firm on the strength of that representation. *See Tower Cabinet Co.* v. *Ingram* (1949).

(c) Estoppel through conduct may arise through silence; but mere silence without some other conduct will not amount to a representation unless there is some duty to make disclosure:

Greenwood v. *Martins Bank* (1933).

(*d*) Representation will not give rise to estoppel if it is merely a representation as to the law or as to future intention: *Jorden* v. *Money* (1854).

(*e*) Estoppel is a "shield not a sword", i.e. a defence, not to be used as the *cause* of an action. But where the estoppel's effect is the creation of a proprietary interest, it can give rise to a cause of action where proceedings to enforce the interest are concerned: *see Ramsden* v. *Dyson* (1866); *Inwards* v. *Baker* (1965); *E. R. Ives Investment* v. *High* (1967); *Crabb* v. *Arun D.C.* (1975) (in which it was held that a landowner who induces another to believe that a right of access will be given over the landowner's land, can be estopped from denying that the right exists if that other person has acted to his detriment by relying on the assurance which has been given)—this is an example of so-called "proprietary estoppel".

(*f*) The estoppel cannot be pleaded successfully unless it is clear and unambiguous: *Freeman* v. *Cooke* (1848).

29. Estoppel by negligence. Where the negligence of defendant causes a person to believe in the existence of a supposed fact, and that person subsequently acts on that belief with resultant damage, defendant will be estopped from denying the existence of the supposed fact: *Coventry, Sheppard & Co.* v. *Great E. Railway* (1833). In that case, a railway company negligently issued two delivery orders, which did not purport to be duplicates, in respect of a single consignment of wheat, as a result of which a person, acting fraudulently, was able to obtain two advances of money as if there had been two separate consignments. It was held that the company *was estopped* by its negligence from disputing that there were two consignments. *See* also: *London Joint Stock Bank* v. *Macmillan* (1918); *Wilson and Meeson* v. *Pickering* (1946).

Progress test 11

1. Define *estoppel*. (3)
2. Enumerate the general conditions applying to estoppels. (5)
3. Consider the argument that estoppel is merely a rule of substantive law. (6)

4. How does estoppel by record arise? (**9**)

5. Assume that a grant of probate has been obtained. Can any person be estopped from denying the title of the executor? (**12**)

6. Which persons are bound by a judgment *in personam*? (**13**)

7. Explain what is meant by *action estoppel*. (**14**)

8. What are the requirements of *issue estoppel*? (**14**)

9. Outline the facts of, and the decision in, *Wood* v. *Luscombe* (1966). (**15**)

10. Do estoppels bind the court? (**17**)

11. Explain "action estoppel" in criminal cases. (**18**)

12. What is the situation concerning issue estoppel in criminal proceedings? (**19**)

13. How does estoppel by deed arise? (**20**)

14. Does a receipt for money stated in a deed ever create an estoppel? (**22**)

15. Explain *estoppel by agreement*. (**26**)

16. What are the essential features of *estoppel by representation*? (**27**)

17. Explain *proprietary estoppel*. (**28**)

18. Explain and illustrate *estoppel by negligence*. (**29**)

12

Matters of which proof is not allowed (2): privilege

Preliminary matters

1. General. Privilege is an extraordinary *right of advantage* attached to persons in some special circumstances. Those who possess this right are exempt from some specific duty, obligation or other burden. An American definition speaks of privilege as "a legal freedom on the part of one person as against another to do a given act or a legal freedom not to do a certain act." In this chapter we consider aspects of the doctrine of privilege which may lead to the exclusion of certain types of evidence.

2. The concept of privilege in the law of evidence. Although a witness may be both competent and compellable to give evidence (*see* Chap. 4), he has the right, nevertheless, to decline to answer certain types of question on a number of grounds, e.g. that the answer required relates to affairs of state, disclosure of which would be injurious to public interests (*see Beatson* v. *Skene* (1860)), or that the answer might subject him to a criminal prosecution (*see R.* v. *Boyes* (1861)). The general result is that there exists a number of circumstances in which a party *will not be allowed to prove some fact*, even though that fact be relevant and proof of it could be given. Estoppel (*see* Chap. 11) is one ground for the refusal of proof of relevant evidence; privilege, to be considered below, is another, similar, ground.

3. Examples of privilege in the law of evidence. The following cases should be noted:

(a) *Duncan* v. *Cammell Laird & Co. Ltd*. (1942). In an action brought by the widows of persons drowned in a submarine disaster, it was held by the House of Lords that a statement by the First Lord of the Admiralty that disclosure would be against the public interest had to be accepted by the court as final. (But *see* 9 below.)

(b) *Paddock* v. *Forrester* (1842). The first of a series of letters was headed "Without Prejudice". It was held that the privilege of non-disclosure attached to the correspondence in its entirety. (*See* 23 below.)

4. Some points underlying the concept of privilege. The following points should be noted:

(a) The fact that witness claims a privilege does not, in itself, give rise to any inference adverse to his case: *Wentworth* v. *Lloyd* (1864).

(b) Privilege attaches to a particular person; hence it may be possible to prove the matters apparently shielded by that privilege through the evidence of other witnesses.

(i) In *Calcraft* v. *Guest* (1898) it was held that although privilege was applicable to documents, they were admissible when secondary evidence of them became available.

(ii) In *Rumping* v. *D.P.P.* (1964) part of the evidence for the prosecution admitted at a trial for murder was a letter written by the appellant to his wife on the day after the killing. (The letter had been intercepted and shown to the police.) The question on appeal was whether the letter was rightly admitted as evidence against the appellant. It was held that the letter *was* properly admitted; there is no rule of common law or public policy preventing someone other than a spouse from giving evidence of an intended communication between spouses.

5. Matters to be discussed. The following matters will be discussed in this chapter:

(a) Privilege relating to matters of "public policy" (*see* 6–12 below).

(b) Private privilege (*see* 13–24 below).

(c) Evidence at a trial for rape (*see* 25–26 below).

Privilege arising on grounds of public policy

6. The general principle. In general, relevant evidence will be excluded *where its disclosure would prejudice the public interest*.

(*a*) "The general public interest is paramount to the interests of the suitor": *per* Swinfen-Eady, L. J. in *Asiatic Petroleum Co. Ltd.* v. *Anglo-Persian Oil Co. Ltd.* (1916). *See Waugh* v. *British Railways Board* (1980). Note *Hehir* v. *Metropolitan Police Commissioner* (1982)—*per curiam*, it might be that public interest immunity can never be waived; *Re Highgrade Traders* (1983).

(*b*) "First, the publication of a state document may involve danger to the nation . . . an order for discovery might involve the country in war. Secondly, the publication of a state document may be injurious to servants of the Crown as individuals . . .": *per* Field, J. in *Hennessy* v. *Wright* (1888). *See Buttes Gas* v. *Hammer (No. 3)* (1981).

7. Aspects of the principle. Three aspects of "public policy" are considered below:

(*a*) national security and other matters affecting the state (*see* **8–9** below);

(*b*) detection of crime (*see* **10** below);

(*c*) judicial disclosures (*see* **11** below).

8. National security and other vital matters affecting the state. State interest lay behind the exclusion of evidence in the following circumstances: communications between a Colonial Governor and a Secretary of State (*Chatterton* v. *Secretary of State for India* (1895)); government plans concerning a First World War campaign (*Asiatic Petroleum Co. Ltd.* v. *Anglo-Persian Oil Co. Ltd.* (1916)); confidential reports relating to a detention order under the Defence of the Realm Regulations (*R.* v. *Secretary of State ex p. Lees* (1941)); medical reports on a prisoner who had assaulted another prisoner (*Ellis* v. *Home Office* (1953)); letters from a chief constable to the Gaming Board concerning the reputation of a club licence applicant (*Rogers* v. *Home Secretary* (1973)).

9. The law restated: Conway v. Rimmer (1968). Prior to the decision in this case, the general rule was that a Minister's decision on a question of "public interest" was *absolutely* binding on the courts: *see Duncan* v. *Cammell Laird & Co. Ltd.* (1942) (at **3** (*a*) above). But in *Re Grosvenor Hotel London (No. 2)* (1965) it was held by the Court of Appeal that in some cases the judge had a residual power to inspect documents even where a Minister had objected to their disclosure.

(*a*) In *Conway* v. *Rimmer* (1968), X, a former police probationer, brought an action for malicious prosecution against a superintendent who had caused a charge of theft to be brought against X, following which X had been acquitted. The Home Secretary objected (contrary to the wishes of the parties) to the production of documents relating to X's conduct during his probationary period. *The House of Lords ordered the documents to be produced for inspection,* after which they ordered production to X.

(*b*) "In my view it should now be made clear that whenever an objection is made to the production of a relevant document it is for the court to decide whether to uphold the objection. The inherent power of the court must include a power to ask for clarification or amplification of an objection to production, though the court will be careful not to impose a requirement which could only be met by divulging the very matters to which the objection related. The power of the court must also include a power to examine documents privately—a power which, I think, in practice should be sparingly exercised, but one which could operate as a safeguard to the executive in cases where a court is inclined to make an order for production where an objection is being pressed. I see no difference in principle between the consideration which should govern what have been called the contents cases and the class cases": *per* Lord Morris.

(*c*) *A subsequent case: Norwich Pharmacal Co. Ltd.* v. *Customs and Excise Commissioners* (1974). The plaintiffs held the patent of a chemical compound used in animal foods which they discovered was being infringed by unknown importers. The Commissioners knew the identity of the importers. The plaintiffs brought proceedings against the Commissioners and asked for an order of disclosure of the importers' identity. The judge granted the order, but this was *not upheld* by the Court of Appeal. The plaintiff's appeal to the House of Lords *was allowed.* It was held that the confidential communications in the hands of the Commissioners could be produced; *the interests of justice outweighed any public interest in the confidential nature of that information. See* also *Burmah Oil Co.* v. *Bank of England* (1980); *Science Research Council* v. *Nassé* (1980)—"the courts should and will do all they can to uphold the moral and social duty not to break confidences"; *British Steel Corp.* v. *Granada Television* (1981).

Note also the Contempt of Court Act 1981, s. 10: "No court may require a person to disclose, nor is any person guilty of contempt of court for refusing to disclose, the source of information contained in a publication for which he is responsible, unless it be established to the satisfaction of the court that disclosure is necessary in the interests of justice or national security or for the prevention of disorder or crime." (*See Secretary of State for Defence* v. *Guardian Newspapers* (1984).)

10. The detection of crime. In general, a source of information which has led to the detection of crime will be privileged from disclosure.

(*a*) "Sources of police information are a judicially recognised class of evidence excluded on the ground of public policy unless their production is required to establish innocence in a criminal trial": *per* Lord Simon in *Rogers* v. *Home Secretary* (1973).

(*b*) In *Marks* v. *Beyfus* (1890), a civil action for conspiracy to prosecute maliciously, the plaintiff called the DPP who declined to answer a question relating to the information leading to the plaintiff's prosecution; the refusal was upheld by the Court of Appeal. "I do not say the rule can never be departed from; if the judge should be of opinion that the disclosure of the name of the informant is necessary or right in order to show the prisoner's innocence, then one public policy is in conflict with another public policy, and that which says an innocent man is not to be condemned when his innocence can be proved, is the policy that must prevail. But, except in that case, this rule is not a matter of discretion; it is a

rule of law, and as such should be applied by the judge at the trial":
per Lord Esher.

11. Judicial disclosures. The general rule is that judges *may not be compelled* to give evidence relating to the cases they have tried. "As everything which they can properly prove can be proved by others, the courts of law discountenance and, I think I may say, prevent them being examined": *per* Cleasby, B. in *Buccleuch* v. *Metropolitan Board of Works* (1872).

(*a*) "The authorities establish beyond all question this: that neither party, witness, counsel, jury, nor judge can be put to answer civilly or criminally for words spoken in office; that no action of libel or slander lies, whether against judges, counsel, witnesses, or parties, for words written or spoken in the course of any proceedings before any court recognised by law, and this though the words written or spoken were written or spoken maliciously without any justification or excuse, and from personal ill-will and anger against the person defamed. This absolute privilege has been conceded on the grounds of public policy to ensure freedom of speech where it is essential that freedom of speech should exist, and with the knowledge that courts of justice are presided over by those who from their high character are not likely to abuse the privilege, and who have the power and ought to have the will to check any abuse of it by those who appear before them": *per* Lopes, L. J. in *Royal Aquarium and Summer and Winter Garden Society Ltd.* v. *Parkinson* (1892).

(*b*) The rule has application to evidence of *arbitrators*. They may be compelled to give evidence relating to matters which had occurred during the arbitration; they may *not* be compelled to answer questions concerning the reasons for an award: *Ward* v. *Shell-Mex and B.P.* (1952).

(*c*) At common law a *juror* could not be compelled to give evidence concerning discussions in the jury box or jury room: *Boston* v. *Bagshaw* (1966). The Contempt of Court Act 1981, s. 8, now protects the confidentiality of a jury's deliberations (subject to strict exceptions).

(*d*) Note that no privilege attaches to the documents on which an expert witness (*see* 15:**34**) in either a civil or criminal trial bases his evidence: *R.* v. *King* (1983).

(*e*) No privilege attaches to notes of evidence made by a justices' clerk, who must, therefore, produce them when requested: *Hill* v. *Wilson* (1985). This is, however, restricted to cases where the clerk is *under a duty* to make notes (which is comparatively rare): *see R.* v. *Clerk to the Lancaster Justices, ex p. Hill* (1984).

12. Claiming the privilege. The following points should be noted:

(*a*) *If the Crown is a party*, objection to the production of documents will generally be taken when the order for discovery of documents is made, or at the trial. (Note the Crown Proceedings Act 1947, s. 28.)

(*b*) *If the Crown is not a party*, objection may be taken before the trial (by the appropriate Minister), or at the trial (by the government official who has answered the *subpoena* to give evidence, by counsel instructed by the Crown, or by the judge).

Private privilege

13. The general principle. Under certain circumstances, a rule of evidence will operate whereby a witness may justifiably refuse to answer questions or interrogatories or produce documents. The principle of private privilege differs from that attaching to matters of public policy on the following grounds:

(*a*) Private privilege may be waived by the person who is claiming it; only the Crown may waive a claim to privilege attaching to matters of state policy. *See Great Atlantic Insurance Co.* v. *Home Insurance Co.* (1981).

(*b*) Secondary evidence (*see* 2:22 (*b*)) may be given for some fact relating to which private privilege can be claimed; secondary (and primary) evidence will be excluded totally in the case of privilege arising on grounds of public policy.

14. Principal occasions on which private privilege will arise. The following circumstances are considered below:

(*a*) Incrimination (*see* **15–16** below).

(b) Legal professional privilege (*see* **17–20** below).

(c) Documents of title (*see* **21–22** below).

(d) Communications made "without prejudice" (*see* **23–24** below).

NOTE: So-called "marital privilege"—the right of spouses not to disclose communications made between them during the subsistence of a marriage and not to give evidence that marital intercourse did or did not take place between them during a given period—was abolished in *civil cases* by the Civil Evidence Act 1968, s. 16(3), (4), and in *criminal cases* by the Police and Criminal Evidence Act 1984, s. 80(9).

15. Incrimination. The general rule is that a person *may not be compelled* to answer a question or produce a document as a result of which he will incriminate himself. *See Re Westinghouse* (1978).

(a) An answer is considered "incriminating" if it involves the person who makes that answer in the possibility of facing a criminal charge. *See Blunt* v. *Park Lane Hotel* (1942).

(b) An extension of the general rule is seen in the Civil Evidence Act 1968, s. 14 (1) (b): "The right of a person in any legal proceedings to refuse to answer any question or produce any document or thing if to do so would tend to expose that person to proceedings for an offence or for the recovery of a penalty . . . shall include a like right to refuse to answer any question or produce any document or thing if to do so would tend to expose the husband or wife of that person to proceedings for any such criminal offence, or for the recovery of any such penalty."

(c) The fact that the person concerned swears that an answer would incriminate is not conclusive; *the judge must decide* in the light of all the circumstances whether there is, in fact, a danger of incrimination: *R.* v. *Boyes* (1861).

(d) The privilege cannot be claimed where an answer would expose the witness merely to an action for debt or to some liability which did not constitute a penalty.

(e) Under the Criminal Evidence Act 1898, s. 1 (e): "A person charged and being a witness in pursuance of this Act may be asked any question in cross-examination notwithstanding that it would tend to criminate him as to the offence charged." For problems arising from the interpretation of s. 1, *see* 15:**14**.

(*f*) Note, also, the Theft Act 1968, s. 31 (1): "A person shall not be excused, by reason that to do so may incriminate that person or the wife or husband of that person of an offence under this Act: (*a*) from answering any question put to that person in proceedings for the recovery or administration of any property, for the execution of any trust or for an account of any property or dealings with property; or (*b*) from complying with any order made in any such proceedings; but no statement or admission made by a person in answering a question put or complying with an Order made as aforesaid shall, in proceedings for an offence under this Act, be admissible in evidence against that person or (unless they married after the making of a statement or admission) against the wife or husband of that person." (*See* also the Criminal Damage Act 1971, s. 9.)

16. Incrimination and the right of silence. In general, a person has the "right of silence" when being questioned by someone attempting to investigate an offence (but *see*, for exceptions, the Official Secrets Act 1920, s. 6, the Road Traffic Act 1972, s. 162). Nor may his failure to reply to the questions be made the subject of any adverse comment. *See R.* v. *Chandler* (1976); *Parkes* v. *R.* (1976) (in which the Privy Council advised that the silence of a defendant in the face of an accusation made among persons speaking on equal terms may properly be taken into account with other evidence in considering whether he has committed the offence with which he was charged).

Legal professional privilege

17. Legal professional privilege. The general rule is that privilege may be claimed in relation to legal professional confidences. Two aspects of this are considered below:

(*a*) Communications between solicitor and client (*see* **18** below).

(*b*) Communications made in pursuance of pending or anticipated litigation (*see* **19** below).

18. Communications between solicitor and client. In general, communications between solicitor and client made in confidence are privileged.

(a) The privilege is that of the client, so that he may waive it if he so chooses: *Minet* v. *Morgan* (1873). If, however, the opposing party has secondary evidence concerning the professional communication in question, he can give this in evidence: *Calcraft* v. *Guest* (1898).

(b) No privilege arises where the communication was made in pursuance of some criminal intention: *see R.* v. *Cox and Railton* (1884).

(c) "Once privileged, always privileged." The client's privilege continues after the ending of the lawyer–client relationship.

(d) The privilege is overruled by the general principle, based on "natural justice", that if there are documents in the possession or control of a solicitor, which on production might help the defence of an accused person in a criminal trial, no legal professional privilege attaches to them: *R.* v. *Barton* (1972).

19. Communications made in pursuance of pending or anticipated litigation. A communication made in pursuance of pending or anticipated litigation is privileged and may not be disclosed in that (or any other) litigation. *See*, e.g., *McAvan* v. *London Transport Executive* (1983).

(a) The privilege attaches also to communications between counsel and solicitor, solicitor and prospective witnesses. Note *Buttes Gas* v. *Hammer (No. 3)* (1981)—legal professional privilege extends to a situation where two persons with a common interest in litigation share a solicitor and exchange documents in connection with that anticipated litigation.

(b) The principle may be waived by the client in respect of some of a series of communications, but he retains the right to claim privilege for the remaining communications: *Lyell* v. *Kennedy* (1884). *See Nea Karteria Maritime Co.* v. *Atlantic Steamship Corp. (No. 2)* (1981).

(c) The privilege arises only where the legal adviser has been consulted in a professional capacity (not merely as a friend): *Smith* v. *Daniell* (1874).

(*d*) In *Wheeler* v. *Le Marchant* (1881) reports made by a surveyor, sent to defendant's solicitor, were held to be not privileged, since no litigation was in prospect when they were drawn up.

(*e*) In *Alfred Crompton Amusement Machines Ltd.* v. *Customs and Excise Commissioners* (1974), the Commissioners claimed privilege relating to: (*i*) communications with their legal advisers to obtain appropriate advice; (*ii*) communications with their legal advisers to obtain appropriate evidence for use in an arbitration in prospect; (*iii*) internal communications with their own officers concerning the company's tax position; (*iv*) documents from third parties concerning the company's sales. The House of Lords held that privilege *was* attached to (*i*) and (*ii*), but *not* to (*iii*) or (*iv*), which were not intended to assist the Commissioners' arguments in the anticipated arbitration (on the matter of the company's payment of purchase tax).

(*f*) "Where a confidential relationship exists . . . and . . . disclosure would be in breach of some ethical or social value involving the public interest, the court has a discretion to uphold a refusal to disclose relevant evidence provided it considers that, on balance, the public interest would be better served by excluding such evidence": *per* Lord Edmund-Davies in *D.* v. *N.S.P.C.C.* (1978). *See Gaskin* v. *Liverpool C.C.* (1980) (confidentiality of child care documents in city council's possession preserved); *Campbell* v. *Tameside M.B.C.* (1982).

(*g*) For the "continuing privilege" of a document in a second action, *see The Aegis Blaze* (1986).

20. A note on other professional confidences. The privilege outlined above does *not* extend to doctors (*see R.* v. *Smith* (1979)), agents (*see Slade* v. *Tucker* (1880)), priests (apparently) or journalists and informants (*see A.-G.* v. *Mulholland* (1963)). *See* also the Patents Act 1977, s. 104.

NOTE: Under the Police and Criminal Evidence Act 1984, s. 19 (6), the powers of seizure exercisable by the police do not extend to items which they have reasonable grounds for believing to be subject to "legal privilege". Such items are defined in s. 10 (1) as "communications between a professional legal adviser and his client or any person representing his client made in connection with the giving of legal advice to the client . . . or in contemplation of legal proceedings . . ." The definition embraces items enclosed with or referred to in such communications.

Documents of title

21. The general rule. A witness could, in general, refuse to produce documents which related to his own title only and which additionally, did not support his adversary's case: *Morris* v. *Edwards* (1890). But *see now* 22 (*b*) below.

22. Further points. The following points should be noted:

(*a*) The privilege was not considered to extend to cases in which an adversary's title was in dispute, where production would have supported the title: *Morris* v. *Edwards* (1890).

(*b*) By the Civil Evidence Act 1968, s. 16 (1) (*b*) the privilege "whereby in any legal proceedings, a person other than a party to the proceedings cannot be compelled to produce any deed or other document relating to his title to any land" was abrogated except in relation to *criminal proceedings*.

Communications made "without prejudice"

23. The general rule. The phrase means "without any prejudice to the legal rights of the person(s) who made the statements." Where a communication, oral or written, has been made "without prejudice" in the course of some attempt to settle a dispute before the commencement of, or during, the action, it is *not* generally admissible in evidence; it should not, therefore, be brought to the attention of the court except with the consent of both parties.

24. Aspects of the rule. The following points should be noted:

(*a*) It is the *essential nature of the communication* which is significant, not merely its description, so that, for example, a letter headed "without prejudice" will not excuse any libel or threat contained therein: *Kurtz & Co.* v. *Spence & Sons* (1887).

(*b*) The privilege relates only to those communications made in an attempt to settle a dispute; it does not extend to a document containing the terms of those negotiations actually ending in some contractual settlement: *Tomlin* v. *Standard Telephones and Cables* (1969)—correspondence relating to damage for personal injuries, resulting in a binding agreement on liability.

(c) Should the first of a collection of documents be headed "without prejudice", the privilege may apply to *all* the documents: *Paddock* v. *Forrester* (1842).

(d) Letters may be inadmissible even though not headed "without prejudice", if it can be inferred from the circumstances that they referred to negotiations "without prejudice": *Oliver* v. *Nautilus S.S. Co. Ltd.* (1903).

(e) The privilege extends to communications made by estranged spouses to a conciliator: they may be disclosed only with the consent of both parties: *Henley* v. *Henley* (1955); *Mole* v. *Mole* (1951).

(f) *See also Walker* v. *Wilsher* (1889); *R.* v. *Nottingham County Justices ex p. Bostock* (1970); *Norwich Union* v. *Waller* (1984); and *Cutts* v. *Head* (1984), a case about "without prejudice" letters dealing with the costs of litigation, and in which the authorities were reviewed; *S. Shropshire DC* v. *Amos* (1986).

A note on evidence at a trial for a rape offence

25. Sexual Offences (Amendment) Act 1976. This Act applies to a trial for a *rape offence*, which is defined in s. 7 (2) as "rape, attempted rape, aiding, abetting, counselling and procuring rape or attempted rape, and incitement to rape."

26. Restriction on evidence. At a trial for a rape offence to which defendant has pleaded not guilty, except with leave of the judge *no evidence and no question in cross-examination may be adduced or asked, by or on behalf of defendant, relating to any sexual experience of complainant with a person other than defendant.* Leave may be given only on application, in the absence of the jury, by or on behalf of defendant, and only if the judge is satisfied that it would be unfair to defendant to refuse to allow the evidence to be adduced or the question to be asked: s. 2. *See R.* v. *Mills* (1978); *R.* v. *Viola* (1982).

Progress test 12

1. What is meant by "privilege" in the law of evidence? (**1, 2**)

2. Explain "privilege arising on grounds of public policy". (**6**)

3. Comment on the decision in *Conway* v. *Rimmer* (1968). (**9**)

4. What is the nature of the privilege attaching to information which has led to the arrest of a thief ? (**10**)

5. May a juror be compelled to disclose the nature of a discussion in the jury room? (**11**)

6. How does private privilege differ from that attaching to matters of public policy? (**13**)

7. What is the essence of the privilege relating to answers likely to result in incrimination? (**15**)

8. Are communications between solicitor and client always privileged? (**18**)

9. Is there ever any privilege attaching to communications between (*a*) solicitor and prospective witnesses; (*b*) doctor and patient? (**19, 20**)

10. Is a letter headed "without prejudice" invariably inadmissible as evidence? (**23, 24**)

13

Matters which may be proved (1): facts in issue; facts relevant to the issue

Preliminary matters

1. General. Previous chapters (9 and 10) outlined those *matters of which proof is not required* and (11 and 12) those *matters of which proof will not be allowed*. In this and the following chapter we consider those *matters of which proof is allowed*. Evidence may be given of two types of fact:

(a) *facts in issue* (see 2:4); and
(b) *facts relevant to the issue* (see 2:5).

Generally, evidence of (a) is "direct evidence" (see 2:14–15); evidence of (b) is "circumstantial evidence" (see 2:14 and 2:16).

2. Matters to be covered. The following topics are covered:

(a) Relevance and admissibility (see 3–5 below).
(b) Facts in issue (see 6–11 below).
(c) Facts relevant to the issue (see 12–28 below).

Relevance and admissibility

3. The general rule. *In order to be receivable by the court, evidence has to be both sufficiently relevant and admissible.* Irrelevant evidence, or evidence which is not sufficiently relevant, is generally excluded.

But not all relevant evidence is necessarily admissible (*see* the rule relating to hearsay (16:**8**)). "Our law undoubtedly excludes evidence of many matters which anyone in his own daily affairs of moment would regard as important in coming to a decision": *per* Darling, J. in *R.* v. *Bond* (1906).

4. Relevance. Known also as "logical relevancy". The term is used in the law of evidence to refer to connections, relationships between facts and events which will ordinarily tend to render one probable from the very existence of the other. (Stephens' definition is: "Any two facts to which [the term 'relevant'] is applied are so related to each other that according to the common course of events one either taken by itself or in connection with other facts proves or renders probable the past, present, or future existence or non-existence of the other.") Note the comments of Lord Simon in *DPP* v. *Kilbourne* (1973): "Evidence is relevant if it is logically probative or dis-probative of some matter which requires proof."

(*a*) Questions of relevance are usually determined "on the basis of rational inference and human experience".

(*b*) In general, hearsay, witness's opinions, conduct on other occasions and character are matters which, although possibly relevant, are excluded.

(*c*) Evidence which is too remote, or which may raise too many side issues is generally not admissible.

(*i*) In *Hollingham* v. *Head* (1858) the question turned on whether P had sold guano to D on certain special terms. The fact that P had sold guano to X and Y on such terms was not admissible in evidence. "It may be often difficult to decide upon the admissibility of evidence where it is offered for the purpose of establishing probability, but to be admissible it must at least afford a reasonable inference as to the principal matter in dispute. . . . The admission of such evidence would be fraught with the greatest inconvenience": *per* Willes, J.

(*ii*) In *Holcombe* v. *Hewson* (1810) in an action by a brewer against a publican, on an agreement by the latter to buy all his beer from the former, it was held that, in relation to the question of whether the brewer had supplied bad beer, the evidence of other publicans that he had supplied them with good beer should be rejected. "This is *res inter alios acta*. We cannot here enquire into the quality of different beer furnished to different persons. The plaintiff might deal well with one, and not with the others": *per* Lord Ellenborough.

(*iii*) In *Agassiz* v. *London Tramway Co.* (1872) X, a passenger on a tram which was in collision claimed damages for injuries alleged to have been caused by the negligence of the driver, Y. X said that she had heard another passenger tell the conductor that Y should be reported, and that the conductor had said, in reply, that Y had been reported already—"for he has been off the lines five or six times today." It was held that the evidence should be rejected because it would have created a number of collateral issues relating to Y's conduct.

NOTE: In the literature and in the decisions of the courts "material" is often used synonymously with "relevant".

5. **Admissibility.** The term "admissibility" in the law of evidence refers to evidence which is *legally receivable whether it is logically probative or not*. (In general, admissible evidence is that which is relevant and not excluded by rules of law or practice.) Unlike *relevance*, which is a matter of *logical inference* making the evidence of some fact probable or improbable, *admissibility* is a matter of *law*, for the *judge*. See *Bartlett* v. *Smith* (1843). Thus, one fact may be relevant for the understanding of another, on grounds of *logic*; it may nevertheless be held inadmissible on grounds of *law* (because it does not comply with some exclusionary rule, for example). In *R.* v. *Turner* (1975), information relating to the mental condition of the accused (charged with murder), based on information from medical records, was excluded by the trial judge as irrelevant and inadmissible. On appeal by the accused it was held that there is no general rule that psychiatric evidence is admissible to prove that a defendant is likely to be telling the truth.

NOTE: "The terms 'relevance' and 'admissibility' are frequently, and in many circumstances legitimately, used interchangeably; but I think it makes for clarity if they are kept separate, since some relevant evidence is inadmissible and some admissible evidence is irrelevant . . .": *per* Lord Simon in *DPP* v. *Kilbourne* (1973).

Facts which may be proved: facts in issue

6. General. Facts in issue (*see* 2:4) are those facts necessary in order to prove or disprove, to establish or refute, a case.

(*a*) Any fact admitted expressly or by implication is *not* in issue.

(*b*) Whether facts *are* in issue will be determined by reference to the substantive law, the pleadings, or the charge.

7. The problem of surrounding circumstances. In general, the facts which make up the surrounding circumstances of a central fact in issue may be admissible if they are relevant. This topic is discussed under the heading of *res gestae* (*see* 8–11 below).

Res gestae

8. Meaning of the phrase. *Res gestae*=things done, events which happened. A fact in issue may be made up of a number of subsidiary facts, known collectively as a "transaction". *Where a transaction is in issue, all those facts which comprise the transaction or accompany and explain it are known as res gestae and are generally admissible. See* also 19:18. Note Kenny's comment: "The words [*res gestae*] are a term of art restricted to events which happened in the affair which is now being considered by the court . . . *Res gestae* therefore comprise all relevant facts or events which are either in issue, or which, though not themselves in issue, yet accompany some fact which is in issue so as to constitute circumstantial evidence which goes to explain or establish that fact."

(*a*) In the case of criminal proceedings, for example, all the acts done by the accused or by any person in his presence or acting under his directions, and all the statements (oral or written) made by him or by a person in his presence at the time of the transaction, or before or after it, will be relevant if they can be shown to be connected with the specific transaction with which accused is charged.

(*b*) The inclusionary nature of the *res gestae* principle (i.e. the receiving as part of the *res gestae* of facts as an exception to the hearsay rule (*see* 16:8)) should be noted. "In its operation the principle renders acts and declarations which constitute a part of the things done and said admissible in evidence, even though they would otherwise come within the rule excluding hearsay evidence": Black.

(*c*) *Res gestae* has been described as "a phrase adopted to provide a respectable cloak for a variety of courses to which no formula of precision can be applied": *per* Lord Tomlin in *Homes* v. *Newman* (1931).

9. Statements used to prove conduct. Where a statement is established in order to prove conduct, it is considered as part of the *res gestae*.

(*a*) *The Dysart Peerage Case* (1881). In this action, the question was whether W was lawfully married to H. Evidence of a marriage in 1845 was given, of which Lord Blackburn said: "Where there has been such evidence given, and you are to see whether or not it is true, you look at what the parties did; what is technically called the *res gestae*, viz., their conduct at the time, their conduct before, their conduct afterwards, and all that they may do and say, as tending to show that they did really enter into this contract, or as tending on the other side to show that they did not enter into this contract."

(*b*) *Lloyd* v. *Powell Duffryn Steam Coal Co. Ltd.* (1914). In an action in which X claimed workmen's compensation on behalf of an illegitimate child, she (X) gave evidence of a conversation in which Y, the deceased, had promised to marry her immediately on learning of her pregnancy. It was held by the House of Lords that the evidence was a part of the *res gestae*. "To treat the statements made by the deceased (Y) as statements made by a deceased person against his pecuniary interest, is wholly to mistake their true character and significance. This significance consists in the improbability that any man would make these statements, true or false, unless he believed himself to be the father of the child of whom (X) was pregnant": *per* Lord Atkinson. Y's promise to marry X constituted conduct and his later conversations were a part of that conduct.

(*c*) *See* also *O'Leary* v. *R.* (1946) in which otherwise inadmissible evidence was received because it was evidence of "facts and matters which form constituent parts or ingredients of the transaction itself or explain or make intelligible the course of conduct pursued." *See* also *Martin* v. *Osborne* (1936); *Woodhouse* v. *Hall* (1980).

10. The criteria for admissibility of a statement: some leading cases. A statement, to be admissible, must explain some fact in issue. Other criteria, relating to the contemporaneity required of a statement, were emphasised in the following cases:

(*a*) *R.* v. *Bedingfield* (1879). X staggered from a room in which she had been with Y, with her throat cut, exclaiming: "See what (Y) has done to me!" It was held that this was no more than a narration of a transaction (*see* **8** above) which was completed, and it was *not admissible* as part of the *res gestae*. There was nothing to show that X "was under the sense of impending death" so the statement was not admissible as a dying declaration. (Note, however, the observations of Lord Wilberforce in *Ratten* v. *R.* (1972) concerning *R.* v. *Bedingfield*: "There could hardly be a case where the words uttered carried more clearly the mark of spontaneity and intense involvement.") *See* also 19:**12** (*e*) (*ii*).

(*b*) *R.* v. *Christie* (1914). The House of Lords did not regard as part of the *res gestae* a statement by a child made to his mother a few minutes after an alleged assault, describing the circumstances of the event. "The statement under review formed no part of the incidents constituting the offence. It was not made whilst the offence was being committed or immediately thereafter. It took place after Christie had left the boy, and the mother had found him and taken him across the fields and had spoken to another man. In my view it was not so immediately connected with the act of assault as to form part of the *res gestae*. In the words of Cockburn, C. J., in *R.* v. *Bedingfield* [*see* (*a*) above] 'It was not part of anything done, or something said while something was being done, but something said after something done. It was not as if, while being in the room, and while the act was being done, she had said something which was heard' ": *per* Lord Reading.

(*c*) *Davies* v. *Fortior* (1952). The spontaneous statements of a workman who had fallen into a bath of acid, relating to the cause of the accident, made within a few seconds of having been helped from the bath, were *admissible* as part of the *res gestae*.

(*d*) *Teper* v. *R.* (1952). A police officer's evidence that he had heard a woman exclaim to the driver of a car, "Your place burning and you going away!", was held to be *inadmissible* evidence of defendant's having been present at a fire (which he was accused of starting) twenty-five minutes earlier. *See* 16:**10**.

11. A consideration of the criteria for admissibility of a statement: *Ratten* v. *R.* (1972). This judgment seems to have stated the test for admissibility of a statement (which explains a fact in issue) as whether the statement was *"made in circumstances of spontaneity or involvement in the event that the possibility of concoction can be disregarded"*, as opposed to the former requirement of its having been made "by way of narrative of a detached prior event."

(*a*) *The facts.* X was charged with the murder of his wife. His defence was that she was accidentally shot while he had been cleaning his gun in the kitchen of their house. The important evidence in question was of a telephone operator who stated that, about the time the wife was shot by X, a telephone call was made from X's house by a woman in a hysterical state, who asked for the police. X objected to this evidence. The Privy Council dismissed X's appeal, stating that the evidence was not hearsay, but that, even if it were, it would be nonetheless admissible as part of the *res gestae* since there was ample evidence of a close connection between the words constituting the telephone message ("Get me the police, please!") and the shooting which occurred shortly afterwards.

(*b*) *Per* Lord Wilberforce: "The possibility of concoction, or fabrication, where it exists, is . . . probably the real test which judges in fact apply. In their Lordships' opinion this should be recognised and applied directly as the relevant test: the test should not be the uncertain one whether the making of the statement was in some sense part of the event or transaction. This may often be difficult to establish: such external matters as the time which elapses between the events and the speaking of the words (or vice versa), and differences in location being relevant factors but not, taken by themselves, decisive criteria. As regards statements made after the event, it must be for the judge, by preliminary ruling, to satisfy himself that the statement was so clearly made in circumstances of spontaneity or involvement in the event that the possibility of concoction can be disregarded. Conversely, if he considers that the statement was made by way of narrative of a detached prior event so that the speaker was so disengaged from it as to be able to construct or adapt his account, he should exclude it. And the same must in principle be true of statements made before the event. The test should not be the uncertain one, whether the making of the statement should be regarded as part of the event or transaction. This may often be difficult to show. But if the drama, leading up to the climax, has commenced and assumed such intensity and pressure that the utterance can safely be regarded as a true reflection of what was unrolling or actually happening, it ought to be received. The expression *res gestae* may conveniently sum up these criteria, but the reality of them must always be kept in mind: it is this that lies behind the best reasoned of the judges' rulings." *See* also *R.* v. *Nye and Loan* (1977); *R.* v. *Turnbull* (1984), in which the Court of Appeal stated that the "concoction or distortion", the danger of which must be avoided, is a concoction or distortion by a person to exculpate himself or incriminate someone else or adapt the matter favourably to himself and against another.

NOTE: The case of the "self-serving statement", whereby a defendant seeks to adduce a statement (cautioned or uncautioned) which amounts to a full denial of the offence, or which admits the offence while offering some explanation, was considered recently in *Leung Kam-Kwok* v. *R.* (1985) by the Privy Council. "If an accused person in a statement not made on oath in Court denies his guilt, saying, for example, 'I am not guilty: I was not there', and no more, that statement is not evidence of the truth of his absence from the scene of the crime and thus of the truth of his alibi. But if such a statement consists partly of an admission and partly of an explanation, for example, 'I shot him: it was an accident', or 'I shot him: I was provoked', the admission is plainly admissible and common fairness requires that the entirety of the statement should be admitted so as to show the precise context in which the admission was made, even though what is said by way of explanation or excuse is not evidence of its truth": *per* Lord Roskill.

Facts which may be proved: facts relevant to the issue

12. General. Facts relevant to the issue (*see* 2:5) are *those facts which make probable the existence or non-existence of some fact in issue* (or some other relevant facts).

13. Facts which may be relevant to the issue. These are considered under the following headings:

(*a*) Facts probative of some fact in issue (*see* **14–22** below).

(*b*) Facts tending to show identity or connection of parties (*see* **23–24** below).

(*c*) Facts showing states of mind (*see* **25–28** below).

(*d*) Similar facts (*see* Chap. 14).

(*e*) Character (*see* Chap. 14).

Facts probative of some fact in issue

14. Nature of these facts. These are facts which "*have a natural and logical tendency to prove or disprove some fact in issue or which experience ordinarily shows to have that effect.*" They are generally admissible.

(*a*) Circumstantial, as well as direct, evidence may be given in this context.

(*b*) The following classes of fact (which are relevant in circumstantial proof of some other fact) are considered below, relating to:

(*i*) existence, previous and subsequent, of facts (*see* **15** below);

(*ii*) course of business (*see* **16** below);

(*iii*) person acting in a public capacity (*see* **17** below);

(*iv*) habit (*see* **18** below);

(*v*) comparative standards (*see* **19** below);

(*vi*) acts of ownership and title (*see* **20** below);

(*vii*) conduct of a third person (*see* **21** below);

(*viii*) complaints (*see* **22** below).

15. Existence, previous and subsequent, of facts. The previous and subsequent existence of facts may be of relevance (see the presumption of continuance at 10:33) when particular conditions (e.g. marriage, life) are in issue.

(*a*) The presumption can be rebutted by contrary evidence or by some contrary presumption.

(*b*) If a long period of time has weakened the presumption the judge may exclude evidence of previous states.

(*c*) Examples: *Brown* v. *Wren Ltd.* (1895)—existence of partnership proved by evidence of its existence six months prior to the action; *Macdarmaid* v. *A.–G.* (1950)—continuance of life for further three years of a healthy person of twenty-eight was inferred. *See* also *R.* v. *Lumley* (1869); *Re Watkins* (1953).

16. Course of business. It is permissible, to show that some act has been done, to prove the general practice of an office or business.

(*a*) There is, in such cases, a probability that the general practice is applicable to specific cases.

(*b*) Examples: *Butler* v. *Allnut* (1816)— proof of endorsement of a lost licence was inferred from evidence that the course of business would not have permitted entry of the goods in question without an endorsement; *McGregor* v. *Keily* (1849)—proof of delivery of a letter was inferred from proof that it was handed to the addressee's employee. *See* also *Trotter* v. *McLean* (1879); *Watts* v. *Vickers* (1916).

17. Acting in a public capacity. Where there is proof of a person having acted in a public capacity, for example, as holder of a public office, this fact has relevance as evidence of his title to that office.

(*a*) The relevant principle here is *omnia praesumuntur rite et solemniter esse acta* (*see* 10:26).

(*b*) The principle relates only to those appointments of a public nature, i.e. affecting the public at large.

(*c*) *See R.* v. *Langton* (1876); *R.* v. *Boaler* (1892).

18. Habit. The fact that X has been in the habit of acting in a particular way will be relevant to the question of whether he acted in that way on the occasion which is presently the subject of enquiry.

(a) *Hales* v. *Kerr* (1908). P wished to prove that D had shaved him with a dirty razor, leading to P's contracting ringworm. P was allowed to prove that X and Y had contracted ringworm after being shaved by D, since this fact tended to prove D's habitual use of dirty razors.

(b) *Joy* v. *Phillips, Mills & Co. Ltd.* (1916). A stable lad, was found in a stable, dying. Apparently, he had been kicked by a horse. Evidence was admitted to show that he had the habit of teasing the horse. "Wherever an enquiry has to be made into the cause of death of a person and, there being no direct evidence, recourse must be had to circumstantial evidence, any evidence as to the habits and ordinary doings of the deceased which may contribute to the circumstances by throwing light upon the probable cause of death is admissible, even in the case of a prosecution for murder": *per* Phillimore, L. J.

19. Comparative standards. If it becomes necessary to establish that a party's conduct has been reasonable in all the circumstances, evidence of what others might have been expected to do in similar circumstances may be admissible.

(a) In *Noble* v. *Kennoway* (1780), where the question related to delay in discharging a cargo in Labrador, evidence was allowed to show that a delay in similar circumstances was acceptable in the Newfoundland trade.

(b) In *Boldron* v. *Widdows* (1824), where the question related to the treatment of school pupils, evidence was admitted concerning the general treatment of pupils at other schools of the same type.

20. Acts of ownership and title. From acts of ownership may be inferred title to property. The underlying presumption is "lawful origin" (*see* 10:**29**). *See Doe d. Graham* v. *Penfold* (1838); *Jones* v. *Williams* (1837).

21. Conduct of a third person. The general rule was based on the maxim *res inter alios alteri nocere non debet* (no person should be prejudiced by a transaction between strangers). (For example, an admission generally limits only its maker, not third parties.) Thus, in *Wright* v. *Doe d. Tatham* (1838) it was held that the mere fact that letters were written to T would be inadmissible evidence of T's sanity, although they were of a nature suggesting that they would only be written to a person believed to be sane.

(*a*) There are, however, many exceptions to this general rule, some of which are mentioned below:

(*i*) An admission by a predecessor in title acts to bind his successors in title: *Woolway* v. *Rowe* (1834).

(*ii*) An agent's admission can bind his principal: *Re Devala Gold Mining Co.* (1883).

(*iii*) Evidence showing that a company had long been accepted by the banking community and government departments as having the status of bankers was accepted in proof of the company's attempt to show it was a bank: *United Dominions Trust* v. *Kirkwood* (1966).

(*b*) In general, a person is not liable in criminal law for the acts of others (but *see R.* v. *Stephens* (1866); *R.* v. *I.C.R. Road Haulage Ltd.* (1944)).

22. Complaints. *See* 7:38. The general rule is that a complaint relating to sexual offences may be proved as evidence-in-chief provided that: it was made voluntarily; it was made as swiftly as was reasonable in the circumstances.

(*a*) The complaint is *not* evidence of the facts on which it was based: *see R.* v. *Osborne* (1905). "The judge [must be] careful to inform the jury that the statement is not evidence of the facts complained of, and must not be regarded by them if believed, as other than corroborative of the complainant's credibility, and, where consent is in issue, of the absence of consent": *per* Ridley, J.

(*b*) Where consent is not in issue, the terms of a complaint will not be allowed as evidence if the victim gives no evidence: *R.* v. *Wallwork* (1958). But if the victim gives evidence, the terms will be admissible only to establish the consistency of complainant's conduct in relation to that testimony.

(*c*) *See R.* v. *Lillyman* (1896); *R.* v. *Whitehead* (1929); *R.* v. *Cummings* (1948).

Facts tending to show identity

23. The general rule. Where there is a question of personal identity, it can be proved or disproved by direct testimony and by evidence of similarity or dissimilarity of relevant personal characteristics. (Methods of proof of identity by *circumstantial evidence* may include, for example, comparison of handwriting (*see* 15:32 (*b*)), comparison of finger prints and blood group identification.) For problems arising in identification parades, *see:* Home Office Circular 109/1978; Code of Practice issued under the Police and Criminal Evidence Act 1984; *R.* v. *John* (1965); *R* v. *O'Brien* (1982); *R.* v. *Creamer* (1985)—evidence of identity given *after* a parade might be admissible provided that witness could satisfy the court that he really had identified the accused and had good reason for refraining from making that identification in his presence. Note also *R.* v. *Grimer* (1982)—video recording admissible as evidence of identification; *R.* v. *Dodson* (1984)—photograph of robber taken by automatic security camera held admissible (and photographs of the same person taken at other times are permissible aids in this process of identification). For fingerprinting, *see* the Police and Criminal Evidence Act 1984, ss. 27, 61, 64.

24. Identification by conduct on previous occasions. An example is provided by *R.* v. *Straffen* (1952) in which S was charged with the murder of a small girl, Z.

(*a*) *The facts.* At his trial, S was found guilty of strangling Z, a small girl. The prosecution were allowed to prove that S had previously been charged with the similar murders of X and Y, to which he had been found unfit to plead by reason of insanity. S argued before the Court of Criminal Appeal that this evidence ought not to have been admitted.

(*b*) *Judgment of the Court of Criminal Appeal.* S's appeal was dismissed. *Per* Slade, J.: "The grounds on which the admissibility of evidence was urged by the Solicitor-General in the court below was the similarity surrounding the murders in the cases of [X and Y] on the one hand and the . . . murder [of Z] on the other. He stated the similarities to be, firstly, that each of the victims was a young girl; secondly, that each was killed by manual strangulation; thirdly, that in none of the cases was there any attempt at sexual interference or any apparent motive for the crime; fourthly, that in no case was there evidence of a struggle; and fifthly, that in none of the three cases was any attempt made to conceal the body, though that could easily have been done . . . It is an abnormal propensity to strangle young girls and to do so without any apparent motive, without any attempt at sexual interference, and to leave their dead bodies where they can be seen and where, presumably, their deaths would be detected. In the judgment of the court, that evidence was admissible because it tended to identify the person who murdered [Z] with the person who confessed in his statements to having murdered the two other girls a year before, in exactly similar circumstances. [Counsel] asked: 'How far does the admissibility of such evidence go? Would it extend to the case of a burglar, housebreaker, thief, and so on?' Speaking for myself, I think that if the question of identity arose in a case of housebreaking and it were possible to adduce evidence that there was some hallmark or other peculiarity in relation to earlier housebreakings which were also apparent in the case of the housebreaking charged, so as to stamp the accused man, not only with the housebreaking charged but with the earlier housebreakings, and there was a confession or other evidence that he had committed the earlier housebreakings, that would fall within the same principle of admissibility, not to prove his propensity for housebreaking, but to prove that he was the person who had committed the housebreaking charged."

(c) Note also *Thompson* v. *R.* (1918) (at 14:**18** (a)); *R.* v. *Chandor* (1959); *R.* v. *Morris* (1970).

Facts tending to show states of mind

25. The general rule. In some cases a party's state of mind will be a fact in issue. *See* 19:**20**. The existence of *mens rea* in circumstances in which, for example, theft or murder is alleged, provides an example. Three matters relating to states of mind are discussed below to illustrate circumstances in which those states may be proved, as a rule, from facts from which their existence can be inferred:

(*a*) Knowledge and notice (*see* **26** below).

(*b*) Good and bad faith (*see* **27** below).

(*c*) Intention (*see* **28** below). "Intention" refers in criminal law to a mental state in which a person foresees and wills those consequences which may possibly flow from his conduct. It was defined in *R*. v. *Mohan* (1975) as "a decision to bring about, insofar as it lies within the accused's power, [a particular consequence], no matter whether the accused desired that consequence of his act or not." *See* also *Cunliffe* v. *Goodman* (1950); *Lloyds Bank* v. *Marcan* (1973); *R*. v. *Hancock and Shankland* (1986).

26. Knowledge and notice. Actual knowledge can be proved by direct evidence, as where it may be proved circumstantially by inference from the fact that accused had, at the time in question, reasonable means of obtaining knowledge, e.g. through access to documents. *See Roe* v. *Naylor* (1918); *Lloyds Bank* v. *Dalton* (1942).

(*a*) Where a party has a duty to know, knowledge may be imputed to him.

(*b*) A party's conduct may provide evidence from which his knowledge can be inferred. Thus, under the Theft Act 1968, s. 27 (3), on a charge of handling stolen goods, evidence may be given that accused "has had in his possession, or has undertaken or assisted in the retention, removal, disposal or realisation of stolen goods from any theft taking place not earlier than twelve months before the offence charged . . . and . . . evidence that he has within the five years preceding the date of the offence charged been convicted of theft or of handling stolen goods."

(*c*) Where a person has had constructive notice (e.g. where a purchaser of land fails to make a reasonable investigation of title deeds, etc.: *see* the Law of Property Act 1925, s. 44 (1)) presumption of knowledge cannot be rebutted: *Plumb* v. *Fluitt* (1791)— "[Constructive notice is] in its nature no more than evidence of notice, the presumptions of which are so violent that the court will not allow even of its being controverted": *per* Eyre, C. B.

27. Good and bad faith. Where this is in issue in relation to a party, for example, as in a defence to an action for defamation, it can be proved by evidence showing presence or absence of knowledge on defendant's part at the time in issue.

28. Intention. *See* 25 (*c*) above. In general, a person's intention or motive is not material. "It is the act, not the motive for the act that must be regarded. If the act, apart from motive, gives rise merely to damage without legal injury, the motive, however reprehensible it may be, will not supply that element": *per* Lord Macnaghten in *Bradford Corporation* v. *Pickles* (1895).

(*a*) When intention is a fact in issue or relevant to some fact in issue, it may be proved, for example, as in malicious prosecution, defamation, slander of title.

(*b*) In criminal proceedings intention may be a fact in issue, for example, where intent to defraud or injure or deprive is significant and it can be proved directly (as by the accused's admissions or conduct).

(*c*) The declarations of a testator in relation to his intention made before, or at, or following, the execution of his will may be admissible as presumptive evidence indicating his state of mind. *See Re Slinn* (1890) (evidence was admitted that testatrix had declared a wish to settle her affairs).

Progress test 13

1. What is meant in the law of evidence by "relevance"? (**4**)

2. Explain the difference between "relevance" and "admissibility" (**5**)

3. What is meant by *res gestae*? (**8**)

4. What is the importance of the decision in *Lloyd* v. *Powell Duffryn Steam Coal Co. Ltd.*? (**9**)

5. Comment on *R.* v. *Bedingfield* (1879). (**10**)

6. Outline the facts and decision in *Ratten* v. *R.* (1972). (**11**)

7. May the general practice of business be proved in evidence? (**16**)

8. Explain the decision in *Joy* v. *Phillips, Mills and Co.* (1916). (**18**)

9. What is the importance of the maxim *res inter alios alteri nocere non debet*? (**21**)

10. When may complaints relating to alleged sexual assaults be proved as evidence-in-chief? (**22**)

11. What are the methods of proof of identity by circumstantial evidence? (**23**)

12. Comment on *R*. v. *Straffen* (1952). (**24**)

13. When may a party's state of mind be a fact in issue? (**25**)

14. What is the importance of the Theft Act 1968, s. 27 (3) in relation to the "inferring of knowledge"? (**26**)

15. When may evidence relating to intention be admissible? (**28**)

14

Matters which may be proved (2): similar facts and character

Preliminary matters

1. General. This chapter continues the examination, begun in Chap. 13, of *matters of which proof is allowed*. Two problems are touched upon in relation to proof of *facts which may* be relevant to the issue (*see* 13:**13**):

    (*a*) Similar facts;
    (*b*) Character.

2. Matters to be discussed. The following points will be covered below:

    (*a*) The meaning of, and general rule relating to, "similar facts" (*see* **3–6** below).
    (*b*) The admissibility of similar fact evidence (*see* **7–20** below).
    (*c*) The meaning of "character" in relation to the law of evidence and the appropriate general rule (*see* **21** below).
    (*d*) Exceptions to the general rule (*see* **22–25** below).

Similar facts

3. The nature of "similar fact evidence". Evidence of this nature is that which is adduced in an attempt to suggest, *through its striking similarity*, that there is an underlying link between the matters with which it purports to deal—which relate essentially to occasions other than those specifically in question—and the matter now being considered in relation to some subject now before the court.

4. Examples of similar fact evidence. The following examples illustrate the concept of "similar facts":

(a) *R.* v. *Smith* (1915). A was accused of the murder of B, his wife, who was found dead in her bath. B had insured her life in A's favour. A claimed that B had died after an attack of epilepsy. Evidence was admitted to show that A had gone through ceremonies of marriage with C and D, both of whom had insured their lives in A's favour, and both of whom had been found dead in their baths. "If you find an accident which benefits a person and you find that the person has been sufficiently fortunate to have that accident happen to him a number of times, benefiting him each time, you draw a very strong, irresistible inference, that the occurrence of so many accidents benefiting him is such a coincidence that it cannot have happened unless it was a design": *per* the trial judge. "I think that puts it very accurately and states exactly the reason why the evidence is admissible": *per* Lord Reading, C.J.

(b) *R.* v. *Mortimer* (1936). X was accused of murdering a lady cyclist by running her down. Evidence was admitted to show that X had driven his car intentionally at other lady cyclists, thus showing that his conduct was not merely negligent, but intentional.

(c) *R.* v. *Hill* (1914). X was charged with living on a certain day upon Y's earnings as a prostitute. Evidence was held admissible relating to similar acts on days before and after the alleged date, explaining the relationship existing on that date between X and Y.

5. The general rule concerning similar fact evidence. In general, similar fact evidence will be *excluded as irrelevant* to prove the occurrence of the fact in issue or the identity of the author of that fact. "It is undoubtedly not competent for the prosecution to adduce evidence tending to show that the accused has been guilty of criminal acts other than those covered by the indictment, for the purpose of leading to the conclusion that the accused is a person likely from his criminal conduct or character to have committed the offence for which he is being tried. On the other hand, the mere fact that the evidence adduced tends to show the commission of other crimes does not render it inadmissible if it be relevant to an issue before the jury, and it may be so relevant if it bears upon the question whether the acts alleged to constitute the crime charged in the indictment were designed or accidental, or to rebut a defence which would otherwise be open to the accused": *per* Lord Herschell in *Makin* v. *A.-G. for N.S. Wales* (1894), the facts of which are given at **16** (*a*) below. (Note that this statement was approved by the House of Lords in *DPP* v. *Boardman* (1974).)

6. The rule in operation. The following cases should be noted:

(*a*) *Harris* v. *DPP* (1952). H, a police officer, was indicted on eight counts of larceny from an office in a market. The counts were tried together and the offences were shown to have been committed in a similar style at times when H would have been on duty in the neighbourhood of the office. H was acquitted on seven counts and convicted on the eighth. The conviction was *quashed* because the summing-up had not included a warning to the jury that earlier events were not relevant to H's guilt on the eighth count. "The fact that someone perpetrated the earlier thefts when the accused may have been somewhere in the market does not provide material confirmation of his identity as the thief on the last occasion": *per* Lord Simon.

(*b*) *R.* v. *Rodley* (1913). X was charged with burglary with intent to rape Y. Evidence that, earlier that evening, X had entered Z's house by the chimney and had intercourse with Z with her consent was held *wrongfully admitted*. "The Court is of opinion that the evidence is not admissible. At the point in the trial at which the evidence was tendered the defences really in issue were: (1) that the appellant never broke into the house at all; (2) that the appellant did not break into the house with any intention of committing a rape; (3) that the prosecutrix's story as to what occurred in the house was not true. The evidence which was objected to was not, in the opinion of this Court, relevant to any of these issues, and was not therefore admissible to rebut any of the above defences": *per* Bankes, J.

(*c*) *R.* v. *Fisher* (1910). X's conviction for obtaining by false pretences a pony and trap was quashed after evidence had been *wrongfully admitted* relating to X's obtaining provender by false pretences. "The principle is that the prosecution are not allowed to prove that the prisoner had committed the offence with which he is charged by giving evidence that he is a person of bad character and one who is in the habit of committing crimes, for that is equivalent to asking the jury to say that because the prisoner has committed other offences he must therefore be guilty of the particular offence for which he is being tried. But if the evidence of other offences does go to prove that he did commit the offence charged it is admissible because it is relevant to the issue, and it is admissible not because but notwithstanding that it proves that the prisoner has committed another offence": *per* Channel, J.

The admissibility of similar fact evidence

7. Role of the judge. In essence, the matter of admissibility of similar fact evidence is a question of law for the judge. In exercising his discretion (*see* **3:16**) he will have in mind the prejudicial tendency of such evidence when weighed against its probative value. "Nothing can so certainly be counted upon to make a prejudice against an accused person upon his trial as the disclosure to the jury of other misconduct similar to that which is the subject of the indictment and, indeed, when the crime alleged is one of a revolting character, such as the charge against Bond in the present case, and the hearer is a person who has not been trained to think judicially, the prejudice must sometimes be almost insurmountable": *per* Kennedy, J. in *R.* v. *Bond* (1906). In a more recent case (*Berger* v. *Raymond Sun Ltd.* (1984)) it was held that the court, in exercising its discretion to exclude similar fact evidence, should consider the probative value of that evidence, the extent to which it might complicate and prolong the trial, whether its inclusion would be "unfair and oppressive" to the other party, and whether that other party had received fair notice of it.

8. Matters involved in the admission of similar fact evidence. The following should be noted.

(*a*) Where the prosecution is able to indicate some aspect of the past character or disposition of the accused which seems to be of probative value in relation to the offence with which he is charged, that evidence will not be rendered inadmissible simply because the jury is, as a result, made aware of his bad character.

(*b*) Similar fact evidence, if admissible, is admissible as part of the case for the prosecution from the beginning of the trial; it is not confined to the rebuttal of a specific defence.

(*c*) The required degree of probative value emerges if the proposed evidence suggests a similarity which goes to the offence itself, not only to side matters. *See*, e.g., *R.* v. *Rodley* (1913) at **6** (*b*) above; *R.* v. *Tricoglus* (1976)—X was accused of raping A after offering her a lift in his car; evidence tending to prove that X had solicited other women in the same area in the same type of car was held to be wrongly admitted. (*See* **20** below.)

(*d*) The required degree of probative value emerges where the proffered similar fact evidence demonstrates a *striking similarity* to significant, and not commonplace, features of the offence in question. "Positive probative value is what the law requires if similar fact evidence is to be admissible. Such probative value is not provided by the mere repetition of similar facts; there has to be some feature or features in the evidence sought to be adduced which provides a link—an underlying link as it has been called in some of the cases. The existence of such a link is not to be inferred from mere similarity of facts which are themselves so commonplace that they can provide no sure ground for saying that they point to the commission by the accused of the offence under consideration": *per* Scarman, L.J. in *R.* v. *Scarrott* (1977).

(*i*) In *R.* v. *Scarrott* (1977) S had been convicted by the Crown Court on an indictment containing thirteen counts charging him with sexual offences involving eight young boys over a period of four and a half years. The trial judge had ruled that evidence given by each of the boys on counts concerning them had a "striking similarity" to the evidence given by the other boys, and that such evidence was admissible on the other counts and could be corroborative (*see* 7:**16**). The judge had left the jury to decide whether there had been a possibility of "ganging-up" among the boys and had directed them that if they found there was no such "ganging-up", the similar facts evidence would be corroborative.

(*ii*) The Court of Appeal dismissed S's appeal. To succeed in quashing the conviction S's counsel would have had to show that the judge was wrong to have treated the similar facts evidence as of a "strikingly similar" nature. "The phrase was no more than a label and was not to be confused with the substance of the law. Positive probative value was what the law required": *per* Lord Scarman. It was for a trial judge to apply the "strikingly similar" test, i.e., whether the similarities were sufficiently striking to justify the evidence being considered by the jury and whether any prejudicial effect outweighed the probative value.

9. Similar fact evidence in civil and criminal cases. "The criminal courts have been very careful not to admit similar fact evidence unless its probative value is so strong that it should be received in the interests of justice and its admission will not operate unfairly to the accused. In civil cases the courts have followed a similar line but have not been so chary of admitting it. In civil cases the courts will admit evidence of similar facts if it is logically probative, that is, if it is logically relevant in determining the matter which is in issue: provided that it is not oppressive or unfair to the other side: and also that the other side has fair notice of it and is able to deal with it. Instances are *Brown* v. *Eastern & Midlands Railway Co.* (1889); *Moore* v. *Ransome's Dock Committee* (1898) and *Hales* v. *Kerr* (1908)": *per* Lord Denning, M.R., in *Mood Music Publishing Co.* v. *De Wolfe Ltd.* (1976). *See Sattin* v. *National Union Bank* (1978), in which the plaintiff, claiming in respect of the loss of a jewel by the defendant, was allowed to adduce evidence of a similar occasion involving a loss of this nature. (The admission of this evidence resulted from the plaintiff's right to rebut a defence that the defendant's safeguards in protecting property were reasonable.) *See* also *Berger* v. *Raymond Sun Ltd* (1984)—similar fact evidence is admissible in *civil proceedings* only if it is relevant to an issue raised in those proceedings.

10. Admission of similar fact evidence in some specific circumstances. In *DPP* v. *Boardman* (1974) (*see* **13** below) it was decided that, assuming there exists an appropriate degree of "striking similarity", similar fact evidence may be admitted in support of the testimony of a prosecution witness, irrespective of considerations arising from the nature of the defence. The separate heads of admissibility mentioned below are useful to draw attention to some precise circumstances in which, as an exception to the general rule of exclusion, similar fact evidence may be admitted. These heads are:

(*a*) to prove a main fact in issue (*see* 11 below);

(*b*) to prove disposition where that is particularly relevant (*see* 12 below);

(*c*) to support the prosecution's evidence where there has been a precise denial of some matter (*see* 13 below);

(*d*) to negative the defence of mistake (*see* 14 below);

(*e*) to negative the defence of lack of knowledge (*see* 15 below);

(*f*) to negative accident and to demonstrate a systematic course of conduct (*see* 16 below);

(*g*) to negative the defence of innocent association in a charge relating to a sexual offence (*see* 17 below);

(*h*) to negative the defence of mistaken identification (*see* 18 below);

(*i*) to negative an innocent explanation of possession of incriminating material (*see* 19 below).

11. Proof of a main fact in issue. ". . . On the other hand the mere fact that the evidence adduced tends to show the commission of other crimes does not render it inadmissible if it be relevant to the crime before the jury, and it may be so relevant if it bears upon the question whether the acts alleged to constitute the crime charged in the indictment were designed or accidental, or to rebut a defence which would otherwise be open to the accused": *per* Lord Herschell in *Makin* v. *A.-G. for N.S. Wales* (1894). Similar fact evidence may be admitted to establish the main fact *and* to show the connection of accused with that fact.

(*a*) *R.* v. *Geering* (1849). W was charged with the murder, by arsenic poisoning, of her husband, H. So as to establish H's death as due to arsenic poisoning, evidence was allowed of the subsequent deaths of their two sons who lived with W, as a result of arsenic poisoning.

(*b*) *R.* v. *Ball* (1911). B and S, brother and sister, were charged with incest at a stated time. To establish the fact of intercourse, evidence was allowed to show that before the time in question they had lived as man and wife and that S had had a child by B. "I agree that the courts of law ought to be very careful to preserve the time-honoured law of England that you cannot convict a man of one crime by proving that he has committed some other crime. That, and all other safeguards of our criminal law, will be jealously guarded, but here I think the evidence went to prove the actual crime for which these parties were indicted": *per* Lord Loreburn.

12. Proof of disposition where that is particularly relevant. Similar fact evidence may be admitted to show a disposition to commit the particular type of offence in a specific way. But in cases of this nature, such evidence must be "exceptional and requires a strong degree of probative force": *per* Lord Wilberforce in *DPP* v. *Boardman* (1974).

13. To support the prosecution's evidence where there has been a precise denial. This may be illustrated by *DPP* v. *Boardman* (1974).

(*a*) *The facts.* B, a headmaster, was charged with three counts of buggery and incitement to commit buggery. His defence to each charge was a bare denial of the alleged events having occurred. B was convicted. The trial judge had held that the evidence of one pupil was admissible on the count concerning another pupil, and vice versa.

(*b*) *Court of Appeal.* B contended on appeal that similar fact evidence was admissible only to rebut a defence of innocent association or in relation to some issue of identity. B's appeal was dismissed, the Court of Appeal holding that the special features mentioned in the trial judge's summing-up were alone sufficient to justify the admissibility of the evidence.

(*c*) *House of Lords.* B's appeal was dismissed, the House of Lords holding that: "The probative force of all the acts together is much greater than one alone; for whereas the jury might think that one man might be telling an untruth, three or four are hardly likely to tell the same untruth unless they were conspiring together."

(*i*) *Per Lord Wilberforce:* "The basic principle must be that the admission of similar fact evidence (of the kind now in question) is exceptional and requires a strong degree of probative force. This probative force is derived, if at all, from the circumstance that the facts testified to by the several witnesses bear to each other such a striking similarity, that they must, when judged by experience and common sense, either all be true, or have arisen from a cause common to the witnesses or from pure coincidence." (Note, also, Lord Wilberforce's comment: "We can dispose at once of the suggestion that there is a special rule or principle applicable to sexual or homosexual offences. This suggestion had support at one time . . . but is now certainly obsolete.")

(*ii*) *Per Lord Cross:* "The question must always be whether the similar fact evidence taken together with the other evidence would do no more than raise or strengthen a suspicion that the accused committed the offence with which he is charged or would point so strongly to his guilt that only an ultra-cautious jury would acquit in the face of it."

(*iii*) *Per Lord Salmon:* "The test must be—is the evidence capable of tending to persuade a reasonable jury of the accused's guilt on some other ground than his bad character and disposition to commit the sort of crime with which he is charged?"

(For a selection of "post-Boardman" cases, *see* **20** below.)

14. To negative the defence of mistake. Where the accused pleads ignorance or mistake, the prosecution may succeed if it can be shown that he had committed similar types of act before the case in question. In *R.* v. *Francis* (1874), X was charged with obtaining money from a pawnbroker by false pretences involving the worth of a ring. X's defence of not knowing the ring was worthless was rebutted by evidence of former representations he had made to other pawnbrokers involving precisely the same kind of ring. "Every circumstance that shows [accused] was not under a mistake on any of these occasions strengthens the presumption that he was not on the last": *per* Coleridge, J. *See* also *R.* v. *Seaman* (1978)—evidence of a thief's *modus operandi*, which established a nexus between the offence charged and earlier offences, was admissible as similar fact evidence to rebut a defence of mistake or accident.

15. To negative defence of lack of knowledge. Similar fact evidence may be admissible in a criminal case where knowledge of some fact is a material component of some offence, and in a civil case where it is material (as in an action for negligence). *See* also the Theft Act 1968, s. 27 (3) (*see* 13:**26** (*b*)).

(*a*) In *Bebee* v. *Sales* (1916), in which the question turned on X's knowing that his son's airgun was dangerous, evidence was allowed to show that X knew that the airgun had caused injuries on other occasions.

(*b*) In *Blake* v. *Albion Life Assurance Co.* (1878) the question was whether P, a principal, knew of the fraudulent activities of his agent, A. Evidence was admitted of A's similar conduct on previous occasions from which P had derived benefit.

16. To negative accident and to demonstrate a systematic course of conduct. *See R.* v. *Smith* (1915) (*see* **4** (*a*) above).

(*a*) In *Makin* v. *A.-G. for N.S. Wales* (1894) X and Y were charged with the murder of Z, an infant they had adopted. Z's body was found buried in the garden of a house occupied by X and Y. Evidence was given showing that other children had been received by X and Y on the same kind of terms implicit in Z's adoption, and that other children's bodies had been found buried in a like manner in other houses occupied by X and Y. It was held that the evidence *was admissible* to show the intention with which the acts constituting the crime were carried out. (It should be noted, however, that the mere repetition of conduct does *not* in itself constitute evidence of a system.) *See* the statement of Lord Herschell at **5** above.

(*b*) "A system is not necessarily criminal: most men carry on business on a system, they may even be said to live on a system. Where, however, acts are of such a character that, taken alone, they may be innocent, but which result in benefit or reward to the actor and loss or suffering to the patient, repeated instances of such acts at least show that experience has fully informed the actor of all their elements and details, and it is only reasonable to infer that the act is designed and intentional, and its motive the benefit or reward to himself or the loss or suffering to some third person": *per* Lawrence, J. in *R.* v. *Bond* (1906).

17. To negative the defence of innocent association in a charge

relating to a sexual offence. *See R.* v. *Ball* (1911) (*see* **11** (*b*) above);
R. v. *Sims* (1946); *R.* v. *Novac* (1977). Note the following cases.

(*a*) *R.* v. *Barrington* (1981). B induced three young girls to come
to his house on the pretext of baby-sitting and indecently assaulted
them there. B denied the offences. The prosecution called three
other girls whose evidence disclosed circumstances similar to those
leading to the alleged assaults. B's appeal against conviction was
dismissed: the evidence of the other girls was admissible to rebut B's
defence of innocent baby-sitting; and, additionally, the circumstances of the relationship of B to the three other girls were
"strikingly similar" to the circumstances which led to the commission of the alleged offences, so that they were of probative value and
admissible as similar fact evidence.

(*b*) *R.* v. *Lewis* (1983). L was charged with indecent assault
against the young twin daughters of the woman with whom he was
living. He denied one of the incidents and put forward defences of
accident and innocent intent for the others. Evidence of L's interest
in paedophilia was admitted. The Court of Appeal held that
evidence of personal predilection was *admissible* to rebut L's defence
even though the defence to another count was a denial.

18. To negative the defence of mistaken identification. *See* 13:**23**.
Where the accused claims that he has been incorrectly or mistakenly
identified, similar fact evidence may be admitted, always subject to
the discretion of the court (*see* **7** above), to rebut that defence.

(*a*) *Thompson* v. *R.* (1918). X was convicted of acts of gross
indecency with two boys. The first acts were alleged to have taken
place on March 16th, and the person who committed those acts was
said to have made a further appointment with the boys for March
19th. The police, having been informed, observed X at the
rendezvous. X's defence was mistaken identity. Evidence was
admitted to show the discovery of indecent photographs, etc., in X's
room. Admission of that evidence was upheld. "What was done on
the 16th shows that the person who did it was a person with
abnormal propensities of this kind. The possession of the articles
tends to show that the person who came on the 19th, the prisoner,
had abnormal propensities of the same kind. The criminal of the

16th and the prisoner had this feature in common, and it appears to me that the evidence which is objected to afforded some evidence tending to show the probability of the truth of the boys' story as to identity": *per* Lord Finlay.

(b) *R.* v. *Hall* (1952). Hall was convicted of acts of gross indecency on a number of occasions with A, B and C. In relation to C, Hall's defence was that he had at no time seen C. Evidence of A and B concerning acts done to them by Hall in incidents closely resembling those mentioned by C was held to have been rightly admitted. "It was for the jury to say whether C was a liar or a witness of truth, and in deciding that question they were entitled to take into account the evidence given by A and B": *per* Lord Goddard.

19. To negative an innocent explanation of possession of incriminating material. Where apparently incriminating material is found in the possession of the accused he may challenge the prosecution to establish that it was not in his possession for some lawful purpose. The prosecution may prove that on past occasions he has used the material in a manner which is similar to that involved in the present case. *See R.* v. *Hodges* (1957).

NOTE: *See* also the Official Secrets Act 1911, s. 1 (2) (*see* **15:9** (*d*)); and the Theft Act 1968, s. 27 (3) (*see* **15:9** (*b*)).

20. Some "post-Boardman" cases. The following cases are of particular note in the light of the extended principles of similar fact evidence as formulated in *DPP* v. *Boardman* (1974) (*see* **13** above).

(a) *R.* v. *Rance* (1975). R, managing director of a building company, was convicted of corruptly procuring a payment of money to H, a local councillor. H was convicted of corruptly receiving the payment. A certificate, authorising payment, was signed by R in which H was described, incorrectly, as a "subcontractor". R stated that he must have been deceived into signing. Evidence was admitted of similar payments made to other councillors, which was supported by false certificates. Leave to appeal against conviction was refused. Citing statements in *DPP* v. *Boardman* (at **13** (*c*) above), Lord Widgery, C.J. stressed that evidence is admissible as similar fact evidence, "if, but only if, it goes beyond showing a tendency to commit crimes of this kind and is positively probative in regard to the crime now charged. That, we think, is the test which we have to apply on the question of the correctness or otherwise of the admission of similar fact evidence in this case."

(b) *R.* v. *Tricoglus* (1976). *See* 8 (c) above. X was convicted of the rape of A. She had given evidence of accepting a lift from a bearded man driving a Mini car in which he had driven her to a cul-de-sac where she was raped. The judge admitted evidence from G that she, too, had been raped, a few days before the rape of A, in a cul-de-sac, by a bearded man who had offered her a lift. The unusual method of rape was almost the same as that in A's case. G identified X's car when shown it. Evidence was also admitted from C and M that a bearded man driving a Mini car in the same vicinity had offered them lifts. X's appeal was allowed. The evidence of C and M had no bearing at all on the manner in which A was raped. "In our judgment it merely went to show . . . that X has unpleasant social habits. Beyond that it does not go. Therefore it ought not, in our judgment, to have been admitted . . . As has been pointed out many times in this Court and in the House of Lords, it is not permissible to call evidence to show that a man has a propensity towards a particular type of crime": *per* Lawton, L.J. (Note that the evidence of G as to the manner in which she was raped "did bear a uniquely and strikingly similar resemblance to the manner in which A was raped. Therefore, prima facie, as a matter of law, Mrs G's evidence as to how she was raped was admissible.")

(c) *R.* v. *Clarke* (1978). D was charged on counts 1–3 with attempted buggery and indecent assault against his stepson, aged 16, and on counts 4–7 with attempting to have sexual intercourse and indecent assault upon his stepdaughter, aged 9. It was alleged that the offences had occurred in the children's home or nearby and that they partook of the same character. The judge directed the jury that if they thought there had been a course of conduct of a similar pattern they could treat each complaint as corroborating the other. He refused to sever counts 1–3 from counts 4–7. D appealed, and it was held that on the facts there were no "striking similarities" between the evidence in relation to each child, so that the judge had erred in refusing to sever the counts and in his direction that the evidence in relation to each child could corroborate the evidence in relation to the other. (As the jury had convicted only where there was an admission, the proviso was applied and the appeal dismissed.)

(*d*) *See* also: *R.* v. *Johannsen* (1977); *R.* v. *Mansfield* (1977); *R.* v. *Hill* (1982); *R.* v. *Butler* (1986).

Character

21. The general rule. In general, the fact that a person's character is "good" or "bad" is not relevant to the question of his having performed the act which is in issue. Evidence of character of parties is, in civil and criminal proceedings, generally not relevant and, therefore, not admissible.

(*a*) "Character" may refer to a person's "reputation", "disposition", or "convictions". *See Selvey* v. *DPP* (1970). *See* 15:**19** (*b*) (*ii*); *R.* v. *Burke* (1986).

(*b*) Where a party's general character, or some aspect of it, is in question, for example, as in a defamation action where a plea of justification is made, evidence of character may be received: *see Scott* v. *Sampson* (1882). "Character" in this connection refers to general reputation; it will not embrace, e.g., rumour.

22. Criminal cases: character of accused. There are exceptions to the general rule, as follows:

(*a*) The accused may prove his *good character*, provided that it is relevant to the specific offence in question.

(*i*) The evidence must be *general* and must not be based on specific matters.

(*ii*) It must have reference to a time proximate to the offence.

(*iii*) Evidence of character may be in the form of accused's own testimony or that of witnesses called by him.

(*b*) When accused attempts to prove his good character he may be "putting his character in issue". One of the results is that the prosecution may seek to rebut this by giving evidence of his *bad character*. *See R.* v. *Butterwasser* (1948); *R.* v. *De Vere* (1981). *See* (*d*) below. *See R.* v. *Lee* (1976).

(*c*) In criminal cases, character usually means "general reputation":

see R. v. *Rowton* (1865).

(*d*) Although, in general, the prosecution may not adduce evidence of the *bad character* of the accused, before verdict is given, there are exceptions, the most important of which are set out below.

(*i*) **Where** accused attempts to show good character, the prosecution may attempt to rebut this. His *general reputation* may be attacked. "There is no such thing in our procedure as putting half a prisoner's character in issue and leaving out the other half": *per* Humphreys, J. in *R.* v. *Winfield* (1939).

(*ii*) **Where** similar fact evidence (*see* 3 above) is admissible, evidence of bad character may be adduced.

(*iii*) *See* also the Criminal Evidence Act 1898, s. 1 (*f*) (discussed at 15:**14**); *R.* v. *Lamb* (1980).

(*e*) A defendant is not allowed at his trial, by any reference to particular acts, to call evidence suggesting that he is of a disposition which makes it unlikely that he would have committed the offence with which he is charged. In *R.* v. *Redgrave* (1982) R was charged under the Sexual Offences Act 1956, s. 32, with importuning for an immoral purpose. The Court of Appeal upheld the trial judge's ruling that the production of evidence by R of his heterosexual relationships, so as to rebut the inference of his having made homosexual approaches, was inadmissible.

23. Criminal cases: character of prosecutor and witnesses. In general, no evidence can be given by accused or the Crown relating to prosecutor's character: *see R.* v. *Wood* (1951). However, *see R.* v. *Krausz* (1973) (prosecutrix's denial that she was a prostitute was allowed to be contradicted by evidence of similar conduct on other occasions). But the party adducing such evidence may be cross-examined as to credit (*see* 5:**12**). Other witnesses, too, may be cross-examined as to credit; in such cases the witness's answers must be accepted as final and evidence may not be adduced in rebuttal: *A.-G.* v. *Hitchcock* (1847). Where, however, a witness denies a previous conviction, or a previous inconsistent statement, evidence may be given of the conviction or statement, under the Criminal Procedure Act 1865, s. 6.

24. Civil cases: character of defendant and third parties. Character is rarely relevant in such cases. Exceptionally, it may be a fact in issue (as in defamation: *see Plato Films Ltd.* v. *Speidel* (1961)). Character of third parties is also rarely relevant (*see Burns* v. *Edman* (1970) where, in a claim under the Law Reform (Miscellaneous Provisions) Act 1934, the court took judicial notice (*see* 9:**14**) of the fact that the life of a third party (a criminal, i.e. the deceased, who had had no honest employment) was an unhappy one).

NOTE: *See* 15:**24–28** for the Rehabilitation of Offenders Act 1974 which may affect evidence relating to convictions.

25. *Lowery* v. *R.* (1974). X, a young girl, was murdered in unusually sadistic circumstances. Y and Z were charged with X's murder. Each stated in evidence that the other had been solely to blame for the killing of X. Y's evidence related to his good character, his happy home life and his lack of motive for killing X. He stated that he was in great fear of Z. Z gave evidence (against Y's objection) from a psychologist who said that an investigation of the personalities of Y and Z showed that Y had a strong aggressive drive with overtones of sadism, but that Z's tendencies were less marked and that he was likely to be led by more aggressive persons. Y and Z were convicted and Y, in his appeal, contended that the psychologist's evidence had been wrongly admitted.

(*a*) The Privy Council dismissed Y's appeal. Y had put his character in issue and although the prosecution could not have called such evidence, since it showed no more than a disposition to commit offences, there was no reason of policy or fairness to exclude it when tendered by a person to demonstrate his innocence.

(*b*) "It is established by the highest authority that in criminal cases the Crown is precluded from leading evidence that does no more than show that the accused has a disposition or propensity or is the sort of person likely to commit the crime charged . . . it is, we think, one thing to say that such evidence is excluded when tendered by the Crown in proof of guilt, but quite another to say that it is excluded when tendered by the accused in disproof of his own guilt. We see no reason of policy or fairness which justifies or requires the exclusion of evidence relevant to prove the innocence of an accused person": from the judgment of the Full Court of the State of Victoria

(sitting as a Court of Criminal Appeal), cited with approval by the
P.C. (Note also *R.* v. *Bracewell* (1978)—in a case where each of two
defendants blamed the other for a crime of violence which must have
been committed by one of them, evidence of the violent propensity
of one may be admissible at the instance of the other.)

Progress test 14

1. What is the meaning of "similar fact evidence"? (**3**)

2. What is the general rule relating to the admissibility of similar
fact evidence? (**5**)

3. Outline the facts and decision in *Harris* v. *DPP* (1952). (**6**)

4. Explain the significance of judicial discretion in relation to the
admissibility of similar fact evidence. (**7**)

5. Comment on the decision in *R.* v. *Scarrott* (1977). (**8**)

6. Comment on the concept of similar fact evidence in civil
cases. (**9**)

7. What is the importance of *DPP* v. *Boardman* (1974)? (**13**)

8. May similar fact evidence be adduced to rebut a defence of
mistake or lack of knowledge? (**14, 15**)

9. Comment on *R.* v. *Barrington* (1981). (**17**)

10. Comment on *R.* v. *Rance* (1975). (**20**)

11. What is the general rule relating to the admissibility of
"character evidence"? (**21**)

12. Is the accused allowed to attempt to prove his "good character"? (**22**)

13. May the Crown give evidence relating to the character of a
prosecutrix? (**23**)

14. Comment on *Lowery* v. *R.* (1974). (**25**)

15

Matters which may be proved (3): convictions; opinions; beliefs

Preliminary matters

1. General. This chapter concludes the examination, begun in Chap. 13, of matters of which proof is allowed. It examines the circumstances in which proof of previous convictions may be admissible and considers the occasions on which the opinions of persons, and their beliefs, may be given in evidence.

2. Matters to be covered. The following points are considered below:

(a) The problem of evidence of previous convictions (*see* **3–13** below).

(b) The interpretation of the accused's "shield" provided by the Criminal Evidence Act 1898, s. 1 (*f*) (*see* **14–20** below).

(c) Judicial findings as evidence (*see* **21–23** below).

(d) The importance of provisions relating to evidence of previous convictions contained in the Rehabilitation of Offenders Act 1974 (*see* **24–28** below).

(e) The admissibility of opinions and beliefs (*see* **29–35** below).

Evidence of previous convictions

3. The general rule. In general, just as evidence of character (*see* 14:21) and similar facts (*see* 14:3) is excluded, so evidence of a person's previous convictions is not admissible. Exceptions to this wide, general rule are considered later in this chapter.

4. The exclusionary rule in criminal cases. In general, a previous conviction was no more than evidence of the fact that the person concerned has been convicted by the court: it was *not* accepted as evidence that he carried out those acts which form the basis of his conviction. The effect of this highly restrictive rule was commented on by Blackburn, J. in *Castrique* v. *Imrie* (1870): "A judgment of conviction on an indictment for forging a bill of exchange, though conclusive as to the prisoner being a convicted felon, is not only *not conclusive*, but is *not even admissible evidence* of the forgery in an action on the bill."

5. The former exclusionary rule in civil cases: *Hollington* v. *Hewthorn & Co.* (1943). In this running-down action, P sued on behalf of his son's estate. The son had been killed in the accident in question and there was no other direct evidence by which P could establish what took place at the time of the collision. An attempt was made to introduce evidence of the conviction of a second defendant for careless driving at that same place and time; the attempt was rejected.

(*a*) "In truth, the conviction is only proof that another court considered that the defendant was guilty of careless driving . . . It frequently happens that a bystander has a complete and full view of an accident. It is beyond question that, while he may inform the court of everything he saw, he may not express any opinion on whether either or both of the parties were negligent. The reason commonly assigned is that this is the precise question the court has to decide, but, in truth, it is because his opinion is not relevant . . . So, *on the trial of the issue in the civil court, the opinion of the criminal court is equally irrelevant*": *per* Lord Goddard.

(*b*) The decision was criticised by Lord Denning, M.R. in *Goody* v. *Odhams Press Ltd.* (1967) and in *Barclays Bank* v. *Cole* (1967), as "a strange rule of law" and as "an unfortunate decision". In *Hunter* v. *Chief Constable of West Midlands* (1982), the House of Lords commented that the decision in *Hollington* v. *Hewthorn & Co.* was incorrect. The Police and Criminal Evidence Act 1984, s. 74 (*see* **12** below) effectively abrogates the rule in that case.

6. General relaxation of the rule. It will be seen below that in both civil and criminal proceedings, a party's previous convictions may now be proved, e.g. under statute or, more generally, whenever they are in issue.

7. In relation to civil proceedings: Civil Evidence Act 1968. The following statutory provision, which amounts to a reversal, for some kinds of civil case, of the exclusionary rule, and its effects, should be noted carefully.

(a) "In any *civil proceedings* the fact that a person has been convicted of an offence by or before any court in the U.K. or by a court-martial there or elsewhere shall (subject to subsec. (3)) be admissible in evidence for the purpose of proving, where to do so is relevant to any issue in those proceedings, that he committed that offence, whether he was so convicted upon a plea of guilty or otherwise and whether or not he is a party to the civil proceedings; but no conviction other than a subsisting one shall be admissible in evidence by virtue of this section": s. 11 (1). *See* also O. 18, r. 7A (which sets out procedural requirements related to s. 11).

(b) The above must be read in the light of the Rehabilitation of Offenders Act 1974, ss. 4 (1) (a), and 7 (3), by virtue of which such evidence may not be admissible if the conviction in question is "spent" (*see* **24** (b) below) unless the interests of justice require its admittance (*see* **27** below).

(c) It should be noted that although such evidence is admissible it is not conclusive, except in the case of an action for defamation. "In an action for libel or slander in which the question whether a person did or did not commit a criminal offence is relevant to an issue arising in the action, proof that, at the time when that issue falls to be determined, that person stands convicted of that offence; and his conviction thereof shall be admissible in evidence accordingly": s. 13 (1).

(d) Note that s. 13 (1) must be read in the light of the Rehabilitation of Offenders Act 1974, s. 8, in which evidence of "spent" convictions will not be admissible in a defamation action brought by a rehabilitated person (*see* **24** (a) below) and based on the publication of some imputation that he has been tried or sentenced for a spent offence.

(e) In matrimonial proceedings in the county court and High

Court, if a person is found to have committed adultery, then in other civil proceedings that fact will be admissible in evidence where the adultery is a relevant issue: Civil Evidence Act 1968, s. 12.

8. Convictions and character. Where a person's character is admissible in evidence *in its entirety*, this will generally be taken to include evidence of past convictions. But if it is his *reputation alone* which is relevant, then evidence relating to past convictions will not be admissible.

9. Evidence of previous convictions in relation to an accused person. Evidence of this nature may be admissible in the following circumstances:

(*a*) Where the accused raises a plea of *autrefois convict* (*see* 11:**18** (*b*)), in which case the conviction has specific relevance as a fact in issue.

(*b*) In proceedings under the Theft Act 1968, s. 27 (3) (handling of stolen goods), evidence is admissible (after seven days' written notice has been given) to prove a conviction of the accused of theft or handling within the five years preceding the date of the offence presently charged. Such evidence may be admitted to prove guilty knowledge, not possession, and where both matters are in issue, great care must be taken to direct the jury about such evidence and its probative value: *R*. v. *Wilkins* (1975).

(*c*) In proceedings under the Prevention of Crimes Act 1871, s. 7, under which certain acts may be punished if committed after two previous convictions and within seven years of the last. In such a case proof of the earlier convictions is necessary and, therefore, admissible.

(*d*) In proceedings under the Official Secrets Act 1911, s. 1 (2), it is possible to infer from the accused's "known character as proved" that his purpose was prejudicial to the safety and interests of the state. Evidence of earlier convictions is admissible.

(*e*) If accused puts his character in issue in an attempt to establish "good character", the prosecution may be allowed to prove his previous convictions as a part of his bad character. But *see R*. v. *Butterwasser* (1948); *R*. v. *Lee* (1976).

(*f*) In relation to cross-examination of the accused and previous convictions, *see* the Criminal Evidence Act 1898, s. 1 (at **14** below). (It should be noted that the Court of Appeal emphasised recently that a defendant can be cross-examined about his previous convictions *only* if the situation falls within the 1898 Act, s. 1 (*f*): *R.* v. *Weekes* (1984).)

(*g*) After conviction, but before sentence, details of the accused's character and antecedents are received.

10. Evidence of previous convictions in relation to parties in civil cases. Previous convictions of a party in a *civil case* may be proved only where the very fact of a conviction is a relevant fact, or where it is admissible under the Civil Evidence Act 1968 in proof of a relevant fact.

(*a*) If convictions are denied in cross-examination to credit, they may be proved in rebuttal.

(*b*) In *London Computer Operators Training Ltd.* v. *BBC* (1973) it was held that where an alleged libel could be interpreted as suggesting that a company was being administered by persons of doubtful honesty, the convictions of the company's founder *were admissible* as particulars of justification (and even though that person was not a plaintiff in the action in question).

11. Evidence of previous convictions in relation to witnesses (except the accused). Any witness may, in the course of cross-examination as to credit, be examined as to a previous conviction so as to show that he is a person who should not be believed.

(*a*) Note, however, the restrictions (in the majority of types of civil proceedings) relating to "spent" convictions under the Rehabilitation of Offenders Act 1974, s. 4 (1) (*b*) (*see* **24** (*b*) below).

(*b*) Where a witness denies a previous conviction it may be proved in cross-examination under the Criminal Procedure Act 1865, s. 6. (This provision applies also to civil proceedings.) "A witness may be questioned as to whether he has been convicted of any felony or misdemeanour, and upon so being questioned, if he either denies or does not admit the fact, or refuses to answer, it shall be lawful for the cross-examining party to prove such conviction . . ."

Convictions as evidence of the commission of offences: the 1984 legislation

12. The Police and Criminal Evidence Act 1984, s. 74. Under this section of the Act, the earlier conviction of a person will suffice to prove that he did commit the offence for which he was convicted. (For pre-1984 cases, *see*, e.g., *R*. v. *Hassan* (1970); *R*. v. *Spinks* (1982).) The following points indicate the essence of s. 74.

(*a*) Where some person *other than the accused* has been convicted of an offence, that fact (where relevant) may be given in evidence so as to prove that the person did commit that offence, and no other evidence of his having committed that offence need be given: s. 74 (1).

(*b*) In any proceedings in which by virtue of s. 74 a person *other than the accused* is shown to have been convicted of an offence, that person will be taken to have committed that offence, unless the contrary is proved: s. 74 (2).

(*c*) Where it is relevant to any matter in issue at his trial, proof of a previous conviction *of the accused* will suffice to establish that he has committed that offence, unless the contrary is proved. But a previous conviction of the accused cannot be given in evidence for the purpose of establishing that he has a disposition to commit the kind of offence with which he is charged: s. 74 (3). (*See* 14:**12**.)

(*d*) Section 74 will not prejudice the admissibility in evidence of any conviction which would be admissible apart from the section, or any pre-existing enactments making previous convictions or finding of fact in any proceedings conclusive evidence for the purpose of other proceedings: s. 74 (4). (Thus, the Powers of Criminal Courts Act 1973, s. 13, will not affect the 1984 Act, s. 74: s. 75 (3) (*a*).) In effect, therefore, s. 74 supplements, rather than limits, the scope of pre-existing legislation concerning proof of previous convictions.

13. Supplementary provisions to s. 74. The following points should be noted.

(*a*) A conviction is admissible under s. 74 only if it is "a subsisting one": s. 75 (4).

(*b*) Under s. 75 (1) the court may allow evidence to be given concerning the identification of the facts on which a previous conviction was based. Specifically, evidence may be given of the contents of any documents admissible as evidence of the conviction and of the contents of the information, complaint, indictment or charge sheet on which the accused, or some other person, was convicted: s. 75 (1) (*a*), (*b*).

(*c*) Where a document is admissible under s. 75 (1), a copy which is authenticated by the court having possession of the document is admissible in evidence as a true copy, unless the contrary is shown: s. 75 (2).

NOTE: Even though a conviction may be admissible under statute, a judge may exercise his discretion so as to exclude it, under s. 78. *See* also *R.* v. *Perry* (1984), where the question was whether evidence of P's previous conviction for theft provided assistance to the jury which was outweighed by the prejudice of that evidence.

Criminal Evidence Act 1898, s. 1 (*f*)

14. General. Under the Criminal Evidence Act 1898, s. 1 (*a*), the accused cannot be called as a witness "except upon his own application". In effect, he is, under the 1898 Act, a competent, though not compellable, witness. Should the accused decide to give evidence, the following important points apply:

(*a*) He "may be asked any question in cross-examination notwithstanding that it would tend to criminate him as to the offence charged": s. 1 (*e*).

(*b*) He may not generally be attacked by a cross-examination aimed at establishing that he has a bad character. The important "shield of the accused" is set out at **15** below, and is considered in detail at **16–20** below.

NOTE: Section 1 (*b*) of the 1898 Act provides that where the accused *fails* to give evidence, this shall not be made the subject of comment by the prosecution. *See R.* v. *Bathurst* (1968); *R.* v. *Sparrow* (1973).

15. Section 1 (*f*). "A person charged and called as a witness in pursuance of this Act shall not be asked, and if asked shall not be required to answer, any question tending to show that he has committed or been convicted of or been charged with any offence other than that wherewith he is then charged, or is of bad character, unless—

(*i*) the proof that he has committed or been convicted of such other offences is admissible evidence to show that he is guilty of the offence wherewith he is then charged; or

(*ii*) he has personally or by his advocate asked questions of the witnesses for the prosecution with a view to establish his own good character, or has given evidence of his own good character, or the nature or conduct of the defence is such as to involve imputations on the character of the prosecutor or the witnesses for the prosecution; or

(*iii*) he has given evidence against any other person charged in the same proceedings." (Note that the final four words were substituted by the Criminal Evidence Act 1979, s. 1 (1), for "with the same offence". This effectively reversed the decision of the House of Lords in *R.* v. *Hills* (1980).)

16. General effect of s. 1 (*f*). This section has the following general effects:

(*a*) It acts as a "shield" for the accused person against a cross-examination relating to character and convictions.

(*b*) The shield can be thrown away, and when that occurs accused can be cross-examined as to character and previous convictions. (Note here the Practice Direction (1975) concerning spent convictions, at **28** below.)

(*c*) Should the shield be cast away, judicial discretion may be exercised to disallow questions considered as being unduly prejudicial.

17. Preliminary interpretation of s. 1 (*f*). Three phrases call for particular interpretation:

(*a*) *"Tending to show."* In *Jones* v. *DPP* (1962) the phrase was construed as meaning "tending to reveal" or "tending to make known". Hence it would seem that questions on matters *already revealed to the court* will not be excluded under s. 1 (*f*). In that case, the cross-examination of Jones tended to show that (because he had previously been in trouble with the police) he was of bad character, but the fact of his previous conviction was not touched upon. The House of Lords held that the cross-examination did not tend to show (i.e. to "reveal") that Jones had been in trouble with the police since he had already revealed this at an earlier stage in the proceedings.

(*b*) *"Charged"*. This means "charged in court": *Stirland* v. *DPP* (1944). In that case it was held that s. 1 (*f*) did not let in evidence that the accused had been *questioned* about a criminal offence with which he had never been charged formally. Further, "charged" has no reference generally to a previous charge resulting in an acquittal.

(*i*) In *Maxwell* v. *DPP* (1935), M was charged with manslaughter by an illegal operation. He had given evidence of his own good character and in cross-examination was asked about a previous acquittal on a similar charge. It was held that the question was not relevant to the present issue and was not relevant to credit. (*See R.* v. *Palmer* (1983).)

(*ii*) "In general no question whether a prisoner has been convicted or charged or acquitted should be asked or, if asked, allowed by the judge, who has a discretion under proviso (*f*) unless it helps to elucidate the particular issue which the jury is investigating, or goes to credibility, that is, tends to show that he is not to be believed on his oath; indeed the question whether a man has been convicted, charged or acquitted ought not to be admitted, even if it goes to credibility, if there is any risk of the jury being misled into thinking that it goes not to credibility but to the probability of his having committed the offence of which he is charged. I think that it is impossible in the present case to say that the fact that the prisoner has been acquitted on a previous charge of murder or manslaughter was relevant, or that it tended in the present case to destroy his credibility as a witness": *per* Viscount Sankey in *Maxwell* v. *DPP* (1935).

(*c*) *"Bad character"*. "Character" in this expression seems to include reputation and disposition. *See Malindi* v. *R.* (1967); *Selvey* v. *DPP* (1970).

18. Section 1 (*f*) (*i*). Under s. 1 (*f*) (*i*) the accused may be questioned about other offences and convictions when proof that he has committed them or been convicted of them is admissible to show that he is guilty of the offence with which he is being charged.

(a) It is not permissible under the exception in s. 1 (f) (i) to question accused in regard to some charge of which he had been acquitted: R. v. Cokar (1960).

(b) A question which tends to show bad character is not admissible under s. 1 (f) (i). In Malindi v. R. (1967) X was charged with conspiracy to commit arson. In cross-examination questions were put to X concerning his private writings of a year earlier in which he had justified the use of violence. It was held that the questions were improper: X had not thrown away his shield under s. 1 (f). See R. v. Nightingale (1977); R. v. Varley (1982), in which the authorities are reviewed and guidelines set out, e.g., that mere denial of participation in a joint venture is not of itself sufficient to rank as evidence against the co-defendant, that it has to be objectively decided whether the evidence either supports the prosecution case in a material respect or undermines the defence of the co-accused (and a hostile intent is irrelevant).

19. Section 1 (f) (ii). This is probably *the most important exception*. It refers to two cases in which the accused's shield is cast away: where accused has put his character in issue; imputations cast on the character of the prosecutor or witnesses for the prosecution.

(a) *Character in issue.* Once the accused puts his character in issue, evidence intending to show his bad character, including convictions, is permitted. Note that "character" means here "reputation" or "disposition". The shield was considered to have been thrown away in the following cases, for example:

(i) R. v. Baker (1912), in which accused had stated that for a long period of time he had been earning an honest living.

(ii) R. v. Samuel (1956), in which accused, charged with larceny by finding, had given evidence relating to previous occasions on which he had returned lost property.

(iii) R. v. Beecham (1921), in which accused, charged with a road traffic offence, had stated that he did not approve of speeding and disliked travelling or driving fast.

(*b*) *Imputations on the character of prosecutor or his witnesses.* It should be remembered that "character" includes reputation and disposition: *see R.* v. *Dunkley* (1927), and that, as soon as the exception is activated, that which emerges in cross-examination goes to the credibility of the accused: *R.* v. *Longman and Richardson* (1969). Attacks on the character of other persons, for example, the deceased in a trial for murder, do not activate the exception. The following cases are of relevance:

(*i*) *R.* v. *Bishop* (1974). D was charged with burglary and explained the presence of his finger prints in P's room by alleging a homosexual relationship between himself and P. It was held that, notwithstanding that such behaviour no longer constitutes an offence, the allegation was an imputation on character, so as to justify D's having been cross-examined on previous convictions for dishonesty.

(*ii*) *Selvey* v. *DPP* (1970). X was charged with a sexual offence against Y. It was put to Y that he was a male prostitute who had had relations with another person earlier in the day in question and that he was merely blaming X who had refused to give him money. The prosecution cross-examined X on previous convictions for indecent assault. It was held by the House of Lords that X's attack on Y's character had resulted in his shield under s. 1 (*f*) being thrown away. There was *no rule* that judicial discretion is excluded merely because imputations were needed to develop the defence properly. The words of the 1898 Act had to be given their ordinary, natural meaning: *per* Lord Dilhorne.

(*iii*) *R.* v. *Lee* (1976). D was charged with theft from the bedroom of a house in which he had been living. It was put to the owner of the stolen goods that two other persons, who visited the house (but who did not give evidence for the prosecution) had convictions for dishonesty. The trial judge ruled that D was attempting to show that the two men, by reason of their convictions, were more likely to have committed the theft and, therefore, that the prosecution could cross-examine D as to his convictions. On appeal by D, it was held, allowing the appeal, that the questions were put to establish the bad character of the two persons, but nothing else; the questions had nothing to do with D's character.

(*iv*) *See also R.* v. *Gunner and Lye* (1977); *R.* v. *McGee* (1979);

R. v. *Watts* (1983); *R.* v. *Fentiman* (1984).

NOTE: (1) Accused should be warned by the judge as soon as it appears that he may be running some risk of his being cross-examined under s. 1 (*f*) (*ii*). Leave to cross-examine under s. 1 (*f*) (*ii*) must be sought from the judge.

(2) Where a defendant loses the protection of s. 1 (*f*), previous convictions which occurred *after* the case in question may be put to him: *R.* v. *Coltress* (1978).

(3) Where the necessary inference behind an attack on a prosecution witness is fabrication of evidence, a defendant cannot protect his character from being introduced by alleging mistake: *R.* v. *Britzman* (1983). (In this case guidelines were suggested for the exercise of a judge's discretion in proceedings involving denials of conversations with the police. "First, it should be used if there is nothing more than a denial, however emphatic or offensively made, of an act or even a short series of acts amounting to one incident or in what was said to have been a short interview . . . Second, cross-examination should only be allowed if the judge is sure that there is no possibility of mistake, misunderstanding or confusion and that the jury will inevitably have to decide whether the prosecution witnesses have fabricated evidence": *per* Lawton, L.J.)

20. Section 1 (*f*) (*iii*). This exception is activated where the accused has given evidence against any other person who has been charged in the same proceedings (*see* 15 above). The criterion of giving evidence "against another" is whether that evidence tends to make the other person's acquittal less likely: *R.* v. *Hatton* (1976). The following cases should be noted:

(*a*) *R.* v. *Davis* (1975). X and Y, who had visited a house together, were charged with theft from that house of a gold cross and tureen. At the trial, on a joint charge, X denied the allegation in his examination-in-chief. When cross-examined on Y's behalf, he said, "I'm not suggesting Y took the cross. As I never, and it's missing, he must have done. But I'm not saying that he did." Evidence of X's previous convictions was admitted under s. 1 (*f*) (*iii*) and X was convicted of stealing the tureen. X appealed, contending that the evidence was inadmissible, since a mere denial was not evidence against a co-accused. It was held, dismissing the appeal, that, in all the circumstances, which were such that one or other must have committed the offence, X's denial had undermined Y's defence and, therefore, amounted to evidence against Y under s. 1 (f) (iii) of the 1898 Act.

(*b*) *R.* v. *Hatton* (1976). X, Y and Z were charged with stealing scrap metal. Y denied that there was a plan to steal the scrap; X and Z agreed that there was a plan but denied dishonesty. The trial judge allowed counsel for Y to examine X on the ground that X had given evidence against Y within the meaning of s. 1 (f) (iii), since X's evidence undermined Y's story. On appeal, X contended that the evidence was not necessarily "against" Y. X's appeal was dismissed; it was held that as X's evidence had supported a vital part of the prosecution's case, which Y had denied, it rendered Y's conviction more likely, thus reducing his chance of acquittal.

(*c*) *See* also *Murdoch* v. *Taylor* (1965); *R.* v. *Bruce* (1975); *R.* v. *Rockman* (1978); *R.* v. *Varley* (1982)—where one defendant asserts (or will assert in due course) a view of a joint venture which the other contradicts directly, the contradiction may amount to "evidence against" that defendant; *R.* v. *Rowson* (1985); *R.* v. *Powell* (1985)— a jury is entitled to know about defendant's previous convictions when he has deliberately attacked the conduct of a witness for the prosecution, and, further, while the similarity of defendant's convictions to the essential subject-matter of the trial is a matter which the judge must consider when deciding on the exercise of his discretion, it will not oblige the judge to disallow the cross-examination of defendant.

A note on judicial findings as evidence

21. General. In civil or criminal proceedings a previous judgment may be admissible as evidence and, if admissible, will be conclusive evidence as to the fact that it was pronounced, the court which pronounced it, the date and the parties. It will *not* be conclusive of anything not appearing on the record. *See R.* v. *Turner* (1832). Note now, however, the Civil Evidence Act 1968, s. 11 (*see* **7** above). *See* also O. 18, r. 7A.

22. Questions of adultery and paternity. Two subsections of s. 12 of the Civil Evidence Act 1968 are of importance:

(*a*) "In any civil proceedings the fact that a person has been found guilty of adultery in any matrimonial proceedings; and the fact that a person has been adjudged to be the father of a child in affiliation proceedings before any court in the U.K. shall . . . be admissible in evidence for the purpose of proving, where to do so is relevant to any issue in those civil proceedings, that he committed the adultery to which the finding relates, or, as the case may be, is (or was) the father of that child.": s. 12 (1).

(*b*) "In any civil proceedings in which by virtue of this section a person is proved to have been found guilty of adultery as mentioned in subsection (1) . . . or to have been adjudged to be the father of a child as mentioned in subsection (1) . . . he shall be taken to have committed the adultery to which the finding relates, or, as the case may be, to be (or have been) the father of that child, unless the contrary is proved on the balance of probabilities": s. 12 (2).

(*c*) *See Taylor* v. *Taylor* (1970); *Sutton* v. *Sutton* (1970).

23. Proof of judgments and convictions. The following rules apply:

(*a*) *Criminal cases.* Previous convictions or acquittals may now be proved by the production of an appropriate certificate of conviction or acquittal: *see* the Police and Criminal Evidence Act 1984, s. 73 (1). The following points should be noted.

(*i*) Proof will be required that the person named in the certificate is the person whose conviction or acquittal has to be proved: s. 73 (1).

(*ii*) The certificate must be signed by the clerk of the court (or his deputy) in which the conviction or acquittal took place: s. 73 (2) (*a*), (3).

(*iii*) Where the certificate refers to a summary trial, it must include a copy of the conviction or dismissal of the information: s. 73 (2) (*b*).

(*iv*) Where the certificate refers to conviction or acquittal on indictment, it must include the substance and effect of the indictment, conviction or acquittal: s. 73 (2) (*a*).

(v) The method of proving acquittal or conviction, as set out in s. 73, is in addition to, and does not exclude, any other authorised procedures: s. 73 (4). Note also, in this context, proof of identity by fingerprints (Criminal Justice Act 1948, s. 39) and written statements and written admissions (Criminal Justice Act 1967, ss. 9, 10 and the Magistrates' Courts Act 1980, s. 102).

(b) *Civil cases.* Judgments of the county court and magistrates' court may be proved on production of an appropriate extract from the court's books. Judgments of the High Court and Court of Appeal may be proved on production of an office copy. Judgments of the House of Lords may be proved on production of the Journal of the House. A foreign judgment requires production of a copy sealed with the seal of the foreign court. Oral evidence may also be needed to identify the parties to the judgments with those involved in the present action.

The Rehabilitation of Offenders Act 1974 in relation to evidence of convictions

24. The general effect of rehabilitation under the 1974 Act. The Act allows a "rehabilitated person" to be treated for all purposes in law as though he had not committed or been charged with or prosecuted for or convicted of or sentenced for the offence which was the subject of that conviction: s. 4 (1).

(a) A "rehabilitated person" is one who, having been convicted of an offence, has satisfied certain conditions (*see* s. 1) after the applicable rehabilitation period.

(b) No evidence of matters relating to a "spent conviction" (i.e. one which is treated as "spent", after the appropriate rehabilitation period (*see* s. 5)) may be admitted in any proceedings, nor may a person be asked questions in proceedings which he can answer only by reference to a spent conviction: s. 4 (1) (a) (b).

(c) Certain sentences are excluded from the provisions, under s. 5 (1), e.g. sentence of imprisonment for life, or of imprisonment for a term exceeding thirty months.

25. The Act and criminal proceedings. The Act's provisions regarding the effect of rehabilitation (s. 4 (1)) do *not* affect "the

determination of any issue, or prevent the admission or requirement
of any evidence, relating to a person's previous convictions or to
circumstances ancillary thereto—(a) in any criminal proceedings
before a court in Great Britain (including any appeal or reference in
a criminal matter) . . ." ("Circumstances ancillary thereto" refers
to: the offence which was the subject of the conviction; the conduct
constituting that offence; any proceedings preliminary to that
conviction: s. 4 (5).)

26. Questions relating to spent convictions. These are *inadmissible*
in any proceedings before a judicial authority (*see* **24** (*b*) above).
("Judicial authority" means any ordinary court of law (s. 4 (6)), but
includes also any tribunal, body or person having power by virtue of
some provision to determine questions affecting rights and obligations
and to receive appropriate evidence: s. 4 (6).)

27. Evidence admitted in the interests of justice. If at any stage in
proceedings before a judicial authority, the authority is satisfied, in
the light of any considerations which appear to it to be relevant
(including any evidence which has been or may thereafter be put to
it), that justice cannot be done in the case except by admitting or
requiring evidence relating to a person's spent convictions or to
circumstances ancillary thereto, that authority may admit or require
the evidence in question, notwithstanding the statutory provisions
relating to the effect of rehabilitation: s. 7 (3).

28. Practice Direction 1975. "During the trial of a criminal charge
reference to previous convictions, and therefore to spent convictions, can arise in a number of ways. The most common is when the
character of the accused or a witness is sought to be attacked by
reference to his criminal record, but there are, of course, cases
where previous convictions are relevant and admissible, as, for
instance, to prove system. It is not possible to give general directions
which will govern all these different situations, but it is recommended that both court and counsel should give effect to the general
intention of Parliament by never referring to a spent conviction
when such reference can be reasonably avoided . . . After a verdict
of guilty the court must be provided with a statement of the

defendant's record for purposes of sentence. The record supplied should contain all previous convictions, but those which are spent should, so far as practicable, be marked as such. No one should refer in open court to a spent conviction without the authority of the judge, which authority should not be given unless the interests of justice so require. When passing sentence the judge should make no reference to a spent conviction unless it is necessary to do so for the purpose of explaining the sentence to be passed": *per* Lord Widgery, C.J. in Practice Note [1975] 2 All E.R. 1072.

Opinions and belief

29. The general rule. In general, a witness may testify only to facts which he has perceived directly. As a result, his opinions, i.e. beliefs founded on inference from facts or from his impressions, are, in general, not admissible as evidence. Reasons for this exclusionary rule are said to include the following:

(*a*) Opinion evidence is largely irrelevant: *Hollington* v. *Hewthorn & Co.* (1943).

(*b*) The reception of opinion evidence has been considered as, in effect, a usurpation of the court's functions: *North Cheshire & Manchester Brewery Co.* v. *Manchester Brewery Co.* (1899). ". . . Upon the one question which your Lordships have to decide, whether the one name is so nearly resembling another as to be calculated to deceive, I am of opinion that no witness would be entitled to say that, and for this reason: that that is the very question which your Lordships have to decide . . .": *per* Lord Halsbury.

(*c*) A witness who speaks only to his private opinion may not be prosecuted later for perjury: *Folkes* v. *Chadd* (1782).

30. Opinion as a fact. Where an opinion, as such, is a relevant fact, it *can be proved*. Thus, the "opinion" of accused as to the age of a girl would be a fact in a charge under the Sexual Offences Act 1956, s. 6 (3), of having unlawful intercourse with a girl under sixteen. (Note, however, the distinction between "opinion" and a "question of fact". "A question of fact is one capable of being answered by way of demonstration; a question of opinion is one that cannot so be answered. The answer to it is a matter of speculation which cannot be proved by any available evidence to be right or wrong": Salmond.)

31. Exceptions to the general rule. The following exceptions are considered below:

    (*a*) Opinions of ordinary witnesses (*see* **32–33** below).

    (*b*) Opinions of expert witnesses (*see* **34–35** below).

32. The opinions of ordinary witnesses. These may be admissible to prove the following facts:

    (*a*) *Identity.* "There are many cases of identification where the law would be rendered ridiculous if positive certainty were required from witnesses": *per* Pollock, C.B. in *Fryer* v. *Gathercole* (1849). (For problems arising from identification parades, etc. *see* **13:23**.) *See Du Bost* v. *Beresford* (1810); *Lucas* v. *Williams & Sons* (1892).

    (*b*) *Handwriting. See* **8:19**. A witness's opinion may be given in proof of the genuineness of a party's handwriting if he has seen the party write on some occasion or has corresponded with him: *Doe d. Mudd* v. *Suckermore* (1837).

    (*c*) *Age.* A witness may testify to his own age. In some cases the court may form its own opinion, however, of the age of a witness. *See R.* v. *Cox* (1898); *Wallworth* v. *Balmer* (1966).

    (*d*) *Other matters.* The opinion of ordinary witnesses has been received in relation to questions concerning e.g.: the value of articles (*R.* v. *Beckett* (1913)); affection for a spouse (*Trelawney* v. *Coleman* (1877)); dislike of a child (*R.* v. *Hagan* (1873)).

    (*e*) *See* also *R.* v. *Loake* (1911); *R.* v. *Chard* (1971).

33. Civil Evidence Act 1972, s. 3 (2). "It is hereby declared that where a person is called as witness in any civil proceedings, a statement of opinion by him on a relevant matter [which includes an issue in the proceedings in question: s. 3 (3)] on which he is not qualified to give expert evidence, if made as a way of conveying relevant facts personally perceived by him, is admissible as evidence of what he perceived."

34. The opinions of expert witnesses: the general principle. "If matters arise in our law which concern other sciences or faculties we commonly apply for the aid of that science or faculty which it concerns. This is a commendable thing in our law. For thereby it appears that we do not dismiss all other sciences but our own, but we approve of them and encourage them as things worthy of commendation": *per* Saunders, J. in *Buckley* v. *Rice-Thomas* (1554). *See Dawson* v. *Lunn* (1984).

The duty of expert witnesses is "to furnish the judge or jury with the necessary scientific criteria for testing the accuracy of their conclusions so as to enable the judge or jury to form their own independent judgment by the application of these criteria to the facts proved in evidence": *per* Lord Cooper in *Davie* v. *Edinburgh Magistrates* (1953).

35. Expert witnesses: further details. The following points should be noted carefully.

(*a*) In matters of science or art, concerning which the court may have no specialised knowledge, an expert witness may give his opinion of relevant facts: *Folkes* v. *Chadd* (1782). His expertise can be challenged in cross-examination.

(*b*) The judge will decide whether a witness is "expert" in a particular subject by considering, for example, his experience and field of study. *See Longley & Co.* v. *SW Regional Health Authority* (1984). It is not necessary, however, that an expert witness be accepted by his profession as an "expert". *See R.* v. *Silverlock* (1894); *R.* v. *Somers* (1963). An expert need not be technically or professionally qualified—considerable practical experience may suffice: *R.* v. *Murphy* (1980). He must confine himself, however, to his area of competence, and argument on fact is not expert evidence: *Hinds* v. *LTE* (1979).

(*c*) The expert is a compellable witness (*see* 4:9), even if he has previously advised the other side: *Harmony Shipping* v. *Saudi Europe Line* (1979).

(*d*) The opinion of an expert is not admissible where the court is as capable of forming an opinion as is the expert witness, or where the court has the assistance of assessors. *See R.* v. *Stamford* (1972); *R.* v. *Anderson* (1972); *R.* v. *Turner* (1975) (*see* 13:5).

(e) The court need not adopt the views of an expert witness: *R.* v. *Secretary of State for Home Affairs* (1941). Expert opinion is, in general, not conclusive on any matter: *R.* v. *Lanfear* (1968).

(f) Demeanour may be important in an expert witness: *Joyce* v. *Yeomans* (1981).

(g) In the case of foreign law, expert evidence may be given by "a person who is suitably qualified to do so on account of his knowledge or experience . . . irrespective of whether he has acted or is entitled to act as a legal practitioner": Civil Evidence Act 1972, s. 4 (1).

(h) Under O. 38, the number of medical or other witnesses called in actions for damages for personal injuries may be restricted. Further, except when the court gives leave or all the parties agree to the introduction of the evidence, no expert evidence may be adduced at proceedings unless the party wishing to adduce it has made application for appropriate directions: 0.38, r. 36 (1).

(i) Under O. 40 a "court expert" may be appointed on a party's application, e.g., in a non-jury case based on a High Court civil action. *See* also the Supreme Court Act 1981, s. 70, dealing with the appointment by the High Court of assessors and scientific advisers.

(j) The expert witness should not generally be asked to answer the precise question in issue. *See*, however, the Civil Evidence Act 1972, s. 3 (1), (3): "Where a person is called as a witness in any civil proceedings, his opinion on any relevant matter on which he is qualified to give expert evidence should be admissible in evidence . . . In this section 'relevant matter' includes an issue in the proceedings in question."

(k) An expert witness is entitled to draw upon the work of others in his specialist field when forming an opinion; he may, therefore, look at data compiled by others: *R.* v. *Abadom* (1983) (expert was allowed to refer to Home Office statistics).

(l) Where two experts differ and there is no apparent reason for the difference, the jury is entitled to accept the evidence of either of them: *R.* v. *Elliot* (1976). *See* also *R.* v. *Platt* (1981).

(m) *See* also 8:**19** (d); 12:**11** (d); *DPP* v. *A&BC Chewing Gum Ltd.* (1968), where, exceptionally, a jury was assisted by expert evidence on the likely effect of reading material on young children; *R.* v. *Skirving* (1985), in which expert evidence concerning the effect of drugs mentioned in allegedly obscene books was held admissible, the Court of Appeal holding that such evidence was not a usurpation of the functions of the jury.

(*n*) Under the Police and Criminal Evidence Act 1984, s. 81 (1), the Crown Court Rules Committee may make rules which will require the prosecution or defence to disclose to the other side the expert evidence which they propose to adduce at the trial. A party failing to comply with this requirement may be prohibited from adducing that evidence without permission of the court. Under s. 81 (2) the rules may specify the types of expert evidence to which they apply, and may exempt certain facts or matters from disclosure under those rules.

Progress test 15

1. What is the general rule relating to the admissibility of a person's previous convictions?   (**3**)

2. What was the importance of the decision in *Hollington* v. *Hewthorn & Co.* (1943)?   (**5**)

3. What is the effect of the Civil Evidence Act 1968, s. 11 (1)?   (**7**)

4. Enumerate some of the ways in which evidence of previous convictions can be given in relation to an accused person.   (**9**)

5. When may evidence be given of previous convictions in relation to parties in civil cases?   (**10**)

6. Outline the main points of the Criminal Evidence Act 1898, s. 1 (*f*).   (**15**)

7. What is the meaning of "tending to show" and "charged" in the 1898 Act, s. 1 (*f*)?   (**17**)

8. Consider the importance of the 1898 Act, s. 1 (*f*) (*ii*).   (**19**)

9. Outline the facts and decisions in *R.* v. *Bishop* (1974) and *Selvey* v. *DPP* (1970).   (**19**)

10. What is the importance of the Civil Evidence Act 1968, s. 12 (1)?   (**22**)

11. How are the judgments of the High Court proved in evidence?   (**23**)

12. What is meant in the Rehabilitation of Offenders Act 1974 by (*a*) a rehabilitated person; (*b*) a spent conviction?   (**24**)

13. What is the importance of the 1974 Act, s. 7 (3)?   (**27**)

14. Is the opinion of a non-expert witness ever admissible in cases of identity and age? (**32**)

15. Must the court accept the opinions of an expert who gives evidence? (**35**)

16. May a non-legal practitioner give evidence of French law? (**35**)

Part four
Hearsay

16
The hearsay rule: its nature and scope

Preliminary matters

1. The concept of "hearsay". The general rule relating to oral evidence (*see* 2:17) is that it must be *direct*. Thus, X, a witness, may speak only of those facts which he has perceived with any of his five senses. He may not generally repeat words spoken by Y with the intention of proving the truth of what Y stated. Assume that the fact in issue is whether P assaulted Q by beating him. It would not be permissible to call R to testify that S had said that P had beaten Q; it would be necessary to call S to give evidence on that specific matter.

2. The place of hearsay in the law of evidence. At one time the concept of hearsay was considered, along with the jury system, as being among the hall-marks of the English law of evidence. The exclusionary rule relating to hearsay (*see* **8** below) dominated the early law of evidence.

(*a*) In the thirteenth century Bracton had expressed strong disapproval of *testimonium de auditu alieno*.

(*b*) Lord Jeffreys, C.J. in *R.* v. *Braddon and Speke* (1684) had given a ruling to the effect that what a witness had heard a woman say was not evidence: "If she were here herself, if she did say it and would not swear to it, we could not hear her; how then can her saying be evidence before us?"

(*c*) "By the general rule of law, nothing that is said by any person can be used as evidence between contending parties, unless it be

delivered on oath in the presence of these parties. Some inconvenience no doubt arises from such rigour. If material witnesses
happen to die before the trial, the person whose case they would
have established may fail in the suit. But although all the bishops on
the bench should be ready to swear to what they had heard these
witnesses declare (and should add their own belief in the truth of the
declarations), the evidence could not be received": *per* Mansfield,
C.J. in *The Berkeley Peerage Case* (1811). The practice grew up, as
the importance of the jury increased, whereby *oral or written
statements made by persons not called as witnesses were not receivable to
prove the truth of the facts stated. This remains the essence of the attitude
of the courts to hearsay evidence.*

This principle has most recently been re-affirmed by the House of
Lords in *R.* v. *Blastland* (1985), where the distinction between
evidence of a state of mind and evidence of events (or facts) was also
examined in relation to criminal proceedings.

3. Matters to be dealt with. This final part of the text contains an
examination of hearsay in the law of evidence. Three vital matters
are discussed:

(*a*) The hearsay rule, its formulation, rationale and general scope
(*see* **4–17** below).

(*b*) The hearsay rule in civil proceedings (*see* Chaps. 17 and 18).

(*c*) The hearsay rule in criminal proceedings (*see* Chaps. 19 and
20).

The nature of hearsay evidence

4. Definitions. The following definitions should be noted:

(*a*) "Hearsay evidence in its legal sense is evidence given by a
testifying witness of a statement made on some other occasion when
it is intended as evidence of the truth of what was asserted":
Halsbury's Laws.

(*b*) "In its legal sense 'hearsay' evidence is all evidence which
does not derive its value solely from the credit given to the witness
himself, but which rests also, in part, on the veracity and competence of some other person": Taylor (*On Evidence*).

(*c*) "A statement other than one made by a person while giving oral evidence in those proceedings . . . as evidence of any fact stated therein": Civil Evidence Act 1968, s. 1 (1).

5. What is covered by the statutory definition. The statutory definition (*see* **4** (*c*) above) includes any representation of fact, whether made in words or otherwise: 1968 Act, s. 10 (1). Hearsay is not confined, therefore, to oral statements. Documents, for example, may not be admissible under the hearsay rule. In *Chandra Sekera* v. *R.* (1937) signs made by a dying person pointing to another were considered hearsay evidence of identification of that other. *See* also *Wright* v. *Doe d. Tatham* (1838), in which the conduct of a testator's relatives was considered inadmissible hearsay.

6. "First-hand" and "second-hand" hearsay. This distinction may be illustrated in the following way, keeping in mind the statutory definition at **4** (*c*) above. Where the maker of the "statement" has *some personal knowledge* of those facts contained in his statement, that statement is said to be "*first-hand*" *hearsay*. Where the maker of the "statement" has *no personal knowledge* of the facts contained therein (so that his evidence of the facts was hearsay), evidence of the contents of the statement is said to be "*second-hand*" *hearsay*.

(*a*) *Example:* A and B, manual workers employed by E at his factory, collide accidentally while carrying dangerous material and both are injured. In subsequent proceedings, a report of S, a supervisor at the factory, is tendered by E, as evidence of the precise details of the accident involving A and B.

(*b*) Such evidence would be considered as *first-hand hearsay* if S had *actually witnessed* the accident involving A and B.

(*c*) If, on the other hand, S's report was no more than a statement he had written, based on what C and D, fellow-employees of A and B, had seen of the circumstances of the collision, the report would be *second-hand hearsay*.

7. Examples of hearsay from the cases. The following provide examples of what is considered hearsay evidence:

(*a*) A post office worker was charged with secreting a letter containing a bill of exchange, both of which were found in his possession. There was a statement in the letter that the bill of exchange was enclosed, but this was held *not admissible* in proof of that fact: *R.* v. *Plumer* (1814).

(*b*) The log book of a motor car was held to be *inadmissible* evidence of the number of the car's engine: *R.* v. *Sealby* (1965).

(*c*) X was charged with a false declaration relating to the origin of bags of seed labelled as "Produce of Morocco". It was held that the markings on the labels were *not admissible* as evidence to prove the origin of the bags of seed: *Patel* v. *Customs Comptroller* (1966).

(*d*) A car manufacturer's records showing that cylinder block numbers belonged to cars alleged to be stolen were held to be *inadmissible hearsay evidence: Myers* v. *DPP* (1965). "The entries on the cards were assertions by the unidentifiable men who made them that they had entered numbers which they had seen on the cards" *per* Lord Reid. *See* also the provisions introduced by the Armed Forces Act 1981, s. 9 (now itself repealed); Police and Criminal Evidence Act 1984, s. 68 (at 19:25).

The hearsay rule

8. Statement of the rule. The following statements, relating to the general inadmissibility of hearsay evidence, should be noted:

(*a*) "Oral or written statements made by persons who are not parties and are not called as witnesses are inadmissible to prove the truth of the matters stated": Phipson.

(*b*) "Evidence of a statement made to a witness by a person who is not himself called as a witness may or may not be hearsay. It is hearsay and inadmissible when the object of the evidence is to establish the truth of what is contained in the statement": *Subramaniam* v. *Public Prosecutor* (1956). *See* also **13** below.

(*c*) "Express or implied assertions of persons other than the witness who is testifying and assertions in documents produced to the court when no witness is testifying are inadmissible as evidence of the truth of that which was asserted": Cross.

9. The rule in operation. The strict application of this complex rule may be exemplified by the following cases:

(a) *Jones* v. *Metcalfe* (1967). D was charged with careless driving of a lorry. The prosecution relied, as evidence of identification, first, on the evidence of an independent witness, W, that he had taken the lorry's number and reported it to the police, but he could not now remember it, and, secondly, on a constable's evidence that D had admitted driving at the material time a lorry bearing the number given to the police by W. At the proceedings W forgot the number but the constable gave evidence in which he stated the number. D was convicted and appealed. It was held, allowing the appeal, that the constable could *not* give evidence of what W had told him, for that would be hearsay.

(b) *R.* v. *Gibson* (1887). X was charged with malicious wounding by throwing a stone at Y in the street in which X's house was situated. Y's evidence included the statement that, immediately after he had been hit by a stone, Z pointed to the door of X's house, saying "The person who threw the stone went in there." X's conviction was quashed. "This court has no power to say that the evidence of the identification of the prisoner was sufficient to warrant a conviction without the statement of the woman who was passing at the time the offence was committed . . .": *per* Pollock, B. (But *see* now *Ratten* v. *R.* (1972), at 13:**11**.)

(c) *Sparks* v. *R.* (1964). X, a white man, appealed against a conviction of indecent assault on Y, a small girl, on the ground, *inter alia*, that a statement made by the child to Z, her mother, about an hour and a half after the assault, that "it was a coloured boy", should have been admissible in evidence. It was held that evidence by Z of what Y had said (not being a part of the *res gestae*—*see* 13:**8**) was properly excluded—there is no rule that hearsay evidence is admissible if it goes to identity. "If the girl had made a remark to her mother (not in the presence of the appellant) to the effect that it was the appellant who had assaulted her and if the girl was not to be a witness at the trial, evidence as to what she had said would be the merest hearsay. In such circumstances it would be the defence who would wish to challenge a contention, if advanced, that it would be 'manifestly unjust' for the jury not to know that the girl had given a clue to the identity of her assailant. If it is said that hearsay evidence should be freely admitted and that there should be concentration in any particular case on deciding as to its value or weight, it is sufficient to say that our law has not been evolved on such lines, but is firmly based on the view that it is wiser and better that hearsay should be excluded save in certain well-defined and rather exceptional circumstances": *per* Lord Morris.

(*d*) *R.* v. *Marshall* (1977). X admitted buying goods from Y who told him that they were stolen. This was the only evidence from which the jury might be able to infer that the goods were stolen. It was held that there was no case to answer since X's statement was hearsay as to whether the goods were stolen, and therefore inadmissible.

10. Justification of the rule. Some of the main reasons for the rule against the admissibility of hearsay evidence are contained in a statement by Lord Normand in *Teper* v. *R.* (1952) (*see* 13:**10** (*d*)): "The rule against the admission of hearsay evidence is fundamental. It is not the best evidence and it is not delivered on oath. The truthfulness and accuracy of the person whose words are spoken to by another witness cannot be tested by cross-examination, and the light which his demeanour would throw on his testimony is lost." Further justification of the rule has been sought in the argument that hearsay evidence, by its very nature, must be unreliable because of the high probability of inaccurate repetition, or even of the fabrication of evidence.

11. Abolition of the hearsay rule: the arguments. The *13th Report of the Law Reform Committee ("Hearsay Evidence in Civil Proceedings")* 1966, suggested that there were five outstanding *disadvantages* of the hearsay rule, a rule characterised by Lord Reid in *Myers* v. *DPP* (1965) as "absurdly technical".

(*a*) The rule adds to the technical nature of the law of evidence because of the many exceptions to it.

(*b*) The rule confuses many witnesses and does not allow them to give their story in a natural way.

(*c*) The rule deprives the court of valuable matter.

(*d*) The rule adds to the cost of proving facts which are not actually in dispute.

(*e*) The rule makes for an element of injustice where a witness who could prove some fact in issue is unavailable to be called.

Statements as facts and statements as proof

12. The general position. The rule against hearsay is a rule excluding a means of proof; it is *not* a rule which acts to exclude facts.

(*a*) Evidence of a statement will infringe the hearsay rule only if the statement is offered as a means of proving the truth of the matter which is stated.

(*b*) Where a statement is offered as a fact (rather than as a means of proving that fact) it is not, as such, hearsay evidence.

(*c*) A distinction is occasionally drawn between "admissible hearsay" and "inadmissible hearsay". The former consists of statements which are *facts*; the latter consists of statements proffered *so as to prove other facts*. *See* **14** below.

13. *Subramaniam* v. *Public Prosecutor* (1956). In this case, arising out of the terrorist campaign in Malaya, X was charged with being in possession of a firearm without lawful excuse. In his defence he stated that he was acting under duress following violent threats against him by Malayan terrorists. He was not allowed by the trial judge to state exactly what the terrorists had said.

(*a*) The Privy Council advised that X's conviction be quashed since the reported statements of the terrorists were tendered as original evidence (*see* **14** (*b*) below) and should have been received as such.

(*b*) The report of the P.C., mentioned at (*a*) above, contains the following statement: "Evidence of a statement made to a witness by a person who is not himself called as a witness may or may not be hearsay. It is hearsay and inadmissible when the object of the evidence is to establish the truth of what is contained in the statement. It is not hearsay and is admissible when it is proposed to establish by the evidence, not the truth of the statement, but the fact that it was made. The fact that the statement is made, quite apart from its truth, is frequently relevant in considering the mental state and conduct thereafter of the witness or of some other person in whose presence the statement was made."

(*c*) From the above, it may be inferred that the principal test in deciding the admissibility of evidence of what some person, other than the testifying witness, has said, is a consideration of *the very purpose for which the evidence is put forward*. If the evidence is put forward to prove a fact which is asserted by the statement (either in express form or by implication), then, in general, the statement is not admissible under the hearsay rule. *See Nicholas* v. *Penny* (1950)—the fact that a car's speedometer was in working order could not be proved by the driver's statement of what had been said to him about the result of a test carried out on the previous day.

14. Statements as "original evidence" or "hearsay evidence". *See Subramaniam* v. *Public Prosecutor* (1956) (*see* **13** above). Considerable significance attaches to the classification of a statement as "original" or "hearsay": the former may be admissible, the latter will fall under the general rule of inadmissibility.

(*a*) In *Gilbey* v. *G. W. Railway Co.* (1910), statements by a person relating to his health, state of mind, were accepted as original evidence and were held admissible. "Statements made by a workman to his wife of his sensations at the time, about the pains in his side or head, or what not—whether the statements were made by groans, or by actions, or were verbal statements—would be admissible to prove those statements": *per* Cozens-Hardy, M.R. (It was held also that the workman's statement asserting a *cause* of those sensations, was *not admissible* (*see* also *R.* v. *Nicholas* (1846)), since it was mere hearsay evidence.)

(*b*) There are cases in which the very making of a statement is, in itself, a fact in issue, for example, an offer in an action in contract, or a statement in an action for slander. *See A.-G.* v. *Good* (1825); *Perkins* v. *Vaughan* (1842); *R.* v. *Willis* (1960).

(*c*) There are cases in which statements, which in themselves do not constitute facts in issue, do constitute circumstantial evidence of a fact in issue. Thus, in relation to proceedings arising out of the Sexual Offences Act 1956, s. 6, the accused, X, will be allowed to give evidence of the fact that the girl involved told him that she was over sixteen; such evidence may support the fact in issue, i.e. X's belief that she was over sixteen.

(*d*) Statements accompanying relevant acts or events may be received as original evidence. *See Hayslep* v. *Gymer* (1834); *R.* v. *Foster* (1834). (Prisoner was charged with manslaughter by driving over X. W, a witness, saw the vehicle driving by, but did not see the accident. W immediately went up to X, who then made a statement as to the cause of his injury. The statement was admitted in evidence. *Per* Park, J.: "I am of opinion that his evidence ought to be received. It is the best possible testimony that, under the circumstances, can be adduced to show what it was that had knocked the deceased down.")

Exceptions to the hearsay rule

15. General. There is now a host of exceptions to the rule of inadmissibility of hearsay evidence. (*See* the statement of Lord Morris in *Myers* v. *DPP* (1965).) Some are common law exceptions; others are the consequence of statute. As a result, the importance of the hearsay rule in civil cases has diminished in very considerable measure; in the criminal law the rule remains of great importance in practice.

16. Exceptions to the rule in civil proceedings. These are enumerated and discussed in Chapters 17 and 18.

17. Exceptions to the rule in criminal proceedings. These are enumerated and discussed in Chapters 19 and 20.

Progress test 16

1. Define "hearsay evidence". (**4**)
2. Is hearsay confined to oral statements? (**5**)
3. What is "first-hand hearsay"? (**6**)
4. State the rule relating to the admissibility of hearsay evidence. (**8**)
5. Comment on the decisions in *Jones* v. *Metcalfe* (1967) and *Sparks* v. *R.* (1964). (**9**)

6. Can the hearsay rule be justified? (**10**)

7. Enumerate some of the arguments for the abolition of the hearsay rule. (**11**)

8. Outline the facts and decision in *Subramaniam* v. *Public Prosecutor* (1956). (**13**)

9. What is the importance of the decision in *Gilbey* v. *G.W. Railway Co.* (1910)? (**14**)

10. May a statement accompanying a relevant act be received as original evidence? (**14**)

17

Hearsay in civil proceedings (1): statements admissible under the Civil Evidence Act 1968, Part I

Preliminary matters

1. General. The problem of hearsay in civil proceedings is now dominated by the Civil Evidence Act 1968. The very wide range of exceptions to the hearsay rule (*see* 16:8) given under the Act means that there are now few other significant types of exception to the rules which apply in civil proceedings. (It should be noted that, under s. 18 (5) (*a*), the court retains its power to exclude evidence at its discretion.)

2. Matters to be covered. The following matters relating to hearsay in civil proceedings are considered in this and the following chapter:

  (*a*) Basis and content of the 1968 Act (*see* **3–31** below).
  (*b*) Informal admissions (*see* 18:**3–8**).
  (*c*) Statements by deceased persons (*see* 18:**9–15**).
  (*d*) Statements in public and official documents (*see* 18:**16–23**).

The Civil Evidence Act 1968: general outline

3. Basis and effect of the Act. The Act gave effect, with some modifications, to a number of the recommendations of the *13th, 15th and 16th Reports of the Law Reform Committee*, in relation to evidence in civil proceedings and privilege against self-incrimination. It admits, subject to certain conditions, in civil proceedings, all first-hand hearsay (*see* 16:**6**) and also, in the case of documentary records, second-hand hearsay (*see* 16:**6**). It takes over and preserves certain common law exceptions to the hearsay rule. In essence, therefore, a hearsay statement in civil proceedings is now admissible only:

(*a*) by agreement of the parties; *or*

(*b*) under statute or some rule of court.

4. Content of the 1968 Act. The Act consists of two Parts:

(*a*) *Part I: Hearsay Evidence.* The following should be noted:

(*i*) Section 1 provides that hearsay evidence in civil proceedings is admissible only by virtue of a statutory provision or agreement.

(*ii*) Section 2 concerns the admissibility of out-of-court statements as evidence of the facts stated.

(*iii*) Section 3 admits a witness's previous statements not only to support or impugn his credit, but also as evidence of facts stated therein.

(*iv*) Section 4 admits a witness's previous statements contained in certain documents of record as evidence of facts therein stated.

(*v*) Section 5 makes admissible statements produced by computers.

(*vi*) Section 6 is concerned with provisions supplementary to ss. 2–5.

(*vii*) Section 7 provides for the admissibility of evidence relating to the credit of the maker of a statement admitted under s. 2 or s. 4 should the maker not be called as a witness.

(*viii*) Section 8 provides for appropriate rules of court to be made.

(*ix*) Section 9 concerns the admissibility of certain hearsay evidence formerly admissible at common law.

(*x*) Section 10 concerns definitions and application of the Act to arbitration.

(*b*) *Part II: Miscellaneous and general.* Sections 11–20 are not dealt with in this chapter; some of the sections are mentioned elsewhere at appropriate points in the text.

Section 1

5. The section stated. "1.—(1) In any civil proceedings a statement other than one made by a person while giving oral evidence in those proceedings shall be admissible as evidence of any fact stated therein to the extent that it is so admissible by virtue of any provision of this Part of this Act or by virtue of any other statutory provision or by agreement of the parties but not otherwise. (2) In this section 'statutory provision' means any provision contained in, or in an instrument made under, this or any other Act, including any Act passed after this Act."

NOTE: "Statement" includes any representation of fact whether made in words or otherwise: s. 10 (1).

6. Effect of section 1. As a result of this key section, hearsay evidence in civil proceedings is now admissible only:

(*a*) by virtue of the 1968 Act and other relevant statutory provisions; *or*

(*b*) by agreement of the parties.

Statements admissible under sections 2 and 3

7. Section 2 (1). This provides that: "in any civil proceedings, a statement made, whether orally or in a document or otherwise, by any person, whether called as a witness in those proceedings or not, should, subject to this section and to rules of court, be admissible as evidence of any fact stated therein of which direct oral evidence by him would be admissible." For definition of "document" *see* s. 10 (1), at **8:3** (*b*).

8. Extension of s. 2 (1). Under the Civil Evidence Act 1972, hearsay statements of *opinion* are made admissible in evidence in civil proceedings to substantially the same extent as hearsay statements of *fact* under the 1968 Act. *See Lego System* v. *Lego M. Lemelstrich* (1983)—market research survey held admissible in evidence of public opinion.

9. Effect of s. 2 (1). In effect, s. 2 (1) renders first-hand hearsay (*see* 16:6) admissible in civil proceedings. It should be noted that the statement may be made "orally, or in a document *or otherwise*"; it need not consist, therefore, of words. *See Taylor v. Taylor* (1970); *General Accident Assurance Corp.* v. *Tanter* (1984).

10. Section 2 (2). Under this subsection, where, in civil proceedings a party wishing to give a statement in evidence under the section has called or proposes to call as witness in the proceedings *the person who has made the statement*, the following restrictions apply:

(*a*) The statement must not be given in evidence on behalf of the party unless the court has given leave: s. 2 (2) (*a*).

(*b*) Without prejudice to s. 2 (2) (*a*), the statement must not be given in evidence on behalf of the party before the end of the examination-in-chief of the person who has made the statement, except:

(*i*) where, before that person is called, the court allows evidence relating to the making of the statement to be given on behalf of that party by some other person; *or*

(*ii*) in so far as the court allows the person by whom the statement was made to narrate it in the course of his examination-in-chief, on the ground that to prevent him from doing so will adversely affect the intelligibility of his evidence: s. 2 (2) (*b*).

11. Section 2 (3). This subsection provides that where a statement which was made otherwise than in a document is admissible under the section, only direct oral evidence by the person who made the statement or any person who heard it or otherwise perceived it, is admissible for the purpose of proving it; *provided that* if the statement was made by a person giving oral evidence in other legal proceedings (civil or criminal) it may be proved in any manner which the court authorises. *See Re Koscot Ltd.* (1972)—there is no general rule that hearsay evidence is admissible on a petition for the winding-up of a company.

12. Section 3. This section provides that where, in civil proceedings, a person called as a witness has made a previous inconsistent or contradictory statement which has been proved under the Criminal Procedure Act 1865, ss. 3, 4, 5 or a previous statement made by a person called as a witness has been proved for the purpose of rebutting a suggestion that his evidence has been fabricated, that statement will be admissible as evidence of any fact stated therein of which direct oral evidence by him would be admissible: s. 3 (1).

(a) Nothing in the 1968 Act is to affect any rule of law relating to circumstances in which, where a witness is cross-examined on a document used by him to refresh his memory (*see* 5:**10**), that document may be made evidence : s. 3 (2). *See Senat* v. *Senat* (1965).

(b) Where a document is received in evidence as a result of a rule of law mentioned in (a) above, any statement in that document will be admissible as evidence of any fact stated therein of which direct oral evidence would be admissible: s. 3 (2).

Statements admissible under sections 4 and 5

13. Section 4. This section provides that in civil proceedings, a statement contained in a document (*see* 8:**3** (b)) shall, subject to this section and the rules of court, be admissible as evidence of any fact stated therein of which direct oral evidence would be admissible, *if* the document is, or forms part of, a record compiled by a person acting under a duty from information which was supplied by a person (whether acting under a duty or not) who had or may reasonably be supposed to have had, personal knowledge of the matters dealt with in that information and which, if not supplied by that person to the compiler of the record directly, was supplied by him to the compiler of the record indirectly through one or more intermediaries each acting under a duty: s. 4 (1). *See Taylor* v. *Taylor* (1970)—probability of the transcript of a summing-up being admissible, since it was a record compiled by the court's shorthand writer as such; *H.* v. *Schering Chemicals* (1983)—documents consisting of the results of research and material published in medical journals are not "records" within s. 4; *Knight* v. *David* (1971)—tithe map admissible under s. 4 (1) to support claim of title to land. *See* also the Civil Evidence Act 1972, s. 1 (extending the 1968 Act, s. 4); O. 38, r. 24.

14. "Person acting under a duty". This expression includes a reference to any person acting in the course of any trade, business, profession or other occupation in which he is engaged or employed or for the purposes of any paid or unpaid office held by him: s. 4 (3).

15. Restriction on the calling of evidence: s. 4 (2). Where a party desiring to give a statement in evidence by virtue of s. 4 intends to call, or has called, as a witness the person who originally supplied the information from which the record containing the statement was compiled, that statement must not be given in evidence on behalf of the party without leave of the court and must not, without leave of the court, be given in evidence on behalf of the party before the end of the examination-in-chief of the person who originally supplied the information. Note that the term "record" is not defined in the 1968 Act: *see*, e.g., *Savings and Investment Bank* v. *Gasco Investments* (1984)—report of inspectors appointed under the Companies Act 1948, ss. 165, 172 (now replaced by the Companies Act 1985, ss. 432, 442–3), held *not* to be a record for the purposes of the 1968 Act, s. 4.

16. Admissibility of statements produced by computers: s. 5. A computer is defined as "any device for storing and processing information": s. 5 (6). A statement contained in a document produced by a computer is admissible as evidence of any fact stated therein of which direct oral evidence would be admissible (s. 5 (1)) if certain conditions are fulfilled, namely:

(*a*) that the document containing the statement was produced by the computer during a period over which the computer was used regularly to store or process information for the purposes of any activities regularly carried on over that period, whether for profit or not, by any body, whether corporate or not, or by any individual;

(*b*) that over that period there was regularly supplied to the computer in the ordinary course of those activities information of the kind contained in the statement or of the kind from which the information so contained is derived;

(*c*) that throughout the material part of that period the computer was operating properly or, if not, that any respect in which it was not operating properly or was out of operation during that part of that period was not so much as to affect the production of the document or the accuracy of its contents; and

(d) that the information contained in the statement reproduces or is derived from information supplied to the computer in the ordinary course of those activities: s. 5 (2) (a) – (d).

17. Section 5 (4). Where in civil proceedings it is desired to give a statement in evidence by virtue of this section, a certificate will be accepted as evidence of any matter contained therein, if it identifies the document containing the statement and describing the manner in which it was produced or if it gives particulars of the device involved in production of the document so as to show that the document was produced by computer and it purports to be signed by a person occupying a responsible position in relation to the operation of the computer: s. 5 (4).

18. Section 5 (5). A document is taken to have been produced by a computer whether it was produced by it directly or (with or without human intervention) by means of any appropriate equipment.

19. Second-hand hearsay and ss. 4, 5. It should be noted that ss. 4, 5 effectively permit, in restricted circumstances, second-hand hearsay (*see* 16:6) in civil proceedings.

Section 6

20. Content of s. 6. This section contains provisions supplementary to ss. 2–5, relating specifically to production of documents, weight of evidence, corroboration and false statements in relation to computerised documents.

21. Section 6 (1): production of copies of documents. Where a statement contained in a document is proposed to be given in evidence under ss. 2, 4, 5, it may, subject to rules of court, be proved by production of that document or (whether or not the document is still in existence) by production of a copy of that document, or of the material part, authenticated in a manner approved by the court.

22. Section 6 (2): deciding whether a statement is admissible.
For the purpose of deciding whether or not a statement is admissible
in evidence under ss. 2, 4, 5, the court may draw any reasonable
inference from the circumstances in which the statement was made,
including the form and content of a document.

23. Section 6 (3): weight of evidence. In estimating the weight to
be attached to a statement admissible under ss. 2, 3, 4, 5, regard
must be had to all the circumstances from which any inference can
reasonably be drawn as to the accuracy or otherwise of the statement,
in particular:

(*a*) the question whether or not the statement within s. 2 (1) or s.
3 (1), (2) (*see* **7, 12** above) was made contemporaneously with the
occurrence or existence of the facts stated and whether or not the
maker had any incentive to conceal or misrepresent the facts;

(*b*) the question whether or not, in the case of a statement falling
within s. 4 (1) (*see* **13** above), the person who originally supplied the
information from which the record containing the statement was
compiled did so contemporaneously with the occurrence or existence of the facts dealt with in that information or whether or not
that person or any other person concerned with compiling or
keeping the record had any incentive to conceal or misrepresent the
facts;

(*c*) the question, in the case of a statement falling within s. 5 (1)
(*see* **16** above) whether the information was supplied to the relevant
computer, or recorded for the purpose of being supplied thereto,
contemporaneously with the occurrence or existence of the facts
dealt with in the information, and whether any person concerned
with the supply of information to the computer, or its operation, had
any incentive to conceal or misrepresent the facts.

24. Section 6 (4): corroboration. *See* 7:**16** and 7:**23**(*b*). For the
purpose of an enactment or rule of law or practice which requires
evidence to be corroborated or regulates the manner in which
uncorroborated evidence is to be treated:

(*a*) a statement admissible under ss. 2, 3 shall not be capable of
corroborating evidence given by the maker of the statement;

(*b*) a statement admissible in evidence by virtue of s. 4 shall not be capable of corroborating evidence given by the person who originally supplied the information from which the record containing the statement was compiled.

25. Section 6 (5): false statements relating to computerised documents. Where, in relation to a certificate tendered in evidence under s. 5 (4) (*see* **17** above), a statement is wilfully made by a person who knows it to be false or does not believe it to be true, he may be liable on conviction to a fine or up to two years' imprisonment or both.

Sections 7 and 8

26. Section 7 (1). Subject to rules of court, where, in civil proceedings a statement made by a person who is not called as a witness is given in evidence by virtue of s. 2 of this Act (*see* **7** above):

(*a*) any evidence which, if that person had been so called, would be admissible for the purpose of destroying or supporting his credibility as a witness will be admissible for that purpose; and

(*b*) evidence tending to prove that, whether before or after he made that statement, that person made (whether orally or in a document or otherwise) another statement inconsistent therewith will be admissible for the purpose of showing that he has contradicted himself: s. 7 (1) (*a*), (*b*).

NOTE: The proviso that nothing in s. 7 (1) shall enable evidence to be given of any matter of which, if the person in question had been called as a witness and had denied that matter in cross-examination, evidence could not have been adduced by the cross-examining party. *See* O. 38, r. 30.

27. Section 8: rules of court. Under this section (as amended by the County Courts Act 1984, Sch. 2, para. 33), provision is to be made by rules of court as to the procedure to be followed before a statement can be given in evidence in civil proceedings by virtue of ss. 2, 4, 5. Appropriate rules have been made under O. 38. *See*

Morris v. *Stratford on Avon R.D.C.* (1973); *Nicholls* v. *Williams* (1983).

28. Notices under the Civil Evidence Act 1968 and O. 38. Where a party wishes to put in evidence at the trial statements admissible under the 1968 Act, the party must, within twenty-one days following setting down, serve on the other parties a notice setting out the time, place, circumstances in which the statement was made, the substance of the statement, persons to and by whom it was made: O. 38, r. 22 (1). Where a written statement is to be submitted, a copy of the document must be annexed to the notice and must contain information relating to its compilation: O. 38, rr. 22 (2), 23, 24.

(*a*) Where the party giving notice claims that the maker of a statement cannot be called as a witness because he is unfit, beyond the seas, dead, cannot by reasonable diligence be identified or found, or cannot be expected to recollect matters relating to the accuracy of his statement (*see* the 1968 Act, s. 8 (2) (*b*)), the notice must state this: O. 38, rr. 22–25.

(*b*) *See Rasool* v. *W. Midlands Passenger Transport Executive* (1974): the reasons that can be relied on for not calling a witness under the 1968 Act, s. 8 (2) (*b*) and O. 38, r. 25, are disjunctive, so that if the maker of a statement is shown, on a balance of probabilities to be beyond the seas, it is unnecessary to show, additionally, that by reasonable diligence he cannot be found. *See Piermay Shipping Co.* v. *Chester* (1978)—where a party seeks to give in evidence the statement of a person beyond the seas, the fact that that person is abroad is sufficient reason for admitting the statement and the court has no discretion to exclude it.

(*c*) Note that (under O. 38, r. 29) the court may exercise discretion so as to admit a statement where proper notice has not been served. *See Ford* v. *Lewis* (1971); *Tremelbye Rubber Co.* v. *Stekel* (1971)—the principle upon which discretion ought to be exercised is "the furtherance of justice".

(*d*) No notice need be served on the opposite party where a party to a probate action wishes to prove a statement made by the deceased in evidence of facts stated: O. 38, r. 21 (3).

Statements admissible under section 9

29. General. Section 9 preserves certain common law exceptions to the hearsay rules and provides that statements admissible under those rules are to be admissible by virtue of the Act.

30. Section 9 (1), (2): statements and documents. In civil proceedings the following are admissible by virtue of s. 9 (1): "Any rule of law—

(a) whereby in any civil proceedings an admission adverse to a party to the proceedings, whether made by that party or by another person, may be given in evidence against that party for the purpose of proving any fact stated in the admission;

(b) whereby in any civil proceedings published works dealing with matters of a public nature (for example, histories, scientific works, dictionaries and maps) are admissible as evidence of facts of a public nature stated therein;

(c) whereby in any civil proceedings public documents (for example, public registers, and returns made under public authority with respect to matters of public interest) are admissible as evidence of facts stated therein; or

(d) whereby in any civil proceedings records (for example, the records of certain courts, treaties, Crown Grants, pardons and commissions) are admissible as evidence of facts stated therein."

NOTE: (1) "Admission" in (a) above includes any representation of fact, whether made in words or otherwise: s. 9 (2).

(2) *See Humberside C.C.* v. *D.P.R.* (1977).

31. Section 9 (3), (4): reputation and family tradition. Under s. 9 (3) any statement tending to establish reputation or family tradition with respect to any matter and which, if the 1968 Act had not been passed would have been admissible by virtue of the rules of law mentioned at (a) and (b) below, will be admissible by virtue of s. 9 (3) (a), in so far as it is not capable of being rendered admissible by ss. 2, 4. The rules of law referred to are: "Any rule of law—

(a) whereby in any civil proceedings evidence of a person's

reputation is admissible for the purpose of establishing his good or bad character;

(*b*) whereby in any civil proceedings involving a question of pedigree or in which the existence of a marriage is in issue evidence of reputation or family tradition is admissible for the purpose of proving or disproving pedigree or the existence of the marriage as the case may be; or

(*c*) whereby in any civil proceedings evidence of reputation or family tradition is admissible for the purpose of proving or disproving the existence of any public or general right or of identifying any person or thing": s. 9 (4) (*a*) – (*c*).

Progress test 17

1. What is the general effect of the Civil Evidence Act 1968 on the admissibility of hearsay evidence in civil proceedings? (**3**)

2. Outline the effect of s. 1 (1) of the 1968 Act. (**6**)

3. How has the 1968 Act been modified by the Civil Evidence Act 1972, s. 1 (1)? (**8**)

4. Consider the general effect of s. 2 (2) of the 1968 Act. (**10**)

5. What type of hearsay evidence becomes admissible under the 1968 Act, s. 4? (**13**)

6. What are the circumstances in which a bank's computer print-out will become admissible evidence? (**16**)

7. What is meant under the 1968 Act by a "computer"? (**16**)

8. Consider the effect of s. 5 (4) of the 1968 Act. (**17**)

9. In what ways does s. 6 (1) of the 1968 Act affect the production of copies of documents? (**21**)

10. How does s. 6 (3) of the 1968 Act affect weight of evidence in relation to statements admissible under ss. 2–5? (**23**)

11. Give a general account of notices under O. 38. (**28**)

12. What is the general effect of s. 9 of the 1968 Act? (**29**)

13. Which rules of law become admissible by virtue of s. 9 (1) of the 1968 Act? (**30**)

18

Hearsay in civil proceedings (2): informal admissions; statements by deceased persons; statements in public documents, etc.

Preliminary matters

1. General. Included among those common law exceptions which are taken over and kept by the Civil Evidence Act 1968, s. 9 (2) (*see* **17:30**) are informal admissions, certain types of statements made by deceased persons and certain statements contained in some types of public document. These exceptions to the hearsay rule, which remain of importance in civil proceedings, form the content of this chapter.

2. Matters to be discussed. The following points are discussed below:

(*a*) The exceptions to hearsay based on informal admissions (*see* **3–8** below).

(*b*) The exceptions to hearsay based on statements by deceased persons as to public or general rights (*see* **9–12** below).

(*c*) The exceptions to hearsay based on statements by deceased persons concerning pedigree (*see* **13–15** below).

(*d*) The exceptions to hearsay based on statements in public documents (*see* **16–23** below).

Informal admissions

3. General. Evidence is usually admissible of a party's earlier statements where they are adverse to the maker's interests. Earlier statements of this kind are generally proved by someone other than the maker, so that they are hearsay, but are admissible as exceptions to the rule against hearsay (*see* 16:8). Statements of this nature in relation to civil proceedings may be admissible under the 1968 Act, s. 2, or, on the basis of the former common law exceptions, under s. 9.

4. Formal and informal admissions. The subject-matter of this section is the informal admission, which must be distinguished clearly from the formal admission considered in 9:7–13.

(*a*) Formal admissions are made only in the course of proceedings and dispense with any need for proof; informal admissions do not dispense with a need for proof.

(*b*) Formal admissions are binding and operate only in the proceedings to which they relate; informal admissions can be contradicted by other evidence and are not confined in their scope to the particular proceedings in which they are made.

5. Circumstances under which informal admissions may be admissible. The following circumstances relating to admissibility should be noted:

(*a*) Informal admissions may be oral or written, express or implied; form is immaterial.

(*b*) The party against whom an informal admission is put in is entitled to have the entire statement containing the admission given, although some parts of it may be favourable to him. *See Randle* v. *Blackburn* (1813); *R.* v. *Storey* (1968).

(*c*) In general, it matters not to whom the informal admission has been made. "What a person is overheard saying to his wife, or even saying to himself, is evidence": *per* Alderson, B. in *R.* v. *Simons* (1834). *See*, however, *Shaw* v. *Shaw* (1935).

(*d*) An informal admission will be considered primary evidence (*see* 2:22 (*a*)) against a party and will be admissible to prove the contents of a written document without any notice to produce, or accounting for the absence of, the original: *Slatterie* v. *Pooley* (1840). "The reason why such parol statements are admissible . . . is that they are not open to the same objection which belongs to parol evidence from other sources, where the written evidence might have been produced; for such evidence is excluded from the presumption of its untruth, arising from the very nature of the case, where better evidence is withheld; whereas what a party himself admits to be true may reasonably be presumed to be so": *per* Parke, B.

(*e*) An informal admission may be constituted by conduct alone and it may relate not merely to specific facts, but may show that the party's entire case is bad: *Moriarty* v. *London, Chatham & Dover Railway* (1870).

(*f*) Silence may amount to an admission in those circumstances in which it is natural to expect a reply: *Bessela* v. *Stern* (1877). (In an action for breach of promise of marriage it was proved that P said to D, "You always promised to marry me, and you don't keep your word." D made no answer, but had said that he would give P money to go away. D's silence in relation to the subject of marriage was held to amount to an admission.)

(*g*) Where the circumstances are such that a reply could not reasonably be expected, the silence of a party in face of an accusation will not necessarily constitute an admission: *Wiedemann* v. *Walpole* (1891). (In an action for breach of promise of marriage, D had failed to answer a letter from P calling on him to carry out his promise of marriage, but this was held not to constitute any admission by D.)

(*h*) The informal admissions of a minor bind him in the same way as those of an adult: *Alderman* v. *Alderman and Dunn* (1958).

(*i*) An admission not based on personal knowledge is admissible but may have only a slight evidential value. *See Customs Comptroller* v. *Western Electric Co.* (1966).

6. Statements made "without prejudice". Statements of this nature are not generally admissible in evidence. This matter is discussed at 12:23.

7. Statements made in the presence of a party. Assume that statements have been made in D's hearing and that he has reacted to them in a certain way, for example, by silence or by an expression of anger. Where P alleges that D's reactions amount to an admission, the statements made in D's hearing can be given in evidence to explain D's response to the statements.

8. Admissions ("vicarious admissions") by persons in privity with the party or other third persons. The term "privity" as used in this context refers to persons bound in a relationship arising from an interest in property. Example: principal and agent; predecessors in title and proprietors; persons with joint interests. *See* 11:**13** (*a*).

(*a*) *Principal and agent.* The informal admissions of an agent (A) made to some person other than his principal (P) will be received in evidence against P where A has been expressly authorised to make them or where A has been authorised to represent P in any business and the informal admissions were made in the scope of A's authority and are concerned with the ordinary course of business.

(*i*) In the relationship arising between master and servant, the servant will not usually be authorised to make an admission on behalf of his master even in relation to acts ordinarily within the course of his employment. In *Great Western Railway* v. *Willis* (1865) X sued a railway company for failing to deliver cattle on time; he intended to show that the company's inspector had stated that the cattle had been forgotten. It was held that the inspector was not authorised to bind the company by this admission. *See* also *Kirkstall Brewery* v. *Furness Railway* (1874).

(*ii*) *See* also *Bruff* v. *G.N. Railway* (1858); *Simmons* v. *London Bank* (1890); *Burr* v. *Ware U.D.C.* (1939).

(*b*) *Predecessors in title and proprietors.* The informal admissions of a predecessor in title will be admissible, in general, against, but not in favour of, a proprietor, where they have been made when the predecessor was in possession: *Woolway* v. *Rowe* (1834). "We are of opinion that these declarations are admissible against the plaintiff, on the principle of identity of interest between the plaintiff and the party making the declarations": *per* Lord Denman.

(*c*) *Persons with joint interests.* Where persons have joint interests, an informal admission by one of them may be tendered against the other(s) if made while the joint interest continued. Note that there is no such privity in the case of co-defendants: *see Daniels* v. *Potter* (1830). *See* also *Re Kitchin* (1881); *Myatt* v. *Myatt and Parker* (1962).

Statements made by deceased persons as to public or general rights

9. The general rule. In some circumstances declarations made by deceased persons relating to public or general rights may be admissible as an exception to the hearsay rule. It should be noted that:

(*a*) In civil proceedings, declarations of this nature are admissible as common law exceptions to the hearsay rule if they are incapable of admission under the 1968 Act, s. 2 or s. 4: 1968 Act, s. 9.

(*b*) Should the statement be based on *first-hand hearsay* (*see* 16:**6**) or should it be recorded in some document (and, hence, should it comply with s. 4), it will be admitted if notice of intention appropriate to these sections be given.

10. Public and general rights: the difference. The following points should be noted:

(*a*) *Public rights* affect the *whole* population. Examples: right of ferry; claim to right of tolls on a public highway. *See Brett* v. *Beales* (1830).

(*b*) *General rights* affect some *section or* class of the population. Examples: rights of common; manor boundaries. *See Evans* v. *Merthyr Tydfil U.D.C.* (1899).

11. Mode of declaration. The declaration can be in written or oral form. It may take the form of maps, plans etc. *See Smith* v. *Lister* (1895).

12. Conditions of admissibility. The following points should be noted:

(*a*) The declaration is not rendered admissible merely because it has been made solely for the purpose of avoiding some future dispute: *see The Berkeley Peerage Case* (1811).

(b) The declaration must have been made before the beginning of the present dispute: *The Berkeley Peerage Case* (1811). *See* also *Moseley* v. *Davies* (1822).

(c) Declarations involving only private rights are not admissible: *Dunraven* v. *Llewellyn* (1850).

(d) Declarations must be related in direct manner to the existence of the right itself, not to particular facts which may support or negative it: *R.* v. *Bliss* (1837), in which a statement made by a deceased resident that he had planted a tree so as to mark a road boundary was not admitted where the question was whether the road was public or private.

(e) Persons whose declarations are tendered in evidence must be shown to have been competent declarants, e.g. by residence, duty: *Newcastle* v. *Broxtowe* (1832). In the case of public rights, all persons would be competent declarants.

Statements made by deceased persons concerning pedigree

13. The general rule. In some circumstances declarations by deceased persons relating to the pedigree of relatives may be admissible as exceptions to the hearsay rule. It should be noted that:

(a) "Pedigree" refers to a relationship by blood or resulting from marriage.

(b) In civil proceedings, declarations of this nature are admissible as common law exceptions only if they are incapable of admission under the 1968 Act, s. 2 or s. 4: 1968 Act, s. 9.

14. Mode of declaration. The declaration may take the form of an oral statement, a will, an entry in a bible or prayer book, an inscription on a tombstone, etc. *See Vowles* v. *Young* (1806); *Hubbard* v. *Lees* (1886).

15. Conditions of admissibility. The following should be noted:

(a) The declarant must have been a blood relation or spouse, not merely a friend of the family.

   (i) The declaration of a long-serving housekeeper was rejected in *Johnson* v. *Lawson* (1824).

(*ii*) The relationship must be legitimate: *Doe d. Jenkins* v. *Davies* (1847). *See*, however, *Re Jenion* (1952).

(*b*) Personal knowledge by the declarant of the fact stated is not essential. It may suffice that his information has come from general family repute.

(*c*) The declaration must have been made before the dispute in question: *The Berkeley Peerage Case* (1811).

(*d*) The declaration should relate directly to a matter of pedigree, e.g. matters of birth, legitimacy. In *Haines* v. *Guthrie* (1844), which was an action for the price of goods sold, the defence of infancy was raised. A statement by defendant's deceased father as to the date of birth of defendant was held inadmissible since the action was not a pedigree case. "The exception which applies to this case is that the evidence is admissible in cases where it is a question of pedigree. Here there is no question as to pedigree, no question as to descent, none as to relationship, none as to the position of any person in the family—all these questions are wholly immaterial—so that in this case no question of pedigree could arise, and, therefore, this case does not fall within the recognised exception to the general rule of evidence": *per* Bowen, L.J.

Statements in public or official documents

16. The general rule. In some circumstances statements in public or official documents may be admissible in proof of facts recorded therein, as an exception to the rule against hearsay.

(*a*) Documents, in this context, include:
   (*i*) Statutes, gazettes (*see* **18** below).
   (*ii*) Official certificates (*see* **19** below).
   (*iii*) Public registers and other records (*see* **20** below).
   (*iv*) Public surveys and reports (*see* **21** below).
   (*v*) Company and bankers' books (*see* **22** below).
   (*vi*) Works of reference (*see* **23** below).

(*b*) A statement in a public document may be admissible, if the conditions of admissibility dealt with below *do not apply*, under the 1968 Act, s. 2 or s. 4, subject to the relevant statutory conditions; if they *do apply*, the statement is admissible without reference to those conditions or the rules under O. 38 (*see* 17:**28**). For documentary evidence generally, *see* Chapter 8.

17. "Public documents." *See* 8:**4** (*b*). "I understand a public document . . . to mean a document that is made for the purpose of the public making use of it, and being able to refer to it": *per* Lord Blackburn in *Sturla* v. *Freccia* (1880).

(*a*) "A public document coming from the proper place or a certified copy of it is sufficient proof of every particular stated in it": *per* Phillimore, J. in *Wilton* v. *Phillips* (1903).

(*b*) A matter may be "public" even though it does not concern the public in general: *see Heath* v. *Deane* (1905).

(*c*) A business record is *not* a public record.

(*d*) Where there is no legal duty to record, the document is not classed as a "public" document. *See Doe d. France* v. *Andrews* (1850); *Daniel* v. *Wilkin* (1852).

18. Statutes, gazettes. Recitals in public Acts of Parliament are admissible in evidence: *see R.* v. *Sutton* (1816). In the case of private Acts, they are evidence only against parties to them, not against strangers: *Brett* v. *Beales* (1830). The *London, Edinburgh, Belfast, Gazettes* are *prima facie evidence* of public matters printed therein.

19. Official certificates. A number of statutory provisions render admissible the reception of certificates as evidence of facts contained therein. *See* the Companies Act 1985, s. 13 (7) (replacing earlier legislation), by which a certificate of incorporation is conclusive evidence that the company has been registered (and, where it contains an appropriate statement, that it is a public company). *See* the Capital Transfer Tax Act 1984, s. 254, by which in any proceedings for the recovery of tax, a certificate by an officer of Inland Revenue shall be sufficient evidence that the sum mentioned in the certificate is due, or unpaid. *See* 2:**19** (*c*).

20. Public registers and other records. Registers and records required to be kept by law for public information may be admissible in proof of the facts stated therein, where:

(*a*) the person keeping the register has a public duty to make an entry after he has satisfied himself of its truth: *Doe d. France* v. *Andrews* (1850); *and*

(*b*) the entry has been recorded promptly and by the appropriate person: *Doe d. Warren* v. *Bray* (1828); *and*

(*c*) the register is not only available for public inspection, but exists for that purpose: *see Lilley* v. *Pettit* (1946).

NOTE: In some cases statute renders professional registers admissible as evidence of matters therein (*see* the Solicitors Act 1974, s. 18).

21. Public surveys and reports. Where these relate to matters of public concern or interest, they are admissible in proof of contents if:

(*a*) they are made under public authority (*see Irish Society* v. *Bishop of Derry* (1846)); *and*

(*b*) they are made by a public officer.

22. Company and bankers' books. Entries in a company's books are admissible as evidence in relation to public and private matters. *See* the Companies Act 1985, s. 361 (*see* also 2:**28**). In the case of bankers' books (*see* 8:**16**), copies of entries therein are admissible as prima facie evidence of entries and of accounts recorded therein, provided that the book is an ordinary book of the bank and the entry was recorded in the ordinary course of business. *See* the Bankers' Books Evidence Act 1879.

23. Works of reference. Maps, almanacs, etc., may be used. Dictionaries may be used in proof of the meaning of words. *See Re Ripon Housing Order 1938* (1939) (Oxford Dictionary's definition of "park" adopted); *Thornton* v. *Fisher and Ludlow Ltd.* (1968) (Oxford Dictionary's definition of "passage" not adopted); *Gravesham B.C.* v. *Wilson* (1983) (reference to dictionary meaning of "commodious"); *Stearn* v. *Twitchell* (1985) (reference to Oxford Dictionary's definition of "correspondence").

Progress test 18

1. What is meant by an "informal admission"? **(4)**
2. Is the form of an informal admission important? **(5)**
3. Can conduct alone constitute an informal admission? **(5)**
4. Comment on *Bessela* v. *Stern* (1877). **(5)**
5. Give examples of admissible informal admissions by persons "in privity" with a party. **(8)**
6. What is the general rule regarding statements by a deceased person as to public or general rights? **(9)**
7. Enumerate the principal conditions of admissibility of a declaration by a deceased person relating to a public or general right. **(12)**
8. Is the declaration of the deceased servant of a family admissible in a pedigree case relating to that family? **(15)**
9. Are recitals in public Acts of Parliament admissible in evidence? **(18)**
10. What are the conditions of admissibility of a public register? **(20)**
11. When is a public survey admissible as evidence of matter therein? **(21)**
12. Is a dictionary ever admissible in proof of the meaning of a word? **(23)**

19
Hearsay in criminal proceedings (1): statements by deceased persons; dying declarations, etc.

Preliminary matters

1. General. In criminal proceedings the main exceptions to the hearsay rule (*see* 16:8) are based on statutory provisions and a number of common law sources.

2. Matters to be covered. In this and the next chapter the following exceptions to the hearsay rule in criminal proceedings will be considered:

(*a*) Statements by deceased persons against interest (*see* **4–6** below).

(*b*) Statements by deceased persons made in the course of duty (*see* **7–9** below).

(*c*) Statements by deceased persons in a case of homicide (*see* **10–12** below).

(*d*) Statements by deceased persons as to pedigree (*see* **13** below).

(*e*) Statements by persons as to public and general rights (*see* **14** below).

(*f*) Statements in public documents (*see* **15** below).

(*g*) Statements in former proceedings (*see* **16–17** below).

(*h*) Statements relating to events in issue (*see* **18** below).

(*i*) Statements accompanying and explaining some relevant act (*see* **19** below).

(*j*) Statements concerning the maker's sensations and state of mind (*see* **20** below).

(*k*) Statutory exceptions (*see* **21–25** below).

(*l*) Confessions (*see* Chap. 20).

3. A note as to the cases cited. Some few of the cases which follow involve *civil proceedings*, decided before the 1968 Act. It should be noted, however, that their principles have application also to the admissibility of hearsay evidence in *criminal proceedings*. They should be read with this in mind.

Statements made by deceased persons against interest

4. The general rule. In criminal proceedings, a declaration made by a deceased person against his pecuniary or proprietary interest (a so-called "declaration against interest") is admissible evidence, not only of the facts against that interest, but of all other facts in that declaration: *Higham* v. *Ridgway* (1808) (*see* **5** below).

5. The rule in practice. The following example should be noted: *Higham* v. *Ridgway* (1808). An entry in a book made by X, the deceased, a male midwife, of payment of his charges for a confinement, was admitted as evidence connected with the date of birth of the child. The payment to X was against his interest and the date was connected with that entry. "If the entry had been produced when the party was making a claim for his attendance it would have been evidence against him that his claim was satisfied": *per* Lord Ellenborough.

6. Conditions of admissibility. The following conditions apply:

(*a*) The declarant's death must be shown: *Stephen* v. *Gwenap* (1831).

(*b*) The declaration may be oral or written.

(*c*) The statement in question must have been against the

declarant's pecuniary or proprietary interest at the time it was made. "The rule is that an admission which is against the interest of the person who makes it, at the time when he makes it is admissible; not that an admission which may or may not turn out at some subsequent time to have been against his interest is admissible": *per* Brett, M.R. in *Re Tollemache* (1884).

(*d*) The declarant must have had personal knowledge of the facts declared. *See Lloyd* v. *Powell Duffryn Steam Coal Co. Ltd.* (1914).

(*e*) The declarant must have known that the statement was against his own interest. "Such declarations are admitted on the ground that declarations made by persons against their own interest are extremely unlikely to be false. It followed, therefore, that to support admissibility it must be shown that the statement was to the knowledge of the deceased contrary to his interest": *per* Fletcher Moulton, L.J. in *Tucker* v. *Oldbury U.D.C.* (1912).

Statements made by deceased persons in the course of duty

7. The general rule. In criminal proceedings, a declaration made by a deceased person in the regular course of his business or duty (a so-called "declaration in the course of duty") is admissible evidence of the facts stated therein: *Price* v. *Torrington* (1703).

8. The rule in practice. *R.* v. *Buckley* (1873): X was charged with the murder of Y, a constable. An oral declaration by Y to his superior officer that he was about to leave "to watch X's movements that night" was held *admissible* as evidence of what Y was doing when he was killed. (The evidence thus admitted was interpreted as evidence of the identity of Y's murderer.)

9. Conditions of admissibility. The following conditions generally apply:

(*a*) The declarant's death must be shown.

(*d*) The declaration may be oral or written.

(*c*) The declarant must have been under a specific duty to make the record. "The duty must be to do the very thing to which the entry relates and then to make a report or record of it": *per* Blackburn, J. in *Smith* v. *Blakey* (1867).

(*d*) The declaration is evidence only of the precise facts which it was the writer's duty to record, not of any other matter which is merely collateral even though contained in the same declaration: *Chambers* v. *Bernasconi* (1834).

(*e*) There should be no motive to misrepresent the facts: *The Henry Coxon* (1878) (in an action against ship owners arising out of a collision, entries made in the ship's log book by the first mate, since deceased, were held inadmissible because: they were written two days after the occurrence; the first mate had an interest to misrepresent; the entries referred not only to the mate's acts but to those of the crew).

(*f*) The action recorded by the deceased should have been performed by him: *Sturla* v. *Freccia* (1880).

(*g*) The declaration must be nearly contemporaneous with the performance of the duty: *The Henry Coxon* (1878) (*see* (*e*) above).

Dying declarations as to homicide

10. The general rules. In criminal proceedings *concerning murder or manslaughter only*, the victim's dying declaration relating to the cause of his death made in "the settled hopeless expectation" of death will be admissible: *R.* v. *Woodcock* (1789).

11. The rule in practice. The following cases should be noted:

(*a*) *R.* v. *Perry* (1909). X, the deceased, who was dying as the result of an illegal operation said to her sister: "Oh! I shall go, but keep this a secret . . . let the worst come to the worst." X then told what the accused had done to her. X's statement *was admitted* in evidence.

(*b*) *R.* v. *Mosley* (1825). X, the deceased, died eleven days after he had made a declaration which implicated the accused. X said repeatedly that he was not getting any better, although his surgeon gave him continuing encouragement. X's declaration *was admitted* as evidence.

12. Conditions of admissibility. The following general conditions apply:

(*a*) The declarant's death must be shown.

(*b*) The declaration may be oral or written, or by signs: *Chandra Sekera* v. *R.* (1937).

(*c*) The declaration is admissible only in a trial for murder or manslaughter. Thus, in *R.* v. *Mead* (1824), a dying declaration concerning an event which led to a trial for perjury was not admitted. *See* also *R.* v. *Hind* (1860).

(*d*) The declaration is admissible only if the declarant would have been competent as a witness: *R.* v. *Pike* (1829). In that case the charge was murder of a four-year-old child. A statement of what the child said was tendered in evidence as a dying declaration, but was held inadmissible.

(*e*) The declaration must have been made when the declarant entertained a settled hopeless expectation of death. The following cases exemplify this very strict requirement:

(*i*) *R.* v. *Jenkins* (1869). The prisoner was charged with the murder of X, who, on her death bed, had accused him of that crime. X's declaration was written down by a magistrates' clerk and it included the words that it was made "with no hope of my recovery". X had it altered to "with no *present* hope of my recovery". The declaration was held *inadmissible* in evidence since the alteration suggested some slight hope of recovery. "These dying declarations are to be received with scrupulous, I had almost said, superstitious, care. The declarant is subject to no cross-examination. No oath need be administered. There can be no prosecution for perjury. There is always the danger of mistake which cannot be corrected": *per* Byles, J.

(*ii*) *R.* v. *Bedingfield* (1879). For the facts, *see* 13:**10** (*a*). "Anything uttered by the deceased at the time the act was being done would be admissible; as, for instance, if she had been heard to say: 'Don't, Harry!' But here is something stated by her after it was all over, whatever it was, and after the act was completed. . . . The statement was *not admissible* as a dying declaration because it did not appear that the woman was aware that she was dying": *per* Cockburn, C.J.

(*iii*) *R*. v. *Gloster* (1888). The deceased woman had from time to time made declarations concerning her physical sufferings and their cause. The declarations included statements such as "I do not think I shall recover" and "I shall not be long here". The declarations were *rejected* in that they did *not* show that there was a settled hopeless expectation of death.

NOTE: (1) There is no requirement for corroboration to support a dying declaration: *Nembhardt* v. *R*. (1981).

(2) In *Waugh* v. *R*. (1950), the deceased fell into a coma, so that it became impossible for him to complete his statement, referring to the defendant, which began: "The man has an old grudge for me simply because . . ." The Privy Council held that the declaration should *not* have been admitted because "it was incomplete and no one can tell what the deceased was about to add": *per* Lord Oaksey.

Statements by deceased persons as to pedigree, public and general rights and statements in public documents

13. Pedigree. The rules applying to this exception to hearsay in criminal proceedings are similar to those relating to statements as to pedigree in civil proceedings. *See* 18:**13–15**.

14. Public and general rights. The rules applying to this exception to hearsay in criminal proceedings are similar to those relating to statements as to public and general rights in civil proceedings. *See* 18:**9–12**.

15. Statements in public documents. The rules applying to this exception to hearsay in criminal proceedings are similar to those relating to public documents in civil proceedings. *See* 18:**16–23**. *See R*. v. *Halpin* (1975)—H and others were charged with conspiring to defraud a local authority, and the prosecution produced as evidence the contents of a file from the Companies Register. It was argued, on appeal, that such evidence was not admissible under the "public documents rule" because (*see* 18:**20** (*a*)) the person who had put together the file had no duty to inquire into the contents and satisfy himself of the truth of what was recorded. The Court of Appeal held that the common law must "move with the times". "Where a duty is cast upon a limited company by statute to make accurate returns of company matters to the Registrar of Companies, so that these returns can be filed and inspected by members of the public, the necessary conditions, in the judgment of this court, have been fulfilled for that document to have been admissible": *per* Geoffrey Lane, L.J.

Statements in former proceedings

16. **Evidence given in previous proceedings.** In general, where a witness who has given evidence in previous proceedings is shown to have died or is too ill to attend, a transcript of his evidence is admissible as evidence in subsequent criminal proceedings as an exception to the hearsay rule. *See* Magistrates' Courts Act 1980, s. 105; Children and Young Persons Act 1963, s. 27.

17. **The rule in practice: *R.* v. *Hall* (1973).** X had given evidence for the Crown at a trial which had ended when the jury failed to agree. At the re-trial, X having died, the defence wanted to put in a transcript of X's evidence at the first trial. The judge ruled that this was inadmissible as hearsay. On appeal against conviction, it was held, allowing the appeal, that because the transcript was the sworn evidence of a witness which was given in defendant's presence and was subject to cross-examination, it was admissible in the exercise of the judge's discretion.

Statements relating to events in issue, accompanying and explaining relevant acts and concerning the maker's sensations and state of mind

18. **Events in issue: spontaneous statements made by observers or participators.** *See* the doctrine of *res gestae* at 13:8. The rule is that a statement made by an observer or participant is admissible as evidence in criminal proceedings if made on an approximately contemporaneous occasion so as to exclude any possibility of its

having been concocted to the maker's advantage. *See Ratten* v. *R.* (1972) at 13:**11**; *R.* v. *Foster* (1834).

19. Accompanying and explaining relevant acts. "Though you cannot give in evidence a declaration *per se*, yet when there is an act accompanied by a statement which is so mixed up with it as to become part of the *res gestae*, evidence of such a statement may be given": *per* Grove, J. in *Howe* v. *Malkin* (1878). The declaration, to be admissible, must be:

    (*a*) related closely to the act: *see R.* v. *Bliss* (1837);
    (*b*) made contemporaneously;
    (*c*) made by the actor.

20. Concerning the maker's physical condition and state of mind. *See* 13:**25**. The general rule is that, as an exception to the hearsay rule, a person's declaration concerning his state of mind will be admitted as evidence of the existence of such state of mind and his statement concerning a physical sensation may be admissible as evidence of that sensation.

    (*a*) *State of mind.* In *Thomas* v. *Connell* (1838) it was held that a statement by a bankrupt that he was aware of his insolvency was admissible as evidence of his knowledge of that fact at a time when he paid money to defendant. *See* also *R.* v. *Gandfield* (1846); *R.* v. *Hagan* (1873). It should be noted that the statement, to be admissible, must relate to the maker's contemporaneous state of mind: *see R.* v. *Vincent* (1840). Further, the statement is relevant only where the maker's state of mind is in issue; it will not be admitted as evidence of other facts to which it refers: *see R.* v. *Gunnell* (1886).

    (*b*) *State of physical sensation. See Gilbey* v. *G.W. Rail Co.* (1910) at 16:**14** (*a*). Note, however, the observations of Pollock, C.B. in *R.* v. *Nicholas* (1846): "If a man says to his surgeon 'I have a pain in the head', or 'in such a part of my body', that is evidence, but if he says to the surgeon 'I have a wound', and was to add 'I met John Thomas who had a sword and ran me through the body with it', that would be no evidence against John Thomas." It should be noted, also, that the statement must refer to a contemporaneous physical sensation. See R. v. *Gloster* (1888); R. v. *Black* (1922).

21. Statutory exception: Criminal Evidence Act 1965, s. 1. This Act was passed as a direct result of the decision in *Myers* v. *DPP* (1965) (see 16:7 (*d*)). It provided that hearsay evidence could be adduced where it was in documentary form and formed part of a record relating to a trade or business, and was compiled from a basis of "personal knowledge" of the facts with which it dealt, provided that the supplier of the information was, for some good reason, unable to attend so as to give evidence. The term "document" included "any device by means of which information is recorded or stored." The Act was repealed by the Police and Criminal Evidence Act 1984, Sch. 7, Part III, but some of the cases are noted to show the problems which may arise in this area.

22. Computers and the 1965 Act, s. 1. Some lacunae in the 1965 Act appear to have emerged, as exemplified by the following cases.

(*a*) R. v. *Pettigrew* (1980). The Court of Appeal considered the problem of "personal knowledge" in relation to a computer which recorded the numbers of bank notes. "The numbers of the notes [which were rejected as defective] can never be said to be in the personal knowledge of the operator or in the mind of anybody. They are recorded purely by the operation of the machine. The operator could never be said to have personal knowledge of these rejected notes, and knowledge of the numbers of the rejected notes is essential to know the serial numbers of the notes in the bundles to which the computer print-out refers": *per* Bridge, L.J. Information recorded on the print-out was *not* admissible under s. 1 (1).

(*b*) R. v. *Wood* (1983). The Court of Appeal held that where a computer was used "as a calculator" and its programming and use were both covered by oral evidence, a print-out *was* admissible as real evidence, not hearsay.

(*c*) R. v. *Ewing* (1983). The Court of Appeal held that a print-out was part of a device by means of which information is recorded or stored, and that the trial judge had been entitled to rule that the person who fed information into the computer could not reasonably be expected to have any recollection of it.

In consequence of the Police and Criminal Evidence Act 1984, Sch. 7, Part III, the 1965 Act is *repealed in its entirety. See* now the 1984 Act, ss. 68, 69, at 23 below.

23. Statutory exception: computers and the Police and Criminal Evidence Act 1984, s. 69. The following points should be noted.

(*a*) A statement in a computer record is admissible as evidence of the facts contained in it *only if* certain criteria are fulfilled:

(*i*) There must be no reasonable grounds for believing that the statement is inaccurate because of improper use of the computer.

(*ii*) It must be shown that at all material times the computer was operating properly, or if not, that the production of the document and the accuracy of its contents are unaffected.

(*iii*) Any rules of the court must have been complied with: s. 69 (1).

(*b*) Any party wishing to adduce a computer document may give in evidence a certificate identifying it, describing its production, giving particulars of the equipment used to produce it, signed by a person occupying a responsible position in relation to the operation of the computer: Sch. 3, Part II, para. 8. But the court may require oral evidence on these matters: Sch. 3, Part II, para. 9.

(*c*) The court shall take into account, in considering the weight to be given to a computer record: all the circumstances from which an inference might be drawn as to the accuracy of the document; whether or not the information in the record was supplied to the computer contemporaneously with the occurrence or existence of the facts dealt with in the information; and whether or not the computer operator had any incentive to conceal or misrepresent the facts: Sch. 3, Part II, para. 11.

24. Statutory exception: Criminal Justice Act 1967, s. 9. "(1) In any criminal proceedings, other than committal proceedings, a written statement by any person shall, if such of the conditions mentioned in the next following subsection as are applicable are satisfied, be admissible as evidence to the like extent as oral evidence to the like effect by that person. (2) The said conditions are—

(*a*) the statement purports to be signed by the person who made it;

(*b*) the statement contains a declaration by that person to the effect that it is true to the best of his knowledge and belief and that he made the statement knowing that, if it were tendered in evidence, he would be liable to prosecution if he wilfully stated in it anything which he knew to be false or did not believe to be true;

(*c*) before the hearing at which the statement is tendered in evidence, a copy of the statement is served, by or on behalf of the party proposing to tender it, on each of the other parties to the proceedings; and

(*d*) none of the other parties or their solicitors, within seven days from the service of the copy of the statement, serves a notice on the party so proposing objecting to the statement being tendered in evidence under this section.

Provided that the conditions mentioned in paragraphs (*c*) and (*d*) of this subsection shall not apply if the parties agree before or during the hearing that the statement shall be so tendered."

25. Statutory exception: Police and Criminal Evidence Act 1984, s. 68. The following aspects of s. 68 should be noted.

(*a*) Under s. 68, which replaces the Criminal Evidence Act 1965, s. 1, a statement in a document will be admissible in evidence, *as an exception to the hearsay rule*, if certain conditions, set out below, are fulfilled:

(*i*) The evidence should be of such a nature that direct oral evidence would have been admissible: s. 68 (1).

(*ii*) The document must form part of a record compiled by some person "acting under a duty" from information supplied directly by another who had, or may reasonably be supposed to have had, "personal knowledge" of the matters dealt with in the information: s. 68 (1) (*a*).

(*iii*) The person who supplied the information in the record should be: dead; or unfit to attend as a witness; or outside the U.K., so that it is not reasonably practicable to secure his attendance; or cannot reasonably be expected to recollect the matters dealt with; or cannot be identified or found: s. 68 (2).

(*b*) If the conditions above are satisfied, the document can be proved by production of the original, or a copy authenticated in a manner approved by the court: Sch. 3, Part III, para. 13.

(c) The contents of a document can be proved (if the appropriate criteria have been fulfilled) by production of an enlargement of a microfilm copy: s. 71.

(d) Where a document setting out the evidence which a person could be expected to give as a witness has been prepared (under s. 68 (1)) it may not be admitted unless the court is of the opinion that the interests of justice require this, having regard to: the circumstances in which leave to admit is sought; its contents; the likelihood of the accused being prejudiced by its admission in the absence of the person who supplied the information on which it is based: Sch. 3, Part I, para. 2.

(e) Where evidence based on s. 68 is given, the accused may call evidence concerning the credibility of the supplier of the information. He may also call evidence tending to prove that the supplier of information had made an inconsistent statement, oral or written: Sch. 3, Part I, para. 3.

(f) A statement admissible under s. 68 is not capable of corroborating information given by the supplier of information on which the statement is based: Sch. 3, Part I, para. 4.

(g) The weight to be attached to a document will be determined by: inferences which can be reasonably drawn as to the accuracy of the statement; whether or not the supplier of information contained in the document communicated it contemporaneously with the existence or occurrence of the facts contained therein; whether the compiler or keeper of the document had any incentive to conceal or misrepresent the facts: Sch. 3, Part I, para. 7 (a), (b).

Progress test 19

1. What is meant by a "declaration against interest"? **(4)**
2. Explain the decision in *Higham* v. *Ridgway* (1808). **(5)**
3. What are the conditions of admissibility for a declaration made by a deceased person against interest? **(6)**
4. What are the conditions of admissibility for a declaration made by a deceased person in the course of duty? **(9)**
5. When is a dying declaration admissible in relation to a charge of manslaughter? **(12)**

6. Explain the decision in *R.* v. *Jenkins* (1869).   (**12**)

7. Comment on *R.* v. *Hall* (1973).   (**17**)

8. Is a spontaneous statement by an observer of an event ever admissible as evidence relating to that event?   (**18**)

9. What is the significance of *Thomas* v. *Connell* (1838)?   (**20**)

10. When is a statement in a computer record admissible under the Police and Criminal Evidence Act 1984, s. 69?   (**23**)

11. Outline the essential features of the Police and Criminal Evidence Act 1984, s. 68.   (**25**)

20

Hearsay in criminal proceedings (2): confessions

Preliminary matters

1. General. This chapter concludes the short survey of exceptions to the hearsay rule in criminal proceedings by considering the exceptions provided by admissions and confessions made by the accused. Reference is made to the Police and Criminal Evidence Act 1984 and Codes of Practice issued under the Act.

2. Matters to be covered. The following points are touched upon below:

    (a) Admissions (*see* **3–4** below);
    (b) Confessions of persons charged with crimes (*see* **5–22** below).

Admissions, informal and formal

3. Informal admissions. An informal admission of a party as to matters of fact or law, made to some person in privity with him (e.g., an agent) may be admitted as evidence against him in relation to its contents in criminal proceedings, as an exception to the hearsay rule.

    (a) An admission may be implied from a party's conduct: *R.* v. *Cramp* (1880).
    (b) An admission may be favourable only in part to the person making it, but, nevertheless, the statement in its entirety may be put in. "If the prosecutor makes the prisoner's declaration evidence, it becomes evidence for the prisoner, as well as against him; but still,

ike all evidence given in any case, it is for you to say whether you eally believe it": *R.* v. *Higgins* (1829).

4. Formal admissions. Under the Criminal Justice Act 1967, s. 10: "(1) Subject to the provisions of this section, any fact of which oral evidence may be given in any criminal proceedings which may be admitted for the purpose of those proceedings by or on behalf of the prosecutor or defendant, and the admission by any party of any such fact under this section shall as against that party be conclusive evidence in those proceedings of the fact admitted.

(2) An admission under this section—

(*a*) may be made before or at the proceedings;

(*b*) if made otherwise than in court, shall be in writing;

(*c*) if made in writing by an individual, shall purport to be signed by the person making it and, if so made by a body corporate, shall purport to be signed by a director or manager, or the secretary or clerk, or some other similar officer of the body corporate;

(*d*) if made on behalf of a defendant who is an individual, shall be made by his counsel or solicitor;

(*e*) if made at any stage before the trial by a defendant who is an individual, must be approved by his counsel or solicitor (whether at the time it was made or subsequently) before or at the proceedings in question.

(3) An admission under this section for the purpose of proceedings relating to any matter shall be treated as an admission for the purpose of any subsequent criminal proceedings relating to that matter (including any appeal or retrial).

(4) An admission under this section may with the leave of the court be withdrawn in the proceedings for the purpose of which it is made or any subsequent criminal proceedings relating to the same matter." *See* 9:**4** and 9:**6**.

Confessions: the common law background

5. Essence of a "confession". A confession is essentially an incriminating admission by an accused person which, when put in evidence, supports some part of the prosecution's case. "An admission made by a person charged with a crime, stating or suggesting the inference that he committed the crime": Stephen. "A voluntary statement made by a person charged with the commission of a crime, communicated to another person, wherein he acknowledges himself to be guilty of the offence charged, and discloses the circumstances of the act or the share and participation which he had in it": Black.

6. The common law rules. The following should be noted.

(a) "When a confession is well proved it is the best evidence which can be produced": *per* Erle, J. in *R.* v. *Baldry* (1852).

(b) A confession could be made *in any way, at any time, and to any person. See*, e.g., *R.* v. *Simons* (1834); *Rumping* v. *DPP* (1964). *See* 12:4. It could be implied from the conduct of an accused person who had remained silent in circumstances which might be considered generally as demanding an explanation or denial of some alleged conduct.

(c) A confession could be given in evidence *against the accused* at his trial, because, "what a person having knowledge about the matter in issue says of it is itself relevant to the issue as evidence against him"; *per* Lord Sumner in *Ibrahim* v. *R.* (1914).

(d) A confession was admissible *only if voluntary*. "In order to render a confession admissible in evidence it must be perfectly voluntary; and there is no doubt that any inducement in the nature of a promise or threat held out by a person in authority vitiates a confession": *per* Parke, B. in *R.* v. *Baldry* (1852). ("A person in authority means, generally speaking, anyone who has authority over the accused or over the proceedings or the prosecution against him": *R.* v. *Todd* (1901). "Persons in authority" have been held to include the prosecutor, prosecutor's spouse, police officer, magistrate, magistrate's clerk; but *not* a police officer's wife, fellow prisoner or prison chaplain. *See R.* v. *Cleary* (1963); *Deokinanan* v. *R.* (1969).)

(e) Additionally, a confession was not generally admissible if obtained *improperly* or by *unfair means. See*, e.g., *Callis* v. *Gunn* (1964); *R.* v. *Prager* (1972).

7. The Judges' Rules. Formulated in 1912, and subsequently revised, the Rules constituted a code of practice designed to ensure, as far as possible, that confessions were not obtained from suspected persons by improper means.

(a) The Rules and accompanying Administrative Directions (*see* Home Office Circular 89/1978 [1964] 1 W.L.R. 152) were based on the concept of ". . . a fundamental condition of the admissibility in evidence against any person, equally of any oral answer given by that person to a question put by a police officer and of any statement made by that person, that it shall have been voluntary in the sense that it has not been obtained from him by fear of prejudice or hope of advantage, exercised or help out by a person in authority, or by oppression." The Rules related to the right of the police to question any person, to the necessity for the administration of appropriate cautions to a person to be charged, and to the taking of statements. The Administrative Directions (drafted by the Home Office) concerned dealings with suspects in a police station.

(b) The Rules were rules of practice intended for guidance only; *they were not rules of law, nor did failure to comply with them necessarily render a confession inadmissible: R.* v. *Prager* (1972). A judge could, in his discretion, admit a statement made in infringement of the Rules if it could be shown that it had been made voluntarily: *R.* v. *May* (1952).

(c) The Rules and Directions were criticised because they had been drafted imprecisely and because they ignored certain aspects of the processes of detaining and questioning. The Royal Commission on Criminal Procedure 1981 called for their replacement by "a statutory code of practice." Under the 1984 legislation (*see* below), the Rules and Directions are superseded by Codes of Practice (*see* s. 66 at **16** below) and Parts III–V of the Act.

(d) *See*, further, *R.* v. *Isequilla* (1975); *DPP* v. *Ping Lin* (1975); *Prasad* v. *R.* (1981); *Ajodha* v. *The State* (1981); *R.* v. *Airey* (1985); *R.* v. *Miller* (1986).

Confessions: the 1984 legislation

8. Essence of the legislation. Prior to the coming into force of the Police and Criminal Evidence Act 1984, evidence of a confession in criminal proceedings was inadmissible if it were shown to have been obtained by oppression or other unfair means or in circumstances which suggested that it had been made involuntarily. The 1984 legislation states clearly the *two grounds on which a confession may now be excluded—oppression or unreliability* (*see* 11 below).

9. Confessions: the general rule. In any criminal proceedings a confession made by the accused person may be given in evidence against him in so far as it is relevant to any matter in issue in the proceedings and is not excluded by the court in pursuance of s. 76: s. 76 (1). Note the following points.

(*a*) The evidence referred to may be given *against the accused*, and not against others.

(*b*) Corroboration does not seem to be required where a confession is declared to be admissible.

(*c*) ". . . Relevant to any matter in issue in the proceedings". An example may be seen where the disposition of the accused to commit the type of offence in question has been raised.

10. Confession defined. "A confession includes any statement wholly or partly adverse to the person who made it, whether made to a person in authority or not and whether made in words or otherwise": s. 82 (1). (A "confession" includes a full admission of guilt as well as an admission of particular facts.) Note the following points.

(*a*) ". . . Wholly or partly adverse" to the person making it, indicates that even the favourable parts of a confession may be admitted by the court.

(*b*) The statement comprising the confession may be made to any person—police, friend, workmate, etc.

(*c*) ". . . Or otherwise". This broad phrase could include a nod, or other gesture, made by the accused, signifying approval.

11. Admissibility of a confession: the test. Where the prosecution proposes to put in a confession made by the accused, and representations are made to the court questioning the circumstances in which that confession has been obtained, the court shall not allow the confession to be given in evidence against the accused unless the prosecution proves to the court beyond reasonable doubt that the

onfession (even though it may be true) was *not* obtained by
ppression of the person who made it, or as the result of anything
aid or done which, in the circumstances existing at the time, was
ikely to render the confession unreliable: s. 76 (2). Note the
ollowing points.

(*a*) "Oppression", "unreliable": *see* **12, 13** below.

(*b*) "The court shall not allow . . . ." This is a clear, mandatory
tatement, so that a confession may be inadmissible even though it is
rue.

(*c*) The court may, of its own motion, require the prosecution to
rove that the confession was not obtained as mentioned in s. 76 (2):
. 76 (3).

(*d*) It should be remembered that when a question of admissi-
ility arises, the judge will rule whether the evidence is admissible,
vhile the jury will decide whether it ought to be believed. *See R.* v.
McArthy (1980). *See* 3:5.

(*e*) Note the general terms of s. 76 (7): "Nothing in Part VII of
his Act shall prejudice the admissibility of a confession made by an
iccused person."

12. "Oppression". "In this section 'oppression' includes torture,
nhuman or degrading treatment, and the use or threat of violence
whether or not amounting to torture)": s. 76 (8). The following
ioints should be noted.

(*a*) The comprehensive wording of s. 76 (8) is, nevertheless, not
:xhaustive.

(*b*) "Torture" was described in United Nations Resolution 3452
s "an aggravated and deliberate form of cruel, inhuman or
legrading treatment or punishment".

(*c*) "This word [oppression] in the context of the principles
inder consideration imports something which tends to sap, and has
apped, that free will which must exist before a confession is
voluntary . . . Whether or not there is oppression in an individual
:ase depends on many elements . . . They include such things as the
ength of time of any individual period of questioning, the length of
ime intervening between periods of questioning, whether the
iccused person has been given proper refreshment or not, and the

characteristics of the person who makes the statement. What may be oppressive as regards a child, an invalid or an old man or somebody inexperienced in the ways of the world, may turn out not to be oppressive when one finds that the accused person is of a tough character and an experienced man of the world": *per* Sachs, J. in *R*. v. *Priestley* (1965).

(*d*) "[Oppressive questioning] is questioning which by its nature, duration or other attendant circumstances (including the fact of custody) excites hope (such as the hope of release) or fears, or so affects the mind of the suspect that his will crumbles and he speaks when otherwise he would have stayed silent": observations of Lord MacDermott, cited with approval in *R*. v. *Prager* (1972). (*See* now **16–22** below.) Note, however, the comment of the Court of Appeal in *R*. v. *Gowan* (1982): "Experienced criminals must expect vigorous police interrogation."

(*e*) In the following cases confessions were excluded because of "oppression": *R*. v. *Westlake* (1979), in which W, who was subnormal, was arrested on a charge of attempted murder and held for five days, during which his questioning occupied nearly thirty hours; *R*. v. *Allerton* (1979), in which a nurse, of previous good character, charged on counts relating to possession of cannabis, was offered no food or drink and deprived of her watch during two periods of "rigorous questioning"; *R*. v. *Hudson* (1980), in which H, who had no previous convictions, was asked some 700 questions over a period of five days.

13. "Unreliability". This term is not defined in the 1984 Act. The following points should be noted.

(*a*) The question for the court to decide is whether the *surrounding circumstances* of the confession were such as to be likely to render it unreliable.

(*b*) Some commentators suggest that it is not clear from a perusal of the Act whether the criterion of "unreliability" will be objective, based on those circumstances which *ought* to reduce the reliability of *any* confession, or subjective, based on the effect of *actual circumstances* on the maker of the confession, in relation to his characteristics and personality.

(*c*) In the following cases confessions were excluded because of "unreliability": *R.* v. *Zaveckas* (1970), in which the suspect was urged, during detention, to make a statement "so that you will get bail"; *R.* v. *Glyde* (1979), in which a 16-year old, arrested on suspicion of burglary, made admissions in the absence of any adult other than a police officer; *R.* v. *Platt* (1981), in which a subnormal suspect, with a mental age of 8–11, dictated a confession in the absence of an independent adult.

14. Admissible evidence based on an excluded confession. Although a confession may be excluded partly or wholly, the following kinds of evidence may, nevertheless, be admissible:

(*a*) facts discovered as a result of the confession; and

(*b*) so much of the confession which is necessary to show that the accused "speaks, writes or expresses himself in a particular way": s. 76 (4). (*See*, e.g., *R.* v. *Voisin* (1918).) Note that evidence that a fact to which s. 76 (4) applies was discovered as a result of a statement made by the accused will not be admissible unless evidence of *how* it was discovered is given by the accused or on his behalf: s. 76 (5).

15. Other features of the 1984 legislation. The following should be noted.

(*a*) The court retains its overriding discretion to exclude unfair evidence: ss. 78 (1), 82 (3).

(*b*) In the case of a confession by a mentally handicapped person (defined in s. 77 (3)), where the case against him depends wholly or substantially on that confession, and the court is satisfied that he is mentally handicapped and that the confession was not made in the presence of an "independent person," a warning must be given to the jury of the special need for caution before convicting: s. 77 (1). ("Independent person" does not include a police officer or a person employed for or engaged on police duties: s. 77 (3).)

Detention, treatment and questioning under the 1984 legislation

16. The Act and Codes. The Act deals with pre-trial procedures in detail: Part I is concerned with stop and search powers; Part II with powers of entry, search and seizure; Part III with arrest; Part IV with detention; Part V with questioning and treatment by the police. Part VI deals with Codes of Practice to be issued under the Act. By virtue of s. 66, the Secretary of State has issued codes of practice in relation to police powers of search, detention, treatment, questioning and identification of persons by the police, search of premises and seizure of property.

(*a*) A police officer is liable to disciplinary proceedings for failure to comply with the provisions of a code: s. 67 (8).

(*b*) Failure on the part of a police officer to comply with a code will not in itself render him liable to any criminal or civil proceedings: s. 67 (10).

(*c*) A code is admissible in evidence in all criminal and civil proceedings: s. 67 (11).

Set out at **17–22** below are the relevant provisions of the 1984 Act, concerning treatment and questioning of detainees, and paragraphs from the *Code of Practice for the Detention, Treatment and Questioning of Persons by Police Officers* (as placed before Parliament and published by the Home Office in May 1985) and referred to below as "the Code". The way in which an accused person has been detained and questioned by the police while in detention may be a significant factor to be weighed in any evaluation of the "reliability" of his confession.

17. Limitations on police detention: the 1984 Act. The guiding principle is stated in s. 34 (1): "A person arrested for an offence shall not be kept in police detention except in accordance with the provisions of [Part IV] of this Act." The following points should be noted.

(*a*) A person is "in police detention" for the purposes of this Act if he has been taken to a police station after being arrested for an offence, or he is arrested at a police station after attending voluntarily at the station or accompanying a constable to it, and is detained there, or is detained elsewhere in charge of a constable, except that a person who is at a court after being charged is not in police detention for those purposes: s. 118 (2).

(b) If at any time a custody officer [i.e. an officer of at least the rank of sergeant, appointed under s. 36 (1) for each designated police station] becomes aware, in relation to any person in police detention, that the grounds for detention have ceased to apply, and he is not aware of any other grounds on which continued detention could be justified under Part IV of the Act, he must order that person's immediate release from custody: s. 34 (2). But a person who appears to the custody officer to have been unlawfully at large [e.g., having escaped from lawful arrest or prison] when he was arrested may not be released under s. 34 (2): s. 34 (4).

(c) A person whose release is ordered by a custody officer under s. 34 (2) must be released without bail unless it appears to the custody officer that there is a need to investigate further any matter in connection with which he was detained, or that proceedings may be taken against him in respect of such a matter, in which case he must be released on bail: s. 34 (5).

(d) The duties of a custody officer before charge are stated in s. 37. Under s. 37 (1), where a person is arrested for an offence without a warrant or under a warrant not endorsed for bail (see the Magistrates' Courts Act 1980, s. 117 (2)), or a person returns to a police station to answer bail, the custody officer must determine whether there is sufficient evidence to charge that person with the offence for which he was arrested. In such a case the officer may detain the person at the police station for a period necessary to enable him to do so. Where the custody officer determines that he has no such evidence, he must release the person with or without bail unless there are reasonable grounds for believing that his detention without being charged is necessary to secure or preserve evidence relating to an offence for which he is under arrest or to obtain such evidence by questioning him: s. 37 (2). Where a custody officer determines that he has sufficient evidence to charge the person arrested with the offence for which he was arrested, the person arrested must be charged or released without charge, either on or without bail: s. 37 (7). (A written record of the grounds for detention must be made where a custody officer authorises a person who has not been charged to be kept in detention: s. 37 (4).)

(e) A person shall not be kept in detention for more than 24 hours without being charged: s. 41 (1). A superintendent (or one of higher rank) may authorise an added period (of 36 hours) of detention if he has reasonable grounds for believing that continued detention is necessary to secure or preserve evidence, or that the offence under investigation is a serious arrestable offence, and that the investigation is being conducted "diligently and expeditiously": s. 42 (1). A warrant of further detention may be issued by a magistrates' court: s. 43 (1), and this may be extended further under s. 44 (1), so that detention without charge for up to a total of 96 hours is possible. (Note that "serious arrestable offence" includes arrestable offences specified under Sch. 5, Parts I, II. Treason, murder, manslaughter, rape, kidnapping are among the offences referred to. *See* s. 116.)

(*f*) A person charged with an offence and kept in detention must be brought before a magistrates' court as soon as is practicable "and in any event not later than the first sitting after he is charged": s. 46 (1).

(*g*) The right of any person in police detention to apply for a writ of *habeas corpus* or any other prerogative remedy is not affected by Part IV of the 1984 Act: s. 51 (*d*).

18. Limitations on police detention: Code of Practice. The Code reminds police officers that "all persons in custody must be dealt with expeditiously, and released as soon as the need for detention has ceased to apply": para. 1.1. A copy of the Code must be "readily available" at all police stations for consultation: para. 1.2.

(*a*) A custody record must be compiled for each person brought to a police station under arrest, or arrested at the station, having attended there voluntarily: para. 2.1. A copy of the record must be supplied on request, up to 12 months after release, to a detained person or his legal representative: para. 2.4.

(*b*) Persons in detention must be informed of their rights, e.g. to consult a solicitor and to consult appropriate codes of practice: para. 3.1.

(*c*) If the custody officer authorises a person's detention he must inform him of the grounds as soon as practicable, and in any case before that person is then questioned about any offence: para. 3.3.

(*d*) Any person attending a police station voluntarily for the purpose of assisting with an investigation may leave at will unless placed under arrest. If it is decided that he should not be allowed to leave he must be informed at once that he is under arrest and brought before the custody officer: para. 3.9.

19. Treatment by police of persons in detention: the 1984 Act.
The following points should be noted carefully.

(*a*) If an officer of at least the rank of superintendent has reasonable grounds for believing that a detained person who has been arrested may have concealed on him anything which he could use to cause physical injury and might so use it, or may have a Class A drug concealed on him, he may authorise a search of that person: s. 55 (1). An "intimate search" (defined in s. 118 (1) as "a search which consists of the physical examination of a person's body orifices") may be authorised where there are reasonable grounds for believing that an object cannot be found without such a search: s. 55 (2). (Note *Brazil* v. *Chief Constable of Surrey* (1983)—a person should not be submitted to a search unless he knows the reasons for it; but this will not apply where it is impracticable to give those reasons.) Under s. 62 (10), if a person refuses "without good cause" (which is not defined in the Act) to consent to the taking of an intimate sample, the court, at committal proceedings, or when deciding whether there is a case to answer, or the court or jury in determining guilt at a trial, "may draw such inferences from the refusal as appear proper." Further, the refusal may, on the basis of such inferences, be treated as, or as capable of amounting to, corroboration (*see* 7:**16**) of any evidence against the person in relation to which the refusal is material.

(*b*) A detainee who has been arrested has the right to have someone informed, under s. 56 (1), and delay in allowing the exercise of this right is permitted only in the case of a serious arrestable offence: s. 56 (2). Delay may be authorised only where a police officer has reasonable grounds for believing that telling a named person of the arrest will lead to interference with persons or evidence, or will lead to the alerting of other suspects, or will hinder the recovery of property: s. 56 (5). Exercise of the right must be permitted within 36 hours of arrival at the police station: ss. 41 (2) (*a*), 56 (3).

(c) A person who is detained is entitled to consult a solicitor privately at any time: s. 58 (1). Permission must be given within 36 hours: s. 58 (5). Delay in granting permission applies only in the case of a serious arrestable offence: s. 58 (6). Authorisation for delay will be given only when a police officer believes that exercise of the right may have the effects mentioned in s. 56 (5) (*see* (*b*) above): s. 58 (8). Additionally, delay may be authorised where a police officer believes that exercise of the right might interfere with the gathering of information concerning acts of terrorism, or might alert persons so that it becomes more difficult to prevent such acts: s. 58 (13) (*c*).

20. Treatment by police of persons in detention: Code of Practice. It should be noted that the Code refers specifically to the detainee's right "not to be held incommunicado." The following points should be noted.

(*a*) A detainee may on request have one person known to him or who is likely to take an interest in his welfare informed at public expense as soon as possible of his whereabouts: para. 5.1.

(*b*) A detainee may at any time consult and communicate privately, whether in person, in writing or on the telephone, with a solicitor of his own choice, a duty solicitor, or a solicitor selected by him from a list of those who have indicated that they are available for the purpose of providing legal advice at police stations: para. 6.1.

(*c*) A solicitor may be required to leave an interview [conducted by the investigating officer] if his conduct is such that the officer is unable properly to put questions to the suspect: para. 6.6.

(*d*) A citizen of an independent Commonwealth country or a national of a foreign country (including the Republic of Ireland) may communicate at any time with his High Commission, Embassy or Consulate: para. 7.1.

(*e*) Cells in use must be adequately heated, cleaned and ventilated: para. 8.2. At least two light meals and one main meal shall be offered in any period of 24 hours: para. 8.6.

(*f*) The following direction in the Code is of particular importance: "Reasonable force may be used if necessary for the following purposes—to secure compliance with reasonable instructions, including instructions given in pursuance of a code of practice, or to prevent escape, injury, damage to property or the destruction of evidence:" para. 8.9.

(*g*) If a complaint is made by or on behalf of a detainee about his treatment since his arrest, or it comes to the notice of an officer that he may have been treated improperly, a report must be made as soon as practicable to an inspector (or above) who is not connected with the investigation: para. 9.1.

(*h*) If a detained person requests a medical examination the police surgeon must be called as soon as practicable. He may, in addition, be examined by a medical practitioner of his own choice at his own expense: para. 9.4.

21. Questioning by the police of persons in detention: the 1984 Act. Little is stated in the Act concerning questioning of detainees, save for a reference in s. 60 to the tape-recording of interviews. The Secretary of State is empowered to issue an appropriate code of practice in connection with the tape-recording of interviews with detained suspects.

22. Questioning by the police of persons in detention: Code of Practice. Note a general principle promulgated in the Code: ". . . When a police officer is trying to discover whether, or by whom, an offence has been committed he is entitled to question any person from whom he thinks useful information can be obtained, subject to the restrictions imposed by this Code. A person's declaration that he is unwilling to reply does not alter this entitlement": para. 1B (Notes for Guidance). The Code emphasises that the purpose of any interview is "to obtain from the person concerned his explanation of the facts and not necessarily to obtain an admission": para. 12A (Notes for Guidance).

(*a*) "No police officer may try to obtain answers to questions or to elicit a statement by the use of oppression, or shall indicate, except in answer to a direct question, what action will be taken on the part of the police if the person being interviewed answers questions, makes a statement or refuses to do either. If the person asks the officer directly what action will be taken in the event of his answering questions, making a statement or refusing to do either, then the officer may inform the person what action the police propose to take in that event, provided that that action is itself proper and warranted": para 11.1.

(*b*) "As soon as a police officer who is making enquiries of any person about an offence believes that a prosecution should be brought against him and that there is sufficient evidence for it to succeed, he shall without delay cease to question him": para. 11.2.

(*c*) An accurate record must be made of interviews with suspects: para. 11.3.

(*d*) In any period of 24 hours a detainee must be allowed a continuous period of at least 8 hours for rest, normally at night: para. 12.2.

(*e*) Questions relating to an offence may not be put to a person after he has been charged with that offence, or informed that he may be prosecuted for it, unless they are necessary for the purpose of preventing or minimising harm or loss to some other person or to the public or for clearing up an ambiguity in a previous answer or statement, or where it is in the interests of justice that the person should have put to him, and have an opportunity of commenting on, information concerning the offence which has come to light since he was charged or informed that he might be prosecuted: para. 17.5.

(*f*) In the case of a written statement under caution, the person making it should sign or make his mark on the following certification clause: "I have read the above statement, and I have been able to correct, alter or add anything I wish. This statement is true. I have made it of my own free will": Annex D to Code, para. 6.

(*g*) A person must be cautioned upon arrest unless it is impracticable to do so by reason of his condition or behaviour, or because he has already been cautioned immediately prior to arrest: para. 10.3. The caution must be in the following terms: "You do not have to say anything unless you wish to do so, but what you say may be given in evidence": para. 10.4. Where a person who is given a caution is unclear as to its significance, the officer concerned should explain the matter of self-incrimination and that no adverse inferences from his silence may be drawn at a trial: Notes for Guidance 10D.

Progress test 20

1. Outline the Criminal Justice Act 1967, s. 10. (**4**)
2. What were the common law rules relating to confessions? (**6**)
3. What is a "confession" under the Police and Criminal Evidence Act 1984, s. 82 (1). (**10**)
4. What is the test for admissibility of a confession under the 1984 Act? (**11**)
5. May evidence based on an excluded confession be admitted? (**14**)
6. How does the 1984 Act place limitations on police detention? (**17**)
7. How does the Code of Practice deal with questioning by the police of persons in detention? (**22**)
8. Must a person always be cautioned on arrest? (**22**)

Appendix 1
Bibliography

NOTE: Only the most recent editions should be used.

Reference Works

Archbold's Pleadings, Evidence and Practice (Sweet & Maxwell)

Halsbury's Laws of England, Vol. 17: ed. Lord Hailsham (Butterworths)

Phipson on Evidence: ed. J. H. Buzzard, R. May and M. M. Howard (Sweet & Maxwell)

Cases and Materials on the English Legal System: M. Zander (Weidenfeld and Nicolson)

Texts

Evidence: Law and Practice, E. Cowsill and J. Clegg (Longman Professional)

Cross on Evidence: ed. C. Tapper (Butterworths)

Outline of the Law of Evidence: R. Cross and N. Wilkins (Butterworths)

Phipson and Elliott's Manual of the Law of Evidence: D. W. Elliott (Sweet & Maxwell)

Evidence: Cases and Arguments: P. Murphy and J. Beaumont (Financial Training Publications)

A Practical Approach to Evidence: P. Murphy (Financial Training Publications)

Police and Criminal Evidence Act 1984: A Practical Guide: G. Powell and C. Magrath (Longman Professional)

Casebooks

Cases and Materials on Evidence: J. D. Heydon (Butterworths)
Cases and Statutes on Evidence: ed. P. B. Carter (Sweet & Maxwell)

Appendix 2
Examination technique

1. Examinations in the Law of Evidence. Examinations in this topic usually take place at a period in a candidate's studies when he may be expected to know the general outlines of criminal law, procedure in the courts, etc. Questions are generally designed so as to test a candidate's general understanding of the essence of evidence, its scope and its place in English law. In particular, the examination will seek to test recall of general principles of statute and case law, and understanding of those principles and rules as applied to the analysis and solution of legal problems.

2. Types of examination questions set. In general, three types of question make their appearance in papers on the law of evidence, but considerable overlap should be expected.

(*a*) *The purely factual question:*

(*i*) Outline the effect of the Civil Evidence Act 1968 on the admissibility of hearsay evidence formerly admissible at common law.

(*ii*) Explain and illustrate what is meant in the law of evidence by (1) *res gestae*; (2) judicial notice; (3) extrinsic evidence.

(*b*) *The discussion question:*

(*i*) Discuss the judgment of the House of Lords in *Hoskyn* v. *Metropolitan Police Commissioner* (1979).

(*ii*) "The hearsay rule ought to have been abolished decades ago; its continued existence acts as a fetter on the development of the law of evidence." Discuss.

(*c*) *The questions involving a problem which is to be solved:*

(*i*) X is charged with the murder of a cyclist Y, by running him down with his motor car. The prosecution wishes to put in evidence that, earlier on the day in question, X had collided with two other cyclists. Is such evidence admissible in the circumstances?

(*ii*) X, a police cadet at a training school is charged with, and acquitted of, theft. He brings an action for malicious prosecution against the school commandant who had caused the charge to be brought. The commandant wishes to include in his list of documents reports relating to X's conduct during his first term at the school. The Home Secretary objects to production of the documents. Given the law as it stands today, how is this problem likely to be resolved?

3. The purely factual question. Answers to this type of question must be precise and unambiguous. Thus, 2 (*a*) (*i*) above clearly involves section 9 of the 1968 Act which must be set out in relation to its effect on the admissibility of hearsay evidence.

4. The discussion question. Answers to this type of question must be based solidly on a foundation of fact. In the case of 2 (*b*) (*i*) the judgment must be known and comprehended. A swift recital of the facts of the case will not suffice; a discussion—required by the examiner—necessitates an awareness of the effect of the judgment, and recent statutory modification.

5. The problem question. This is, typically, an exacting test of the ability to comprehend principles, to see into the heart of a legal problem, to apply statute and case law and, above all, to present a considered answer. The following technique is recommended:

(*a*) Read the question through two or three times and underline key words and phrases. Thus, in 2 (*c*) (*i*), "running down", "other cyclists", "earlier that day" are vital phrases. In 2 (*c*) (*ii*), "malicious prosecution", "documents", "Home Secretary objects" are key phrases.

(*b*) Identify very carefully the principles involved and note them. Thus, in 2 (*c*) (*i*) the appropriate principle to be noted is that of similar fact evidence adduced so as to rebut a defence of accident or mistake. In 2 (*c*) (*ii*) the appropriate principle to be noted is the claim of privilege in relation to matters alleged to be of state interest.

(c) Identify relevant cases. (Here, *R.* v. *Mortimer* (1936); *Conway* v. *Rimmer* (1968).)

(d) Apply (b) and (c) to the problem's facts.

(e) Write a considered answer, ensuring that your examiner can see that you have grasped the problem, analysed it in the light of the authorities you have cited and, finally, answered it, giving precise reasons for your answer.

6. In the examination room. The following advice should be considered carefully:

(a) Read the rubric and the questions very carefully.

(b) Plan your time allowance with care, allocating it equally to the questions to be answered. Always allow a few minutes for a swift revision of each answer after you have completed it and, in particular, allow time for a final revision of the entire set of answers.

(c) Plan each answer in outline before commencing the answer to be submitted. Check the order of presentation of facts and the construction of your conclusions.

(d) Avoid irrelevance, padding and mere guesswork, none of which will escape the attention of the expert teachers and practitioners who are your examiners.

(e) Above all, use the examination as an occasion for demonstrating what you have learned, in a fashion which indicates that you have absorbed the *essence* of the law of evidence.

Appendix 3
Specimen test papers

INSTRUCTIONS

Answer *any five questions* in each of the three papers. The time allowed for each paper is *three hours*.

NOTE: All the questions in the papers are taken from examination papers in the Law of Evidence set by the University of London in its LL.B. examination. They are reprinted here by kind permission of the Senate of the University.

TEST PAPER I

1. (*a*) Distinguish between presumptions of law and presumptions of fact. In what category would you place the presumption that a man intends the natural consequences of his acts?

(*b*) Explain the effect of presumptions on the burden of proof.

2. "Evidential rules applicable in cases of rape are in urgent need of reform." Comment.

3. (*a*) Specify the various kinds of evidence which the courts will admit.

(*b*) Consider the admissibility of (*i*) a copy of an account in a ledger kept by a bank; (*ii*) a birth certificate; (*iii*) a copy of a carbon copy of a letter, assuming them all to be relevant.

4. What do you consider to be the rationale for the rule against hearsay? Discuss, with reference to decided cases, whether the rationale is reflected in the application of the rule.

5. (*a*) "It is the duty of the prosecution to prove the prisoner's guilt." Discuss.

(*b*) When can a plaintiff rely on *res ipsa loquitur*? In such cases what burden (if any) lies upon the defendant?

6. "The English courts have failed to deal with the policy issues raised by the question of the admissibility of improperly obtained evidence." Discuss.

7. (a) Summarise the reasons why relevant evidence may be excluded.

(b) A, a fair-haired youth of average height, who had always been clean-shaven, was charged with indecent assault on B, aged four years. B did not give evidence at the trial. C, the mother of B, gave evidence for the prosecution that B had complained to her of the assault shortly after it had occurred, but that B had said that her assailant was a tall man with a black beard. Is C's evidence (i) relevant; (ii) admissible?

8. (a) Discuss briefly the methods by which handwriting may be proved.

(b) A's will was attested by B and C. B is dead and C has been certified to be of unsound mind. In a contested suit for probate of the will, how may its execution be proved?

9. Consider whether any privilege against disclosure will be allowed in the following cases:

(a) In an action against a Ministry, the Minister swears an affidavit that it is contrary to the public interest for certain plans to be produced and for the civil servant dealing with them to give evidence orally.

(b) In an action for slander, a witness objects to answering questions imputing to him adultery and dishonesty.

(c) Before an action for personal injuries a prospective witness signs similar proofs of evidence for both sides. His evidence for the plaintiff departs from his proof. In cross-examination by counsel for the defendants, the witness objects to answering questions as to statements in the proofs, and the plaintiff's counsel objects to the defendants putting in the proof supplied to them by the witness.

TEST PAPER II

1. (a) Explain the distinction between relevance and admissibility.

(b) In a collision between two cars, driven respectively by M and N, M was killed, and his executor brings an action for negligence against N. The proposed evidence for the plaintiff includes an account of the accident in a newspaper, a certificate of N's conviction for dangerous driving, and oral statements connecting the conviction with the collision. Is any of this evidence (i) relevant; (ii) admissible?

2. (a) Comment on the statement that estoppel is a rule of evidence. What is the effect of an estoppel which conflicts with (i) another estoppel; (ii) a statutory rule?

(b) J is the owner of a yacht sailed by K, which collides with a motor boat driven by L. K brings an action against L for personal injuries caused in the collision, but the action fails on the ground that L was not negligent. Later J brings an action against L for damage to his yacht caused by the collision, and L pleads (inter alia) estoppel by the previous judgment. Is J stopped from attempting to prove negligence on the part of L?

3. (a) What do you understand by the parol evidence rule? Explain shortly the principle upon which it is based, and its effect.

(b) In an action on a contract for the sale of land the plaintiff puts in as the necessary memorandum a letter sent to him by the defendant. The letter does not contain the plaintiff's name. The defendant contends (inter alia) that an agreed term as to payment by instalments was omitted from the letter. Both parties wish to adduce oral evidence in amplification of the letter. Is this permissible?

4. A and B (who is A's mistress) are accused of causing C (who is A's wife) to take poison, and A is also accused of theft from D (a mental defective). On the charge in relation to poison against A, the Crown proposes to call as witnesses B and C. On the charge of theft, the Crown proposes to call D and E (a child aged nine years). Discuss.

5. Discuss the functions of the judge with reference to the evidence adduced at a civil trial.

6. (a) Upon what principle is the evidence of experts received in criminal and civil trials?

(b) D is charged with driving a motor cycle dangerously and with exceeding the speed limit. At the trial D proposes to call his brother, a medical student, to testify to D's medical history of sudden epileptic fits and the probable effect of such an attack on his driving. The prosecution call the driver of a police patrol-car who states that a radar speed test showed that D was travelling above the speed limit at the relevant time. Comment.

7. Analyse critically the reasoning of the courts in reported cases when upholding or rejecting claims to "privilege" on the ground of public interest.

8. Dan is charged with the murder, by shooting, of Eric. Is evidence admissible:

(*a*) that Fred, when dying of cancer, confessed that it was he (Fred) who had killed Eric?

(*b*) of a note made by Eric in his diary that he was to meet Dan at a spot near where his body was later found, at a time approximately that when the murder must have occurred?

(*c*) about a motorist, George, who drove past the spot at about the time of death, heard a voice shouting, "Please, Dan, don't shoot!"?

9. Discuss, with reference to decided cases, whether the English courts have manifested a reluctance in the recent past to use the law of evidence as a means of protecting the accused at a criminal trial.

TEST PAPER III

1. What is meant by corroboration? Give examples of cases where it is required (*a*) by law; (*b*) as a matter of practice, and state the duty of the trial judge in directing the jury in such cases.

2. (*a*) Discuss the dictum that "a confession is the species of which an admission is the genus".

(*b*) X was asked to accompany police officers to a police station and did so and was questioned by them about a theft. He asked to see his father, and later had a conversation with him in the presence of the officers at the station. Just before leaving the station, his father advised X "to put his cards on the table and tell them the lot". After his father had left and before any caution was given, X made a statement admitting his presence at the time and place of the theft. Is the statement admissible in evidence? Would the legal position be different if a caution had been given after the father's advice and before the accused made a statement?

3. (*a*) How can the execution of a document be established?

(*b*) Comment on the statement that there are no degrees of secondary evidence.

4. " 'Res gestae' is a blanket phrase, covering the reception of a variety of items of evidence for a variety of purposes. If there is any feature common to all the cases in which evidence has been said to have been received as part of the res gestae, it is that of relevance via contemporaneity." (Cross and Wilkins). Discuss and amplify this statement in the light of the cases.

5. "The Civil Evidence Act 1968 has in fact, insofar as civil proceedings are concerned, practically abolished the exclusionary principles of the hearsay rule." Discuss.

6. (a) "In the present case the defence raised both automatism and insanity. And herein lies the difficulty because of the burden of proof": per Lord Denning in *Bratty* v. *A.-G. for N. Ireland* (1963). Explain the difficulty referred to in the quotation.

(b) "Judicial notice is taken of domestic but not of foreign law." Discuss.

7. On a charge against O of forgery of a cheque, P, a witness for the prosecution, was asked in cross-examination whether he himself had forged the cheque and whether he had expressed hostility to O. P denied both allegations. O gave evidence denying the charge, and was cross-examined as to two previous convictions for rape and an acquittal of forgery, none of which he disputed. O then called as witnesses Q, to prove an admission by P that P had forged the cheque, and also R, to prove that P had threatened to put O in prison. Comment.

8. (a) Briefly explain the means, other than evidence, whereby facts may be established in a court of law.

(b) How may the existence of a state of marriage between A and B be shown in the following circumstances: (i) when the marriage ceremony between A and B took place in Western Germany; (ii) when A and B lived all their lives in England but there is no evidence of a marriage ceremony between them?

9. Discuss the following extracts from the directions of a judge to a jury:

(a) "The story told by the accused in this court was in my view hardly credible compared with the accuracy of evidence of Crown witnesses. However this is a matter for you, and you, members of the jury, must decide whose story you prefer."

(b) "It was pointed out by the defence that the fact that the prosecutrix did not consent to sex with the defendant rests entirely on her uncorroborated evidence. This does not matter as long as you are prepared to accept her testimony on this point, since her testimony is corroborated with regard to the fact that it was the defendant who had sexual relations with her on the day in question."

(c) "The defendant said nothing when he was asked questions by the police about the theft. That is his privilege. Now you would think that if he was innocent as he claimed in court he would at least have denied his guilt."

(d) "Since the defendant did not give evidence in the case, I must ask you to disregard what he said to the police on arrest, namely that the stolen goods were on his premises because a man called Victor put them there."

Index